44TH CONGRESS, 2d Session. | SENATE. | Ex. Doc. No. 21.

REPORT

FROM THE

SECRETARY OF STATE,

WITH

ACCOMPANYING PAPERS,

RELATING TO THE

COURT OF COMMISSIONERS OF ALABAMA CLAIMS.

WASHINGTON:
GOVERNMENT PRINTING OFFICE.
1877.

MESSAGE

FROM THE

PRESIDENT OF THE UNITED STATES,

COMMUNICATING

A report from the Secretary of State, with accompanying papers, relating to the Court of Commissioners of Alabama Claims.

JANUARY 20, 1877.—Ordered to lie on the table and be printed.

To the Senate of the United States:

Herewith I transmit a report from the Secretary of State, with accompanying papers, relating to the Court of Commissioners of Alabama Claims.

U. S. GRANT.

WASHINGTON, *January* 20, 1877.

DEPARTMENT OF STATE,
Washington, January 20, 1877.

To the PRESIDENT:

I have the honor to transmit herewith a report from the clerk of the Court of Commissioners of Alabama Claims, together with several of the opinions of the judges of the court delivered in the more important cases submitted to that body.

The court having examined and decided all claims submitted to it in accordance with the several acts of Congress prescribing its jurisdiction, adjourned on the 29th ultimo.

Respectfully submitted.

HAMILTON FISH.

LIST OF PAPERS.

Mr. Davis to Mr. Fish.

WASHINGTON, *January* 5, 1877.

SIR: The Court of Commissioners of Alabama Claims adjourned on the 29th of December last, having examined and decided all claims submitted to them, in accordance with the several acts prescribing their jurisdiction.

I have the honor to transmit herewith a report of the business of the court, to which I have added several of their opinions in the more important cases in which an opinion was delivered, and in some cases I have inserted a synopsis of the argument of counsel.

In most of the claims the court simply entered judgment for a certain amount, not announcing the manner in which they arrived at their decision.

Some of these cases I have reported, as they appear to be of interest, and have given what, in my opinion, was the ruling of the court upon the questions of law arising in them.

The statements of the principles decided in these cases are my own, and for them I alone am responsible. They are reached after a careful comparison of the amounts claimed, the amounts awarded, and the decisions of the court in other and similar cases. I have little doubt that they are substantially correct; still they are in no sense an official expression of the opinion of the court.

In a court organized as this has been, and required to determine so large a number of cases in a comparatively short time, duties have necessarily been imposed upon me which in courts generally do not fall upon the clerk.

If I have been successful in the performance of these duties, and in my efforts to facilitate the speedy disposal of the cases before the court, a large proportion of the credit is due to my assistants.

I would especially call to your attention the valuable services rendered me by Mr. J. Scott Laughton, Mr. J. C. Poor, Mr. Thornton Carusi, and Mr. Arthur O'Conor. They have been untiring in their industry, and their faithful performance of the services required of them is worthy of high praise.

To Mr. R. W. C. Mitchell, the short-hand reporter of the court, I am also indebted for extended notes of the arguments of counsel and the oral opinions of the court, which he has kindly furnished me, and for assistance rendered by him in various other ways.

In conclusion, I beg to express to you my thanks for the uniform kindness and consideration you have shown me at all times since I had the honor to be placed under your direction.

I have, &c.,

JOHN DAVIS,
Clerk and Disbursing Agent.

REPORT OF MR. JOHN DAVIS, CLERK OF THE COURT OF COMMISSIONERS OF ALABAMA CLAIMS.

Hon. HAMILTON FISH,
Secretary of State:

The sum awarded by the tribunal of arbitration at Geneva to the United States as indemnity for losses sustained by the depredations of certain so-called insurgent cruisers was, in accordance with an act approved March 3, 1873, paid into the Treasury of the United States, and an amount equal to that paid in was invested in 5 per cent. registered bonds of the United States, to be held subject to the future disposition of Congress.

To distribute the money so invested, the Court of Commissioners of Alabama Claims was created by an act approved June 23, 1874. (Section 11, chapter 459 of the Laws of the Forty-third Congress.)

The President, on the 24th of June, 1874, nominated Hezekiah G. Wells, of Michigan, as presiding judge; Martin Ryerson, of New Jersey; Kenneth Rayner, of Mississippi; William A. Porter, of Pennsylvania, and Caleb Baldwin, of Iowa, as judges, and John Davis, of Massachusetts, as clerk of the court, and these nominations were confirmed by the Senate.

In the winter of 1874–'75 Judge Ryerson resigned, and soon after died. Harvey Jewell, of Massachusetts, was appointed to fill the vacancy on the 26th February, 1875. On Friday, the 15th of December, 1876, Judge Baldwin died. No appointment was made to fill this vacancy in the court.

On the 22d July, 1874, the President designated and appointed John A. J. Creswell, a counsellor at law admitted to practice in the Supreme Court of the United States, to appear before the court as counsel on behalf of the United States and to represent the interests of the Government in the court, subject to the supervision and control of the Attorney-General.

Alexander Sharp, marshal of the United States for the District of Columbia, has discharged the duties of marshal of this court, as provided in the act creating it.

R. W. C. Mitchell has acted as the short-hand reporter of the court since its organization.

In accordance with law, the judges met and organized the court at Washington on the 22d day of July, 1874, and since that time have held all their sittings in that city. On the 24th of July they made certain "needful rules and regulations, regulating the form and mode of procedure" before them, and "for carrying into full and complete effect the provisions" of the act, (as provided in section 3 thereof,) which rules and regulations, together with a notice of their next session, were duly published.

The court then adjourned, to enable claimants to prepare their cases for trial.

A house was rented for the use of the court, no accommodation being found in any Government building, and during the summer the clerk adapted the building to the purposes of a court-house, prepared the dockets and endeavored to bring to the knowledge of all claimants the organization of the court, with its rules and regulations.

Counsel were not expeditious in preparing claims for submission to the court, and for some time after it met in October, 1874, but few cases were presented for trial.

In the month of January, the last month in which, under the act, claims could be filed, 312 more petitions were received than in the previous five months together.

On the 22d of January, 1875, the six months within which claims might be filed expired, and on that day there were 1,383 cases on the dockets, in which the gross amount claimed was $12,673,451.44, exclusive of interest. This sum does not include, however, several claims in which a simple statement was made that certain property had been destroyed, its value not being estimated.

It being found impossible to dispose of this large number of claims before the 22d of July, 1875, when the court would have expired under the act creating it, its duration was extended by proclamation of the President to the 22d of January, 1876, and by an act approved December 24, 1875, to the 22d of July, 1876.

On the 6th March, 1876, an act was approved allowing additional claims to be filed within three months after the act should take effect.

The three months expired on the 6th of June, 1876, when 685 claims had been received, in which the sum claimed was $1,825,865.55, not including interest. As these cases could not be heard and decided before the expiration of the court, on the 22d of July following, Congress extended its duration to the 1st day of January, 1877.

The court has passed upon 2,068 cases, in which the amount claimed was about fourteen and one-half millions of dollars, not including interest, and has awarded the sum of $9,316,120.25, including interest.

Three lists of judgments and decisions have been reported to the Secretary of State, as required by law, the first containing judgments entered on or prior to January 22, 1876; the second containing judgments entered between that date and July 22, 1876; and the third containing judgments entered between that date and the expiration of the court.

The amount of the judgments in the first list, including interest, was	$6,641,287 26
The amount in the second list, including interest, was	2,353,634 21
The amount in the third list, including interest, was	321,198 78
Total amount	9,316,120 25

The labors of Mr. Creswell, the counsel on behalf of the United States, in defending this large number of claims, have been most onerous. While represented in many cities of the country by assistant counsel, who were charged with the examination of witnesses on behalf of the Government, and with the cross-examination of those for the claimants, still the task of scrutinizing the voluminous testimony in over two thousand cases, and defending them in court, has devolved upon him personally. In cases of this nature the counsel for the United States is always at a disadvantage, as against private claimants, who possess a full knowledge of their claims, and by reason of their familiarity with all the facts and circumstances are enabled to bring out and fortify the strong points and disguise the weak ones.

In view of the large number of claims disposed of by the court, the time allowed it was very short, and without the untiring industry of Mr.

Creswell, and his constant endeavors to facilitate the speedy disposal of cases, it would have been impossible for the court to have so soon reached the termination of its labors.

Testimony of witnesses was taken on notice, and either on written interrogatories or on oral examination by counsel attending, in almost every State or Territory in the Union, in Great Britain, France, Germany, Japan, China, India, Peru, the West India and Hawaiian Islands, and in numerous other foreign countries.

The jurisdiction of the court was limited to claims (filed within a certain period) directly resulting from damage caused by the so-called insurgent cruisers Alabama, Florida, and their tenders, and the Shenandoah after her departure from Melbourne on the 18th day of February, 1865.

Claims for which the party claimant, his assignee or legal representative, should have received compensation or indemnity from any insurance company, insurer, or otherwise, were by law excluded, except for the difference between the loss or damage actually suffered and the indemnity so received. The act also excluded claims "for or in respect to unearned freights, gross freights, prospective profits, freights, gains, or advantages, or for wages of officers or seamen for a longer time than one year next after the breaking up of a voyage" by the acts of one of the inculpated cruisers; also, claims by or in behalf of any insurance company or insurer, either in its own right or as assignee or otherwise, in the right of a person or party insured, unless such claimant should show to the satisfaction of the court that during the rebellion "the sum of its or his losses, in respect to its or his war-risks, exceeded the sum of its or his premiums or other gains upon or in respect to such war-risks;" also, claims arising in favor of any insurance company not lawfully existing at the time of the loss under the laws of some one of the United States; also, claims arising in favor of any person not entitled, at the time of his loss, to the protection of the United States in the premises; also claims arising in favor of any person who did not at all times during the rebellion bear true allegiance to the United States.

With these limitations upon its jurisdiction, the court was to receive, examine, and decide upon the amount and validity of the claims presented to it in accordance with the provisions of the act of June 23, 1874, the principles of law, and the merits of the several cases.

The court was further empowered to make all "needful rules and regulations regulating the forms and mode of procedure before it," which rules and mode of procedure should conform, as far as practicable, to the mode of procedure and practice of the circuit courts of the United States; and the court was vested with the powers of the circuit and district courts of the United States "to compel the attendance and testimony of parties, claimants and witnesses, to preserve order, to punish for contempts, and to compel the production of books or papers when deemed material to the consideration of any claim or matter pending therein."

Nearly all the claims filed in the court were for the loss of property actually destroyed by one of the cruisers named in the act, or of mariners for loss of wages and personal effects occasioned by the destruction of the vessel on which they were serving. The few exceptions to this rule will be found reported below.

In deciding the cases before it, the court has been obliged to pass upon all the questions of fact, as well as those of law.

I take the liberty of adding to this general statement of the business and powers of the court some remarks upon the principal points decided and a report of the more important cases in which an opinion was delivered by the court.

The able dissenting opinions of members of the court I have not included in this report, for lack of space, although in each case I have indicated who, if any, of the judges dissented.

The first step in the prosecution of a case was the

FILING OF THE PETITION.

Section 11 of the act provides that all claims not filed within six months next after the organization of the court shall be barred.

The petition of William C. Geohegan was not received until after the six months had elapsed; but it appearing that it was posted at such a date that in due course of mail it would have reached the court within the time limited by law, but for an accident to the postal service, the court made the following order:

Ordered, That the claim of William C. Geohegan be filed *nunc pro tunc* as of the day when it would have reached this court in due course of mail, viz, on the 16th January; the court being satisfied by the inspection of the papers, including the post-mark, that the petition failed to reach the office of the clerk merely through an accident.

The earlier questions presented to the court related to the form of the petitions, to the necessity of certain allegations therein, and the effect of their omission. Many of these points were raised by the counsel on behalf of the United States on demurrer.

VERIFICATION OF THE PETITION.

Section 11 of the act provides that "all claims shall be verified by oath of the claimant," and Rule III of the court requires every claim to be stated in a petition.

Counsel requested the court to place a construction upon this section of the act, when Wells, presiding judge, read the following memorandum:

"The court has been asked by counsel to place a construction upon the second sentence embraced in section 11 of the act of Congress approved June 23, 1874, and under which the 'Court of Commissioners of Alabama Claims' was created, and thus determine in advance, and before the question is raised in any given case, whether two or more claimants in the same petition may not have their respective claims verified by any one of such claimants named in said petition. Ordinarily it would be impolitic, if not improper, thus to give an opinion in advance and before such question was raised in the trial of a given case; but in this instance, as many of the cases already on the calendar have several claimants, it may not be amiss at once to dispose of the question for the purpose of facilitating the business of this court. It may be argued in favor of permitting one of several claimants to make the oath in behalf of himself and one or more others in any given case, that the object of the verification by oath is merely to get such case before the court, so that proofs and adjudication may be had; that, in fact, the oath of the claimant does not in any case constitute absolute evidence; that the formality of the law in this requirement is, in fact, complied with by the affidavit of one, although the interests of several were involved.

"Some degree of latitude might be tolerated if the court was called upon to construe one of its own rules, to which it would undoubtedly have the right to make exceptions; but in this case it is a provision of the law itself, and whether a necessary provision or not is not the province of this court to determine. It may be that Congress intended that each claimant, although joining with others in the same case, should make separate verifications under oath of his particular interest in its value, possibly conceiving that estimates of value might be different as presented by the different claimants, and that no one claimant, although presenting his claim jointly with others, could properly make affidavit other than as to his belief in reference to the loyalty of his associate claimant; but this court is impressed with the belief that it is not its province to determine the reasons that induced any particular action on the part of Congress. We find the law plain in its provision 'that all claims shall be verified by oath of the claimant;' and we understand that in the use of the word 'claimant' the law refers specifically to *each claimant*, and that each claimant when associated or joined with others in any given case must verify by his own oath his claim."

In Matthew A. Chadwick *vs.* The United States, the petition was filed and verified by Elizabeth L. Chadwick, the wife and attorney of Matthew A. Chadwick, it being averred that the claimant was absent at sea, and was not expected home until November, 1875, too late to file a petition.

Petition demurred to, "because the claim of the said complainant is not duly verified by the oath of the claimant."

Demurrer overruled, "the court holding that where a party claimant is beyond the limits of the United States, and it is impossible at the time of making the petition to procure his oath, the oath of his authorized attorney is sufficient to make his petition admissible, provided the facts of such absence and inability to procure such oath are set out in the petition, or in an annexed affidavit."

Miguel Ignacio *vs.* The United States was a claim for personal effects and wages, brought by William Gordon, jr., as attorney and next friend of the complainant. It did not appear at first whether Ignacio was alive when the claim was filed; subsequently, and after the time allowed for filing petitions had expired, his death was suggested and a motion made to substitute an administrator as complainant. At the trial of the case it appeared that Ignacio had died at a date prior to that on which the petition was filed. The petition was dismissed; no opinion was delivered; but the court apparently sustained the position of the counsel on behalf of the United States that the claim being filed by a person having no standing in court (the next friend of a deceased person having no authority to act) cannot be amended by bringing in a new party-claimant after the time for filing claims has expired.

But in later cases this decision seems to have been overruled. See William O. Smith, administrator, *vs.* The United States, and several other cases.

In these claims a foreign administrator filed the petition as claimant. The cases came on for trial after the time for filing claims had expired, when the counsel for the United States contended that the complainant had no standing in court. Mr. James Lowndes, counsel for complainant, then asked leave to amend by substituting an administrator appointed by the supreme court of the District of Columbia.

After argument, leave was granted to so amend.

And in Robert Montgomery *vs.* The United States, and other cases, leave was asked to amend by substituting the administrator as claimant when the claim had been brought in the name of a person deceased at the time it was filed.

These motions were allowed, the court remarking that the filing of the claims in the court on behalf of a veritable individual was a satisfaction of the provisions of the act, the object of which was that the Government should have due notice of all claims to be brought against it, (see MacLeane, admx., & Taylor *vs.* the United States,) and that owing to the peculiar circumstances of these claims they should not be allowed to perish through a strict adherence to the technical rules of courts of law. The act merely requires that the claim shall be presented. Porter, judge, dissented from this ruling, holding that the parties in whose names the claims were brought being dead at the time they were filed, the petition was a nullity, and could not be amended.

The court, by the presiding judge, stated its opinion early in its session, that letters of administration or letters testamentary granted in any State of the United States would give authority to sue in this court. In the cases of William O. Smith and others, the court denied the right of a foreign administrator to bring suit.

In Abraham Osborn *vs.* The United States, the claimant (former master of the ship Ocmulgee) prayed damages for the personal effects and wages due to the other officers and seamen of the vessel, and their respective interests in the "catch" in addition to his own claim. He showed no previous authority or subsequent ratification from these officers or seamen, of the names even of some of whom he was ignorant.

The counsel on behalf of the United States demurred to the claim, and, after argument, the petition was dismissed on the ground of the want of authority in the petitioner from the parties for whom he assumed to act.

CATCH.

Many of the seamen sailing on whaling-vessels were paid from the catch, their "lay" depending upon the amount of oil and bone taken by the vessel in which they sailed.

Owing to the difficulty experienced in properly apportioning their claims in accordance with the various contracts entered into by them with the ship-owners, to avoid the danger of a double allowance, to protect sailors absent at sea, and to enable owners to obtain payment of advances made to seamen on the credit of the catch, the court entered judgment in favor of the owners of the vessel for the value of the oil and bone on board the ship at the time of her destruction, which judgment, with the interest thereon, was "to be received and distributed by the said owners according to law, among the respective parties entitled thereto in their due proportion."

The owners, therefore, hold the money awarded by the court in these cases subject to all claims, as they would have held the proceeds of the oil and bone taken, had it arrived at its destination and been sold.

The district court of Massachusetts, acting as a court of admiralty, has, I learn, been applied to to settle questions arising under these awards, and has adjusted them substantially in accordance with the rulings of this court.

In estimating the value of the oil and bone lost on whaling-vessels, the court seems to have taken their average value for the year during which the vessel would have reached home, in the ordinary course of navigation.

The claim of John Stevens, a seaman on the Ocean Rover, for the value of his share of the oil on board of that vessel at the time of her loss, was dismissed by the court, his remedy being against the owners, a judgment having been entered in their favor for the whole value of the catch.

TRUE ALLEGIANCE.—PERSONS ENTITLED TO THE PROTECTION OF THE UNITED STATES.*

The leading cases under this head, involving the question of the right of aliens and persons residing in the insurgent States during the rebellion to recover in this court, are those of Williams against the United States; Rhind, executor, against the United States; Worth against the United States; and Schreiber & Meyer against the United States, reported below.

Joseph Levois, surviving partner of the firm of J. Levois & Co., *vs.* The United States, No. 158.

The firm of J. Levois & Co. was composed of the petitioner and Pierre Ferdinand Mathon, who died in 1869. The partnership was formed in 1862.

The petitioner, a Frenchman, did not reside in the United States during the rebellion; his business in New Orleans being conducted by Mathon, also a French subject. There was no averment in the petition that the complainant bore true allegiance during the rebellion to the United States, or was entitled to its protection at the time of his loss.

The claim was for the value of certain merchandise shipped from New York to the firm in New Orleans, on the steamship Electric Spark, which was destroyed July 10, 1864.

The counsel on behalf of the United States demurred to the petition—

1. Because it does not state that the said petitioner did, at all times during the late rebellion, bear true allegiance to the United States.

2. Because it does not state that the said complainant was entitled, at the time of his pretended loss, to the protection of the United States.

3. Because the said complainant was, at the time of his alleged loss, and still is, an unnaturalized foreigner, and never resided within the United States.

After the demurrer was filed, complainant amended his petition, setting forth that "the firm was entitled, at the time of the loss, to the protection of the United States in the premises, under the terms of the treaty of February, 1855, and former treaties between France and the United States," and "that Levois and Mathon did, at all times during the late rebellion, conduct themselves as neutral foreigners; and that during such time neither of them committed any act detrimental to the Government of the United States, or in violation of their duties as such neutrals."

There was no argument on demurrer, all the questions of law and fact being considered at the final hearing, when it appeared from the testimony that up to the close of 1861, or the beginning of 1862, Levois had been in partnership with one Paul Vidal, also a French subject, residing in New Orleans; that Vidal was engaged in the liquidation of the business of the firm under a general power of attorney from Levois, from the beginning of 1862 to the occupation of the city by the United States troops, and that in the course of liquidation he purchased $10,000 of New Orleans City bonds, paying for them in confederate money.

The court entered judgment for the respondent. A motion for a rehearing was then filed and denied. Subsequently another motion for a rehearing, accompanied by additional testimony, was filed and granted. The additional testimony showed that the firm of J. Levois & Co., the complainants, was a different firm from that of which Vidal was a member; that the account between Vidal and Levois had never been closed;

* Section 12, act of June 23, 1874.

that Levois had never authorized or ratified the purchase of the bonds by Vidal, but considered it a personal affair of the latter; that the price of the bonds had not been placed on the books of the firm to the account of profit and loss.

After rehearing, judgment was entered for the complainant in the sum of $5,033.21, with the usual interest.

No opinion was delivered by the court in this case, and the reasons for its decision can only be inferred.

As the opinions in the cases of Worth *vs.* The United States, and Schreiber & Meyer *vs.* The United States, sustained the right of an unnaturalized foreigner, not a British subject, to sue in this court, it would seem that the judgment at first entered in favor of the respondent was not intended to sustain the third ground of demurrer by the counsel on behalf of the United States, but rather that the purchase of the New Orleans City bonds by Vidal, together with his possession and use of confederate money, was a breach of neutrality toward the United States which deprived him of his right to sue; that this breach of neutrality being committed in his capacity as a member of the firm, was imputed to the surviving partner; and that upon subsequent proof that the transaction of Vidal was not imputable to Levois, he having repudiated it as a firm transaction, the judgment was reversed.

William Hutchinson *vs.* The United States, No. 1797.

The complainant, a native of Ireland, "sailed out of the United States, and lived on shore since 1849," and "resided between April 13, 1861, and April 9, 1865, both inclusive, at sea, sailing on vessels under the flag and register of the United States, and in the city of New York."

The claim was for personal effects and wages lost while on the Electric Spark, July 10, 1864.

It appeared that the complainant declared his intention to become a citizen of the United States in 1857, but was not in fact naturalized until 1865, after the loss was sustained for which he claimed indemnity. Mr. James Lowndes, for complainant, called the attention of the court to section 2174 of the Revised Statutes.

Counsel on behalf of the United States contended that this section of the Revised Statutes, taken from the act of June 7, 1870, not being in force at the time of the alleged loss, the complainant was at that time a subject of Great Britain, and, under the decision of the court in Worth *vs.* The United States, not entitled to recover.

Petition dismissed.

Lord and Munn *vs.* The United States, No. 233: Complainants (copartners, doing business in New York during the war,) claimed the value of some wheat destroyed on the Lafayette.

The complainant, Lord, was born in the United States, but Munn was a native of Ireland, and arrived in the United States in 1860. He was naturalized in 1872.

The petition was demurred to on the ground that an unnaturalized foreigner could not claim indemnity before this court. The demurrer was argued in connection with Worth *vs.* The United States and several other similar claims.

The court delivered an opinion sustaining the demurrer, (see Worth *vs.* The United States.) The case was afterward submitted to the court on the evidence, when judgment was entered in favor of "William G. Lord, one of the said complainants," for a sum which seems to be one-half the entire loss.

Rodocanochi Sons & Co. *vs.* The United States, No. 1883: The principal house of this firm was at Leghorn, with branches in London, Marseilles, and Odessa. The firm claimed for goods destroyed on the Brilliant and the Lamplighter. All the members of the firm were foreigners; two of them resided in London, and one of them, Mr. Michael Em. Rodocanochi, was a British naturalized subject at the time of the loss; the other was naturalized in Great Britain in 1868.

Mr. F. W. Hackett, counsel for complainants, contended that the firm was entitled to a judgment for the value of the goods as an entirety, and that the fact that a member of the firm was a British naturalized subject should not effect a diminution in the award of the court.

The property was Italian property, the domicile of the firm being in Italy. (The Cheshire, 3 Wall., 231; Ang. and Ames on Corp., § 108; Regina *vs.* Arnaud, 9 Q. B., 806.)

While the nationality of a corporation is that of the sovereignty which creates it, and that of a firm is the nationality of its individual partners, still, where a firm has a main house in one country with branches in other countries, the analogy between a corporation and a partnership is complete, and the country where the main house is situated gives the firm the impress of its nationality.

The requirement that a person must be entitled to the protection of the United States is satisfied by a firm's being so entitled, even though a partner might not be. (6 Court of Claims, 360.)

Mr. Michael Em. Rodocanochi is entitled to recover for, his certificate of naturalization excepted, "any rights and capacities of a natural-born British subject out of and beyond the dominions of the British Crown and the limits thereof." He had no right to the protection of the British government as to any property "out of and beyond the dominions of the British Crown," and in that is distinguished from a native-born British subject. He can fairly be considered as a foreigner of some other nation than Great Britain. (App. Rep. Brit. Comm. Natln., 1869, p. 76; Foreign Office Circular, 8 January, 1851; Cockburn on Nationality, pp. 115, 116; United States For. Rel., 1873, part 2, p. 1350; *ibid.*, p. 1351; Schreiber & Meyer *vs.* The United States, *post;* 7 and 8 Vict., c. 66; 10 and 11 Vict., c. 83; Worth *vs.* The United States, *post.*)

Judgment was entered in favor of the firm.

The decisions of the court show that aliens shipping goods on American vessels during the rebellion, or employed at that time as seamen on vessels owned and registered in the United States, (except subjects of Great Britain,) were held to be entitled to "the protection of the United States," and to indemnity for property destroyed by one of the so-called insurgent cruisers named in the act of June 23, 1874.

It seems also to have been held that the allegation required by the statute, that they had "during the late rebellion" borne "true allegiance to the United States," was in the nature of a negative declaration, setting forth that they had not in any manner aided or assisted the rebellion. Proof of the strict neutrality of aliens, resident in the United States, appears to have been held sufficient to sustain this allegation.

Claims of subjects of Great Britain were excluded on special grounds; this exclusion does not seem, however, to have been extended to naturalized subjects of Great Britain, apparently on account of the peculiar provisions of the British naturalization laws.

As to the right of an alien naturalized in a colony of Great Britain to indemnity under the act for merchandise destroyed on a vessel, in fact belonging to the United States but collusively sailing under the flag of Great Britain, see the case of Schrieber and Meyer *vs.* The United States, *post;* Pike, admx., *vs.* The United States, *post.*

PROSPECTIVE PROFITS, FREIGHTS, GAINS, OR ADVANTAGES.

(See the following cases: Hubbell *vs.* The United States; Buck & Spofford *et al. vs.* The United States; Gannett, admx., *vs.* The United States, reported below.)

Henry P. Haven and Charles A. Williams, executors, *et al.*, *vs.* The United States, 992: Complainants were the owners of the bark Alert, which was destroyed by the Alabama on the 9th September, while on a voyage to Kerguelan Land, otherwise called Desolation Island, to procure a cargo of sea-elephant oil. It appeared that this oil was imported almost exclusively from this and Hurd's Island, and the entire business was carried on by the complainants; that in prosecuting these voyages a large ship and one or more schooners were usually employed, and it was alleged that no ship or bark could procure a cargo of this oil without having a schooner to assist her. The schooner E. R. Sawyer was sent out as a companion to the Alert, and arrived in safety at her destination, where it was alleged large numbers of sea-elephants were found, and a cargo of oil could have been taken had the Alert arrived. As soon as the owners heard of the destruction of the Alert, they fitted out the Arab, a smaller vessel, and sent her to Desolation Island, where she procured a cargo of oil. The Alert, before her destruction, had taken two sperm whales and had the oil on board.

The complainants in this case claimed their share ($\frac{7}{48}$) of the bark, cargo, and outfits, and $\frac{7}{48}$ of the difference between the cargo brought home by the Arab and that which the Alert would have procured had she reached Desolation Island.

The court in entering judgment delivered no opinion; but by a comparison of amounts it appears that judgment was entered for the value of the vessel, and the oil actually on board at the time of destruction; and that no allowance was made for the probable catch of sea-elephants.

In calculating the value of the sperm oil on board, the market-rate on the day when it would have arrived home in the usual course of business seems to have been taken as the measure of damage.

Charles L. Colby *vs.* The United States, No. 1187, and sundry other claims: These claims were brought by the owners of the ship Commonwealth, destroyed by the Alabama, for the value of the vessel, outfits, and freight.

The Commonwealth sailed from New York for San Francisco on the 19th of March, 1863, laden with a general cargo. On the 17th of April following she was destroyed.

On the 15th of April, 1863, a charter-party was entered into between the owners of the vessel and the agents of the government of Peru, agreeing that the vessel should proceed from San Francisco to Callao, Peru; thence, on receipt of orders, to the Chincha Islands for a cargo of guano; thence to Hamburg or Rotterdam, calling at Cowes for orders. The complainants claimed net freight on this charter-party, which a comparison of the amount claimed with the amount awarded by the court shows was not allowed.

George B. Upton, jr., *et al. vs.* The United States, No. 960: The complainants were the owners of the ship Nora, her tackle, apparel, outfit, and freight.

The Nora sailed from Liverpool for Calcutta about February 14, 1863, and on the 27th March was destroyed by the Alabama. The value of the vessel was claimed as increased by her vicinity to a point where vessels were in demand. A claim was also made for services and risk of money.

The judgment in the case was for $74,603.10, with the legal interest from the date of destruction.

No opinion was delivered in the case, but a comparison of amounts shows that the court did not allow the claim for enhanced value or for services or risk of money.

Sixty thousand dollars, gold, was stated by the complainants as the value of the Nora when new. This amount reduced to currency, with expenses at Liverpool and freight added, and insurance received subtracted, gives approximately the judgment rendered.

Lorenzo F. Fisler *vs.* The United States, No. 404: The complainant, a photographer, on his way to China in the ship Talisman, was captured by the Alabama, and his clothing, stock-in-trade, &c., was destroyed.

The complainant showed that, at the time of his capture, he had an agreement with a firm in China, the conditions of which were that, in return for his professional services, he was to receive a salary of one hundred Mexican dollars per month, and his expenses paid; or in lieu thereof, one-fourth share in the profits of their business; that, immediately upon his arrival at Shanghai, thirteen months after the date when the Talisman would have reached her destination, had she not been destroyed, he entered into the employment of that firm, with a compensation equal to one-fourth of the profits. It was alleged that on this basis, during the thirteen months he was delayed, his share of the profits would have been about $2,600 gold.

No opinion was delivered by the court. The complainant proved $1,180 gold as the value of his goods actually destroyed. Adding to this sum the premium on gold on the day when the Talisman was destroyed, we have $1,722.80, the amount for which the court entered judgment. It appears, therefore, that the claim for compensation for delay in fulfilling his contract was not allowed.

DAMAGES NOT "DIRECTLY RESULTING," &C.

(See Hynemann *vs.* The United States; Ann Eliza Gannett *vs.* The United States; Phillips *vs.* The United States, reported below.)

CASE OF THE LOUISIANA.

William Henry Haskins *vs.* The United States, No. 208. The complainant was master of the ship Louisiana, a whaling-vessel which was driven into Kotzebue Sound, in her attempt to escape from the Shenandoah, where she struck on a sand-bar, took fire, and was burned, with nearly all her contents. This complainant asked indemnity for loss of personal effects, wages, and share of oil, together with his expenses in returning home.

Counsel on behalf of the United States demurred to the petition.

* * * * * * *

3d. Because the claim of the said complainant is not admissible under the law creating this court.

4th. Because the said claim is not a claim directly resulting from damage caused by the so-called insurgent cruisers Alabama, Florida, and their tenders, or by either of them; nor is it a claim directly resulting from damage caused by the so-called insurgent cruiser Shenandoah after her departure from Melbourne on the eighteenth day of February in the year eighteen hundred and sixty-five.

Argument on the demurrer was had at the final hearing of the cause. Mr. H. H. Wells, for the complainant, contended that the claim was for a loss directly resulting from damage caused by the Shenandoah, and was within the jurisdiction of the court, citing the eleventh section of the act of June 23, 1874, and the following authorities: Waters *vs.* Merchants' Louisville Insurance Co., 11 Peters, 213; David C. Magoun *vs.* New England Marine Insurance Co., 1 Story, 157; 1 Phillips on Insurance, sec. 1132, page 677, 5th edition, 1867; Thomson *vs.* Hopper, 1 Ellis, Blackburn & Ellis, 1038; Hahn *vs.* Corbet, 2 Bing., 205; Patrick *vs.* Commercial Insurance Co., 11 Johnson, 9; Peters *vs.* Warren Insurance Co., 14 Peters, 99; Insurance Co. *vs.* Tweed, 7 Wallace, 44; Dole *vs.* New England Mutual Insurance Co., 2 Clifford 394; Voss *vs.* United Insurance Co., 2 Johnson's Cases, 180; Luckley *vs.* Delafield, 2 Caine's Cases, 222; American Insurance Co. *vs.* Dunham & Wadsworth, 12 Wendell, 463; Havelock *vs.* Hansell, 3 Term Reports, 277; Grim *vs.* Phœnix Insurance Co., 13 Johnson, 451; Montoya *et. al. vs.* London Assurance Co., 4 Eng. Law and Eq., 500; Savage *vs.* Pleasants, 5 Binn, 403; Coolidge *vs.* New York Fireman's Insurance Co., 14 Johnson, 308.

Mr. John A. J. Creswell, counsel on behalf of the United States, *contra.*

The court dismissed the petition.

Ann Eliza Gannett, administratrix of the estate of Abraham Osborn, deceased, *vs.* The United States, No. 1321: The following allegations were made in the petition: Complainants were owners of the ship Mary, of Edgartown, which cleared the 18th of June, 1861, for a whaling-voyage of five years in the Atlantic and Indian Oceans and elsewhere. In November, 1863, the master, to escape the confederate cruiser Alabama, ran into Singapore, and, being blockaded there, shipped his oil on a British ship to England. This was valued in Singapore, as shipped, at $36,852, gold, but netted the owners (in gold) at home, (through England,) only $9,990, making a loss, in gold, of $26,862, which sum was claimed.

This claim was dismissed, together with others similar to it in principle.

In the case of Samuel Osborn, jr., *et al.*, *vs.* The United States, No. 787, the following allegations were made in the petition: That the whale-ship Almira, in the summer of 1865, was fitted out to pursue the while-fishing in the Pacific Ocean for a voyage of four years, and proceeded to the Arctic Ocean. While there she was "pursued by the rebel cruiser Shenandoah, with the purpose of capturing and destroying her; and she was compelled to leave said fishing-grounds, and then and thereafter prevented by said rebel cruiser from returning to said fishing-grounds for a period of more than two months; that, when so compelled to leave, the preparations which had been made and the work which had already been done promised a most successful season's catch." The owners claimed the value of the season's catch so lost.

This claim and others similar to it were dismissed by the court, after extended argument.

The gross amount claimed in this class of cases is estimated at $2,000,000, not including interest.

BONDED VESSELS.

(See *In re* ships James Maury, General Pike, Milo, and the bark Nile,

Moses Hyneman *vs.* The United States, No. 643; William Phillips *vs.* The United States; *In re* bark Richmond, 1228, reported below.)

The brig Baron de Castine on the 20th October, 1862, sailed from Bangor, Maine, with a cargo of lumber, bound for Cardenas, Cuba. On the 30th October she was captured by the Alabama, bonded in the sum of $4,000 on the brig and $2,000 on the cargo, and forty-four prisoners were put on board of her. The brig was obliged to make for Boston, the nearest port, where she arrived on the 2d November. She was detained at Boston about ten days making repairs, when she proceeded to Cardenas.

The brig at the time of capture was sailing under a charter binding her to take a cargo of lumber from Bangor to Cardenas, returning to New York with a cargo of merchandise, thirty lay-days being allowed to receive and discharge cargo; the compensation agreed to being $2,250, currency, and foreign port-charges paid.

Counsel for complainants, Mr. Alexander P. Morse, contended that damages should be estimated by accepting the value of the charter-party, allowing its full value, less any indemnity or compensation paid complainants in consideration thereof. (Rogers *vs.* Beard, 36 Barbour, 31; 20 Howard, Pr. Reports, 102.)

If this basis of compensation should not be accepted by the court, counsel claimed indemnity, to be estimated as follows, viz, by computing the number of days lost by capture and multiplying it by a figure representing a fair compensation on that account.

That an allowance should be made also for provisions consumed and other actual expenses consequent upon the capture. (McAfee *vs.* Crofford, 13 How., 447; 6 Bingham, 716; No. 19, Eng. L. R., 215, *et seq.;* Sedgwick on Damages, pp. 57, 63, (note,) 69, 99.)

Judgment was entered in favor of the complainants. No opinion was delivered. From a comparision of the amounts claimed and awarded, it appears that the court calculated damages in accordance with the second basis of computation suggested by counsel.

In the case of the bark Justina, it appeared that while on a voyage from Rio de Janeiro to Baltimore, she was captured and bonded. Nineteen prisoners were placed on board, and the master was ordered to and did proceed to Baltimore, without stopping at any intermediate port; that the Justina was in ballast, and but for the capture would have stopped at the West Indies for a cargo to Baltimore.

Complainants claimed the passage-money of the nineteen men, at $100, gold, each, amounting in currency to $2,750.25, the value of one crate of bananas, taken by the crew of the Alabama, $25, and the value of the vessel for freighting purposes during the time she was under bond, viz, thirty-six days, at $75 a day, amounting to $2,700; the total amount claimed being $5,475.25.

The court awarded $1,425, with the usual interest. The amount of the judgment can be reached by allowing passage-money at $2 and a small fraction per day per man for the prisoners on board for the thirty-six days they were on the vessel, adding the value of the crate of bananas.

NET FREIGHTS.

(See Hubbell *vs.* The United States; Buck & Spofford *et al. vs.* The United States, reported below; Charles L. Colby *vs.* The United States, No. 1187, *supra.*

The complainants in case No. 1942, William Johnston Taylor *et al. vs.*

The United States, were the owners of the steamship Electric Spark, which sailed July 9, 1864, on a voyage from New York to New Orleans and return under charter of the New York Mail Steamship Company. The vessel was destroyed by the Florida on the 10th July, 1864. The complainants recovered the value of the vessel and outward freight in another petition and now claimed the value of the return freight and passage-money, it being shown that the vessel was engaged full of passengers and freight for the return-trip by the agent at New Orleans of the New York Mail Steamship Company.

The compensation to the owners of the vessel, under the charter, was to be the freight and passage-money less a commission to the New York Mail Steamship Company.

Mr. Throckmorton for complainants contended that an allowance for the return freight and passage-money should be made under the decision in Buck & Spofford *et al. vs.* The United States.

The court ruled that the engagement of the freight and passage-money by the New York Mail Steamship Company's agent did not establish such privity of contract with the owners of the vessel as to enable them to recover therefor, the vessel having been destroyed before arrival at the port where the freight and passage-money was engaged.

INJURIES TO THE PERSON.

(See Martha Noyes Williams *vs.* The United States; William H. Whiting *vs.* The United States; Lawrence M. Brown *vs.* The United States, reported below.)

Several claimants asked indemnity for injury to the health, occasioned by the exposure, fright, and suffering consequent upon the capture, or by harsh treatment after capture, while on board one of the so-called insurgent cruisers. These claims were demurred to, and the demurrer was sustained.

CRUISERS NOT INCLUDED IN THE ACT.

Several claims were presented to the court for loss of property destroyed by cruisers other than the Alabama, Florida, and their tenders, and the Shenandoah after she left Melbourne. These claims were all dismissed by the court as not within its jurisdiction.

WAR-PREMIUM CASES.

Several petitions were filed setting forth that certain moneys were paid to insurance companies for insurance on property against destruction by the so-called insurgent cruisers, and claiming indemnity for the money so paid. The property insured was not destroyed. The court dismissed these cases apparently on the ground that the loss did not directly result from damage caused by the inculpated cruisers. The amount claimed in these cases was not definitely stated, but is estimated at $550,000, not including interest.

INSURANCE COMPANIES.

Six claims of insurers, corporate or private, were allowed by the court, the aggregate of the judgments being $111,055.23, not including interest. All of these claimants alleged and proved not only that they suffered losses by the acts of the inculpated cruisers, but that their losses in the business growing out of war-risks was greater than the aggregate of their premiums and other gains growing out of war-risks taken. (Commercial Mutual Marine and other Insurance Co.'s *vs.* The United States, *post.*)

In the case of the President and Directors of the Insurance Company of North America *vs.* The United States, No. 1342, no such allegation of net loss on the business growing out of war-risks was made, and the petition was dismissed.

CONTESTED CLAIMS.

Counsel in several cases contended that this court was a court of the United States, with full power to compel contending claimants to interplead. For the decision of the court on this question see the cases of William J. Taylor and Agnes C. MacLeane, administratrix, *vs.* The United States, *post.*

In one case where certain claims made by counsel were not allowed, the court delivering no opinion, but the disallowance being apparent from the judgment, counsel requested the court to state its ruling on the points of law involved, contending that it was a court of the United States, and that an appeal from its rulings lay to the Supreme Court.

The motion was not allowed.

WAGES AND EXPENSES OF SEAMEN.

It appears that the court allowed wages to seamen for the time shown to have elapsed from the destruction of the vessel to the date when employment was next secured, not exceeding in any case one year. The wages, up to the date of destruction, appear not to have been allowed, as the seamen have their remedy for this loss against the owners.

The actual expenses of seamen in returning home, or to the place where they next secured employment, appear to have been allowed.

Seamen on whaling-vessels generally sailed under an agreement to receive from the owners as compensation a proportion of the proceeds of the catch of the vessels. For the judgment of the court in these cases, see Catch, *supra.*

TITLE TO PERSONAL PROPERTY AS BETWEEN CONSIGNOR AND CONSIGNEE.

Homer & Sprague *vs.* The United States, No. 840, Spark. It appeared from the evidence in this case that the complainants were, on the 19th January, 1863, doing business as commission-merchants in Boston, under the firm and style of Homer & Sprague. That Venicia, Rodriquez & Co. were Spanish subjects, carrying on business as merchants and planters in Manzanillo, in the island of Cuba; that for years they had shipped merchandise to Homer & Sprague, as their factors and consignees; that a regular account-current had been stated at the end of every year, showing an indebtedness, varying in amount from year to year, from said Venicia, Rodriquez & Co. to said Homer & Sprague; that the balance due to Homer & Sprague only thirty days before the destruction of the Estelle amounted to $138,373.34; that this balance of indebtedness had accumulated on the promise of consignments of produce; that on the 12th day of January, 1863, said Venicia, Rodriquez & Co. shipped on board the Estelle, from Santa Cruz to Boston, an invoice, mainly of sugar and molasses, of the cost-value in gold of

$11,270.55, and at the same time forwarded to Homer & Sprague an invoice and bill of lading, making the goods deliverable to them; that this shipment was made in the general course of credit and payment spoken of; that the same was shipped as the property of said Venicia, Rodriquez & Co., and on their account; that on the 19th of January, 1863, the Estelle, with her cargo, was captured and burnt by the confederate cruiser, the Florida. *Per curiam:* The complainants, Homer & Sprague, consignees of Venicia, Rodriquez & Co., are entitled to judgment for the amount of the invoice and bill of lading.

Rayner, J., filed an opinion concurring with the court on different grounds.

Wells, P. J., dissented.

RIGHT OF ASSIGNEE TO RECOVER.

Osgood and Stetson claimed the value of merchandise owned by Dimon Hubbard, and destroyed by the so-called insurgent cruisers.

The claim was made under an assignment to complainants from Hubbard, made and filed in the Department of State, before the organization of this court. Hubbard also filed a petition claiming indemnity for the same losses and moved that the claims be heard and decided together. This motion was denied and Hubbard's petition dismissed.

In this case and in Taylor and MacLeane's cases, the court seems in substance to have held—

1st. That the assignment settled the legal title in the claim in the assignee.

2d. That its judgment should be for the party holding the legal title.

3d. That it could not adjudicate the rights of parties setting up equities in respect of the claim.

MEASURE OF DAMAGE.

(See George B. Upton, jr., *et al. vs.* The United States, *supra;* Henry W. Hubbell *vs.* The United States, *post;* Wages and expenses of seamen, *supra;* Catch, *supra;* Net freight, *supra;* Prospective freights, gains, and advantages, *supra.*)

NATIONAL LOSSES.

(See George M. Robeson, Secretary of the Navy, *vs.* The United States, *post.*)

A claim was presented by the Secretary of the Navy for the loss of the Hatteras, a vessel of war, sunk by the Alabama, and for the loss of the Greenland, a vessel chartered by the Navy Department as a transport, and destroyed by the Florida. The Department having assumed the risk of her destruction by one of the so-called insurgent cruisers, was obliged to pay her owners for the loss. This was the only claim presented for losses sustained by the Government, and it was dismissed.

CLAIMS OF NAVAL OFFICERS.

(See Butman *vs.* The United States, and other claims, *post.*)

The claimants were officers of the Hatteras, and filed claims for property destroyed on that vessel. These claims were allowed; Rayner, judge, dissenting.

THE REPUBLIC OF PERU.

This republic, by its agent, claimed indemnity for loss of guano shipped in American vessels and destroyed by the insurgent cruisers. These claims were dismissed by the court.

VESSELS UNDER FOREIGN COLORS.

(See Stevens *vs.* The United States; Schrieber & Meyer *vs.* The United States, *post.*)

THE HARVEST.

Mary Eldridge *vs.* The United States, No. 1254: This claim was brought by the mother and attorney in fact of John P. Eldridge, master of the bark Harvest, the latter being absent at sea.

The Harvest, a whaling-vessel, was destroyed when sailing under Hawaiian colors.

This petition and others, for loss sustained by seamen on this vessel, were dismissed.

PRACTICE.

(As to the practice of the court on motions for a rehearing, see case of Ann Eliza Gannett, administratrix, *vs.* The United States, *post.*)

It was further decided in several cases that after judgment and receipt of the money by the claimant, the usual rule would be adhered to, denying motion for a rehearing.

The question of amendments was ruled upon in the case of Schrieber *et al.*, (*post,*) and generally amendments were allowed after the time for filing petitions had elapsed, where they did not have the effect of making a new claim or enlarging the old one. Before the time for filing petitions had elapsed all amendments were allowed.

In no case was the court called upon to punish for contempt or perjury, nor was any process issued to enforce the production of books and papers.

COUNSEL-FEES.

Section 18 of the act of June 23, 1874, provides that "at the time of the giving of the judgment the court shall, upon motion of the attorney or counsel for the claimant, allow out of the amount thereby awarded, such reasonable counsel and attorneys' fees" as the court shall determine "is just and reasonable," which allowance shall be entered as part of the judgment in such case, and shall be made specifically payable "to the attorney or counsel, or both."

Motions under this section were made in several cases. In one instance the motion was made after entry of judgment, but before it had been reported to the Secretary of State. Counsel who made the motion argued that under the words of the statute, viz, "at the time of the giving the judgment," his right to judgment for his fees was not excluded, because, in accordance with a well-known rule of practice, the judgment was under the control of the court during the term of the court at which it was rendered, and the term of the court in this case continued until the judgment had been certified to the Secretary of State. The motion was allowed.

In another case counsel moved for an allowance before entry of judgment for an amount agreed upon between the complainants and himself.

The motion was denied, the court stating that this section of the act seems to refer to cases of disagreement between counsel and claimants, in which injustice is likely to be done to counsel, when the court is authorized to examine the circumstances of his employment the services rendered, and to fix such an amount as the court shall determine to be just and reasonable. That the fact that an attorney may be put to delay in receiving his money cannot be considered by the court, and no relief can be given counsel on that account.

Again counsel moved for an allowance under this section, stating that he had been employed by the attorney for the claimant to argue the cause and had prepared the argument, when other counsel were retained in his stead. The court refused an allowance, not doubting that the counsel had rendered important services in the preparation of the case, but holding that they "under that section have the power to allow compensation only to the counsel or attorney who has actually appeared before the court and rendered services in the case in court, or, at least, who has been authorized by a claimant to appear as his counsel or attorney on the records of the court."

All of which is respectfully submitted.

JOHN DAVIS, *Clerk, &c.*

MARTHA NOYES WILLIAMS *vs.* THE UNITED STATES. } No. 87.

WILLIAM H. WHITING *vs.* THE UNITED STATES. } No. 164.

LAWRENCE M. BROWN *vs.* THE UNITED STATES. } No. 286.

Under the act of Congress creating this tribunal, it can entertain jurisdiction of claims for the loss of *property* only. It has no jurisdiction to hear, determine, and allow claims for damages caused by injury to the *person*.

The facts and proceedings appear in the opinion of the court.

Mr. B. S. Roberts for the complainant Williams.

Mr. J. Daniels for the complainant Whiting.

Messrs. Paine & Grafton for the complainant Brown.

Mr. J. A. J. Creswell for the respondents.

BALDWIN, J., delivered the opinion of the court:

In case No. 87 the petitioner represents that she sailed from the port of Foo-Chow, China, on the 7th of November, 1862, on board of the American ship Jacob Bell; that the said ship was on the 12th of February, 1863, captured by the confederate steamer Florida and burned, and that she lost thereby valuable goods, wares, merchandise, and other personal property. And in a separate and distinct count she asks and prays for judgment for direct damages because of permanent loss of health from exposure, prostration of nervous system, of suffering of mind and body, by reason of the capture on the high seas by pirates, and asks judgment therefor.

In case No. 160 the petitioner represents that he shipped on board of the Levi Starbuck, in the month of October, 1862, for a whaling-voyage of three years, and after crossing the Gulf stream said vessel was captured by the rebel steamer Alabama; that the Starbuck was immediately burned by the Alabama; that the officers and crew of the Starbuck, including himself, were placed in irons and kept in close confinement on board of the Alabama for sixteen days; that during the night-time, for the whole of that period, he was kept in irons—confined in the hold of the vessel, in a small, filthy place, &c. After sixteen days of confinement he was set at liberty in an exhausted and enfeebled condition. And, notwithstanding he has employed the best medical aid within his reach, he has continued and still is in a condition little better than entire helplessness; that is to say, he is crippled in hands and feet for life, as he verily believes. He further states that when he was captured by the Alabama he was in good health, strong and robust; that he is advised that his sickness and present physical condition are the result of and directly chargeable to the treatment he received on board of the Alabama, as aforesaid. And for these injuries he asks judgment.

In case No. 286 the claimant represents that about the 26th of December, 1863, the ship Sonora was boarded in the Straits of Malacca by a boat's crew from the Alabama, who seized and burned the vessel, and cast the petitioner, who was the captain of the ship, and the other officers and crew of the Sonora, adrift at sea, in open boats, without provisions, water, charts, compass, or sails; that the petitioner made for the port of Penang, which he reached on the 30th of December, having suffered great dangers and privations while at sea in the open boat. For this injury he claims compensation.

To each of these petitions a demurrer has been filed by the counsel for the United States, and the objections raised by the demurrer are: First, that the damages claimed do not directly result from acts of the so-called insurgent cruisers Alabama, Florida, and the Shenandoah, or their tenders; and, second, that this court has no jurisdiction to hear, determine, and allow claims or damages for injuries to persons; that it has jurisdiction to allow damages for injury to property only. Holding as we do upon the second question presented by the demurrer, it becomes unimportant for us to consider whether the damages claimed are too indirect or remote to entitle these petitioners to recover. The most important question raised by the demurrer in these cases is whether this court has jurisdiction, under the act of Congress creating it, to hear, determine, and allow claims for personal injuries of the character named in these petitions; that is, for injuries to the health and bodies of the claimants, caused, as it is alleged, by the acts of the officers and crews of the so-called rebel cruisers. Section 11 of the act referred to confers jurisdiction upon this court to hear and determine all claims admissible under the said act. And in section 12 it has defined the claims not admissible in this court. These two sections confer and limit the jurisdiction of this court. Section 11 provides that it shall be the duty of this court to receive and examine all claims admissible under this act that may be presented to it, directly resulting from damages caused by the so-called insurgent steamers Alabama, Florida, and their tenders, and the Shenandoah, after a certain date. The act itself nowhere defines the class of cases that are admissible. The question then arises as to what is the proper consideration to be given to the words "receive and examine *all claims* admissible * * * * * * * directly resulting from damages caused," &c. Could it have been the intention of Congress, in the language here used, for this court to take jurisdiction of and hear and determine all claims growing out of the acts of the said cruisers, whether claims for which Great Britain might have been held liable or not? or for claims that had never been presented or considered by either government, or at the tribunal of Geneva? Or was it intended to include only such claims or classes of claims that had been presented and considered, or had some known character or classification? In order to determine the legislative intent in the language used, we adopt the usual rule in the construction of statutes, and seek to ascertain, if possible, such intent from the subject-matter to which the act relates. What was the subject-matter of this legislation? The creation of a court for the adjudication and disbursement of certain moneys received into the Treasury of the United States under an award made by the Tribunal of Arbitration, constituted by the first article of the Treaty of Washington, &c. To this tribunal were referred certain claims growing out of acts committed by certain vessels, and known as the "Alabama Claims." In pursuance of the award of this tribunal these moneys were paid into the Treasury of the United States. Now, what was the nature and classification of these claims as presented by the counsel for the Government of the United States? In note D, p. 249, vol. III, Papers Releating to the Treaty of Washington, we find the following divisions and classifications of these claims as presented to that tribunal by such counsel. They say:

The claims now under discussion, excluding those for increased war-premiums, may be divided into two general classes: 1. Claims for the alleged value of property destroyed by the several cruisers. 2. Claims arising from damages in the destruction of property, but over and above its value. Under the first class should be included, (*a*) owners' claims for the value of goods destroyed; (*b*) merchants' claims for the value of goods destroyed; (*c*) whalers' and fishermen's claims for the value of oil or fish destroyed; (*d*) passengers', officers', and sailors' claims for the value of personal property destroyed; (*e*) the claims of insurance companies for the values of property destroyed for which they had paid the owners the insurance. Under the second class of claims would be included, (*a*) owners' claims for the loss of charter-parties, freights, &c.; (*b*) merchants' claims for the loss of expected profits on goods; (*c*) whalers' and fishermen's claims for the prospective catch of oil or fish; (*d*) passengers' claims for *various injuries* other than in the loss of baggage; (*e*) officers' and sailors' claims for wages and expenses until their arrival home.

Two of these claimants would fall within class (*e*,) officers or sailors. No claims were presented for this class excepting for the value of personal property destroyed and wages and expenses until they arrive home. The other claimant, being a passenger, would fall in class (*d*,) and the only claims presented for this class were for the value of personal property destroyed, and for various injuries other than the loss of baggage. In the argument that follows, in explanation of the character of claims falling in these several classifications, no claims for injuries are named other than those for personal property, and injuries to persons are not mentioned. And wherever these claims are referred to by counsel in the presentation of their case, and whenever they speak of claims of individuals for personal injuries, they appear to have had in mind and spoke of none other than for injury to property. For instance, by reference to that portion of the argument upon page 185, of vol. I, Papers Relating to the Treaty of Washington, we find the claims, as stated by the American agent, classified as follows:

1. The claim for direct losses growing out of the destruction of vessels and their cargoes by the insurgent cruisers.
2. The natural expenditures in the pursuit of those cruisers.
3. The loss in the transfer of the American commercial marine to the British flag.
4. The enhanced payments of insurance.

5. The prolongation of the war, and the addition of a large sum to the cost of the war and the suppression of the rebellion.

So far as these various losses and expenditures grew out of the acts committed by the several cruisers, the United States are entitled to ask compensation and remuneration therefor before this trbunal.

The claims for direct losses growing out of the destruction of vessels and their cargoes may be further subdivided into, 1st. Claims for the destruction of vessels and property of the Government of the United States. 2d. Claims for the destruction of vessels and property under the flag of the United States. 3d. Claims for damages or injury to persons growing out of the destruction of each class of vessels.

He then proceeds to say that in the accompanying volume, 7, of the proceedings of the Geneva tribunal, will be found ample data for determining the amount of damages which should be awarded in consequence of the injuries inflicted by the destruction of vessels or property, whether of the Government or of private persons. Now, by reference to volume 7, we find the claims of *private persons* to be for losses of vessels, loss of cargo, loss of personal effects, loss of wages, of stores, of freight-money, of commissions, of trunks, wearing apparel, articles of trade, &c. Throughout the whole list thus referred to in volume 7, we find no claims whatever of private persons for injuries for anything else than for property.

Again, the counsel for the claimants refer to that portion of the argument in behalf of the United States (p. 215, 3d vol. Papers Relating to Treaty of Washington) wherein they say that the United States claim indemnity in like manner for vessels and other actual property of the United States destroyed, and for immediate personal injuries to the officers and crew. Now, by reference to the argument on the next page, we find the following language used: "The nature of these reclamations is explained in the American case and in the appendix thereto, especially in the seventh volume; and in supplementary documents there will be found detailed statements, made on oath, with valuations and other particulars for the information of the tribunal." We find nothing in the appendix or in volume 7 giving any information whatever in reference to this kind of claim. In our examination of all the correspondence upon the part of the representatives of our Government, as well as that of Great Britain, in relation to what is known as the "Alabama claims," from their inception down to and during the treaty at Washington, and in the examination of all the papers and correspondence submitted by our Government at the time of the treaty and during the whole of the discussion before the Geneva tribunal, both in the case of the United States and in the counter-case, we have not been able to find any allusion, in any manner whatever, by either government, to claims of the character presented by these claimants. And claims for injuries to the persons of individuals were in no way presented or considered or discussed before or at the time of the final award by the Tribunal of Arbitration. It is conceded that these claims were not presented to or considered by that tribunal.

Now, if this is true that no such class of claims were ever considered or presented at the time of the treaty, or at the time when this final award was made, what, then, must have been the character of claims that Congress intended should be adjudicated by this court? When the proper disposition of this money was considered by Congress, the main controversy appeared to be in regard to the rights of insurance companies to participate in the benefits of this award, and the whole discussion before Congress seemed to turn upon this particular question alone. Neither in the Senate or House of Representatives was there any reference made to claims of the character presented by these complainants.

From the language used in the various sections of the act, it appears to us that Congress had only in view at the time of its passage compensation for loss of property. The words "loss" and "losses" are used in every section of this act where reclamation or indemnity for injuries committed by the so-called confederate cruisers is referred to. And it seems to us that if Congress had intended this court to entertain jurisdiction of any other character of claims than those for the loss of property, it would have used language more clearly expressing such legislative intent.

We fully agree with counsel for claimants, that it is the duty of the Government to protect the person of its citizen as fully and as readily as it should protect his property. At the same time we recognize the fact that this is a court of special and limited jurisdiction, and that it should hesitate long before it exercises a doubtful power, especially when, by so doing, it disposes of a portion of this fund confided to its trust to a class of claimants, as we think, never contemplated by Congress.

Demurrer sustained.

CHARLES PRATT WILLIAMS *vs.* THE UNITED STATES. } No. 45.

The act of Congress of 23d June, 1874, provides that no claim shall be admissible or allowed by this court "arising in favor of any person who did not at all times during the late rebellion bear true allegiance to the United States:" *Held*, That this requirement was in the nature of a condition precedent, and that a claimant, in order to entitle himself to the benefit of the act, must make the averment in his petition of his "true allegiance" during the period specified, and prove the same. An averment which states in substance that the claimant was not guilty of the crime of treason, as defined by the Constitution, is not sufficient.

In a case in which the testimony suggests no doubt on such a point, the claimant's own statement, under oath, will be regarded as sufficient to establish for him a *prima-facie* case of true allegiance.

A statement of the case will be found in the opinion of the court.

Mr. R. B. McMaster for complainant.
Mr. J. A. J. Creswell for respondents.

PORTER, Judge, delivered the opinion of the court:

The claimant seeks, by this proceeding, to recover the value of certain merchandise shipped from New York to San Francisco, in a vessel known as the Crown Point, which was captured in May, 1863, by the rebel cruiser Florida. The counsel of the United States has demurred to the petition, chiefly on the ground that the petitioner has not averred that during the late rebellion he bore true allegiance to the United States. This raises an important question, not in this case only, but in many other cases, which ought to be set at rest once for all.

The petitioner alleges "that he was not, at the times mentioned in the petition herein, nor at any other time or times, actively or otherwise, or in any way, engaged in making or carrying on war against the United States, or in aiding or abetting, in any way, shape, or manner, the so-called southern confederacy, or any person or persons engaged in rebellion or making or carrying on war against the United States aforesaid." The act of Congress of 23d June, 1874, constituting this court, contains the following provision: "No claim shall be admissible or allowed by said court, arising in favor of any person not entitled at the time of his loss to the protection of the United States in the premises, nor arising in favor of any person who did not at all times during the late rebellion bear true allegiance to the United States." It is not necessary, and it would not be seemly in us, to discuss the wisdom of this provision. Every good citizen must admire the benign spirit which pervades the more recent acts of Congress, and the decisions of our highest judicial tribunal, in regard to the legal effects of a participation in the rebellion. (Klein's case, 13 Wallace, 128, and Carlisle's case, 16 Wallace, 148.) Doubtless the time will come when words naturally employed in the legislation of a nation struggling to protect its own life will be dropped from the statutes of the united nation. In construing the present statute we must take such provisions as we find in it, and without unnecessary criticism assign to them their true meaning.

Let not the proper attitude of the claimant to the fund for distribution be misunderstood. Whatever his loss may have been, he had not the power to obtain compensation from Great Britain by his own act. Her army and navy would have proved uncomfortable obstacles in his way to her treasury. Just here, the Government of the United States took up his case, and by the exercise of its powers as a sovereign, after years of patient labor, by the highest skill in diplomacy, without the loss of blood or treasure, obtained the whole amount due for the depredations complained of, thus achieving a triumph which may, in the progress of civilization, take a higher rank than the most profound achievements in arms. How the amount of the award obtained at Geneva was made up, what precise species of losses it was intended to cover, or even how the interest was computed, is not now known, and a careful study of the opinions of the several arbitrators has shown us that it was not intended to be known outside of the tribunal itself. The Government of the United States accepted the sum awarded in full settlement of all the claims comprehended in the terms of the treaty, and soon afterwards Congress passed the act providing for its distribution among the claimants, which is to be our chief guide in the actual work of distribution. It is clear to us that the Government had the right to prescribe the terms on which claimants should present their claims. They were not strong enough to compel payment of the money by Great Britain, and when this Government obtained it the claimants had no power to demand it, and no legal right to it, except that which the Government by its own acts chose to accord. They must, therefore, take their respective shares of it subject to all the conditions which the Government has thought fit to appoint, or not take them at all.

Has the claimant in this case complied with the requirement of that portion of the act which has been quoted? He was expressly required to say that he had borne true allegiance to the United States during the period of the late rebellion. Allegiance is the obligation of fidelity and obedience which every man owes to the government under which he lives in return for its protection. He bears true allegiance to his government when he scrupulously and faithfully keeps this obligation of fidelity and obedience at all times and in all things. The petitioner has not said in direct terms that he did during the rebellion bear true allegiance to the United States. Avoiding this plain and simple language, he has in its place introduced certain negative words. He avers that during the times referred to he was not actively or in any way engaged in making or carrying on war against the United States, or in aiding or abetting the southern confederacy, or any person or persons engaged in rebellion or carrying on war against the United States. In other words, in place of the averment that he bore true allegiance, he states, in substance, that he was not guilty of the crime of treason as defined by the Constitution. Without stopping to inquire whether this is a mere accidental departure from the terms of the act, or whether he may have done acts short of treason but inconsistent with the true allegiance of a citizen, (which it would serve no good purpose for us to specify,) can the claimant thus vary the terms on which he is allowed to participate in this distribution? The act of Congress has conferred on this court almost unprecedented powers, by making us judges both of the law and the facts of every case, and giving no appeal from our judgments to any other tribunal; but the court is nevertheless one, not of general, but of special and limited jurisdiction, and clearly no claimant can bring himself within this jurisdiction without an exact and faithful compliance with the terms of the act. The claimant who chooses to place himself outside of the limits which the act has prescribed stands where our action cannot reach him. We have no power to excuse him from the performance of conditions which Congress has made it necessary for him to perform before he can present his case at all. "No claim shall be admissible or allowed by said court," &c. The term *admissible* is more commonly used with respect to the introduction of testimony. When it cannot be received at all, or permitted to enter into the consideration of the tribunal for any purpose, it is pronounced inadmissible. So a claim cannot be admitted here from which any one of the essential terms of the act have been omitted. If admitted, it is further provided that it shall not be allowed by the court. The averment of true allegiance during the period defined in the act seems to us one of the conditions thus made essential to the admission or allowance of the claim. It is in its spirit akin to the performance of a condition precedent in law, and no court of law or equity in England or America has ever undertaken to relieve any party from the performance of such a condition. Finding this requirement plainly written in the act, and being both indisposed and unable to modify it, we hold that the claimant must prove his true allegiance before he can touch a dollar of the money to be distributed, however meritorious his claim in other respects. If he is required to prove his allegiance he should be required to allege it. It is one of the rules of good pleading that a party should allege that which it is essential for him to prove, so that his opponent may, if he see proper, either traverse it or confess and avoid it. Let it be carefully noted, however, that we are not now called upon to measure the quantity or quality of the proof which the claimant will be obliged to give. In the argument before us it was earnestly and ably insisted that the claimant might well rely on the presumption of his innocence. We admit the value of this principle, and agree that no man can be presumed guilty of treason or any other crime until he has been proved guilty; and when he is obliged to aver affirmatively his innocence to bring his case within the jurisdiction of a tribunal of limited powers, the very slightest proof ought, in reason and justice, to be sufficient *prima-facie* evidence in his favor. We are clear that in a case in which the testimony suggested no doubt on such a point the claimant's own statement, under oath, should be regarded as sufficient to establish for him a *prima-facie* case of true allegiance. For these reasons we sustain the demurrer; but we suspend the entry of judgment until the present claimant, and others who may be affected by this decision, shall have offered to amend their claims, if they shall find themselves able, and deem it good so to do.

CADWALLADER D. C. RHIND, EXECUTOR, &c., *vs.* THE UNITED STATES. } No. 242.

A claimant in this court is required to set forth in his petition that during the late rebellion he bore true allegiance to the United States.
It is not sufficient to aver that for any offenses committed by him during the rebellion, he received a pardon from the President of the United States.

A statement of the case will be found in the opinion of the court. The counsel on behalf of the United States demurred to the petition in that the complainant did not aver that at all times during the late rebellion he bore true allegiance to the United States. Argument was had on the demurrer, when it was withdrawn at the suggestion of the court, all questions growing out of it being reserved for argument when the case should come on for final hearing.

At the final hearing—

Mr. H. H. Wells for the complainants.

Mr. J. A. J. Creswell for the respondents.

PORTER, J., delivered the opinion of the court:

The petitioner, as executor of the will of John J. Kelly, claims to recover for a certain interest which his testator owned in the bark Lamplighter and her freight. The bark was destroyed by the Alabama, on the 11th day of October, 1862, and we assume that the plaintiff's title to the interest which he claims in the ship and the freight has been established. The objection to a recovery grows out of certain averments of other facts made in the petition. He sets forth that "in legal intendment, and under the allegations already made, he has at all times borne true allegiance to the Government of the United States." These allegations are: "That during the late rebellion the said Kelly, although he resided within the limits of the so-called Confederate States, had no connection with the war in any manner whatsoever, being exempt from conscription by reason of possessing a medical certificate of disability, and that, as far as any sympathy he may have had for the cause of the said Confederate States, he has been duly and legally pardoned." He produces before us exemplifications of two pardons issued by the then President of the United States, in the usual form, bearing date, respectively, on the 28th of August and 23d of September, 1865. From the other proofs submitted, it appears that Mr. Kelly took no active part in the war; that he was exempt from military service; that he contributed no pecuniary aid to the confederacy; that he was in his opinions opposed to the war, but that his sympathies were with the southern people. There is no evidence in any part of the proofs of acts of loyalty on his part toward the United States. This is the substance of his claim for re-imbursement. It differs from every other claim yet brought before us. Can we allow it?

The twelfth section of the act constituting this court contains this now familiar provision: "And no claim shall be admissible or allowed by said court arising in favor of any person not entitled, at the time of his loss, to the protection of the United States in the premises, nor arising in favor of any person who did not at all times during the late rebellion bear true allegiance to the United States." In the case of Charles Pratt Williams, No. 45, we held, unanimously, after full argument, that this requirement of the statute was in the nature of a condition-precedent in law, and that every claimant, to entitle himself to the benefit of the act, must make an averment of his true allegiance during the period of the rebellion. This petitioner avers that his testator did bear true allegiance to the United States, but qualifies the averment by describing his conduct and opinions, and then ascribes to the pardons he received the effect of causing him to occupy, in the eye of the statute, the same position he would have occupied, if he had borne allegiance. Before the passage of the act of 23d June, 1874, many of the most important decisions of the Supreme Court of the United States on the subject of pardons, had been announced; *Ex parte* Garland, 4 Wallace, 334; United States *vs.* Klein, 13 Wallace, 136; Carlisle's case, 16 Wallace, 151; and since its passage, Osborn *vs.* The United States has been decided but is yet unreported. These decisions have held, in substance—

1st. That the power of pardon conferred on the President by the Constitution is unlimited, except in cases of impeachment.

2d. That the pardon reaches both the punishment prescribed for the offense and the guilt of the offender, releasing the punishment and blotting out the guilt of the offense.

3d. That Congress cannot in any way limit the effect of a pardon, nor exclude from its exercise any class of offenders.

4th. That a pardon restores to its recipient all rights of property lost by the offense pardoned, unless the property has by judicial process become vested in other persons.

The decisions growing out of the Abandoned and Captured Property Act are not pertinent here, for that act and the several interpretations of it were founded on the theory that the right of a claimant once perfect, was not divested by the sale of the property, and that he was entitled to the proceeds, because he was the owner of that which the proceeds represented. (Armstrong's case, 13 Wallace, 154.)

The several principles relating to the effect of a pardon must be supposed to have been known to Congress when the act constituting this court was passed, and, doubtless, the cases decided up to that time were familiar to the members of the Judiciary Committee in each house, before whom the bill came in its progress. With this knowledge in its mind, Congress enacted, not that a claimant should merely assert his allegiance, or that the absence of it might be supplied by proof of a pardon, but that he should establish that at all times during the rebellion he did bear true allegiance; and thus Congress took from this court jurisdiction of every case in which the fact of true allegiance was wanting, by holding that no such claim should be admitted or allowed.

If the right of the petitioner to a part of the fund received from Great Britain were a right of property legally vested in him, it is clear from the cases which have been cited, that a pardon would restore it, and that any denial of the right by Congress would be unavailing to defeat it. Has he such a right? He had a right of property in the ship which the Alabama destroyed, and he lost it without any act on the part of the Government of the United States which could give him redress against it. The Government of the United States was not obliged to claim from Great Britain payment of the loss, but acted in that regard according to its sovereign pleasure. It did not succeed in obtaining payment of the whole of the claims presented, and the most careful investigation of the proceedings at Geneva has failed to show what claims were included in the award and what excluded therefrom. The award was made in favor of the Government and not in favor of the claimants. The Government thus vindicated the national honor, but it did not assume to pay any particular class of claimants nor any particular claim. Having obtained the money by its own act and at its own cost, it had the right to prescribe the terms on which the distribution should be made. It certainly had the power to exclude certain claimants and to include others less meritorious. In the act now before us, claimants are excluded who believe themselves justly entitled to a part of the fund, but they have no power to assert their right to it. Under the powers committed to us, we have in some instances rejected altogether claims presented at Geneva, and in many more instances we have largely reduced such claims in amount.

The present claimant exhibits in every line of his petition a proper effort to bring himself within the terms which Congress has prescribed. He was obliged to do this, for there was no right which Congress took away, and no right which a pardon could restore. One of the terms thus prescribed is that he shall allege and show his true allegiance. This he has not been able to allege, except in a sense so qualified that it does not meet the positive requirement of the act. He has not been able to prove it, for his sympathies are very candidly stated to have been against the Government in its struggle, and no act on his part tending to establish allegiance has been proved. It only remains for us to employ in our judgment the language of the statute and to say that a claim thus presented cannot be allowed.

Petition dismissed.

BENJAMIN WORTH *vs.* THE UNITED STATES. } No. 91.

And numerous other cases.

The eleventh section of the act under which the court is organized provides that no claim shall be admissible or allowed arising in favor of any person not entitled, at the time of his loss, to the protection of the United States "in the premises," &c.: *Held*, That this provision embraced all persons, whether native-born or of foreign birth, whether naturalized or unnaturalized, except the subjects of Great Britain, who are held to be excluded on other grounds.

A statement of the case will be found in the opinion of the court.

Mr. W. W. Crapo for the complainants Worth, Levois, Dovolo, and West.

Mr. H. C. Bliss for the complainant Gordon.

Messrs. R. M. Corwine & Son for the complainants Lord and Munn.*

Mr. John A. J. Creswell for the respondent.†

---

* Cited the following cases: Opinions of the principal officers of the Executive Departments on the question of Expatriation, 3 Sumner, 115; Woodbury and Minot's Reports, United States *vs.* Petersen, p. 305; Consular Regulations, sec. 128; Revised Statutes, sec. 4612; Lawrence's Wheaton, part 2, chap. 2, p. 214; Arrest of Mason and Slidell, correspondence between Secretary Seward and Earl Russell; vol. 3, Papers relating to Treaty of Washington, pp. 17, 215, 315, 577, 580; vol. 4, Papers relating to Treaty of Washington, pp. 19, 53; vol. 1, Papers relating to Treaty of Washington, p. 17; 7 Cranch, pp. 536–542; 2 Wheaton, Pizarro case, p. 227; 12 Statutes at Large, pp. 589, 820; 6 Opinions Attorney-General, p. 474; Captured and Abandoned Property Act, 4 Opinions Attorney-General, p. 350; 3 Court of Claims, pp. 195, 238; 8 Cranch, p. 285; 16 Wallace, pp. 147–153; Consular Regulations, secs. 4577, 4578, 4579 4580, 4581, 4582.

† Cited section 5596 Revised Statutes; section 4612 Revised Statutes; 1 Kent, p. 153, note; Cushing on the Treaty of Washington, pp. 164, 167; Consular Regulations, sec. 128; Revised Statutes, sec. 2174; 2 Kent, pp. 43, 49; 15 Statutes at Large, p. 223; Treaty between United States and Great Britain, May 8, 1871; 16 Statutes at Large, p. 775; 33 and 34 Victoria, chap. 14; Mixed Commission on British and American Claims, British Reports, Barckley *vs.* United States, p. 267.

RAYNER, judge, delivered the opinion of the court:

In case Benjamin Worth *vs.* The United States, in José Lewis *vs.* The United States, in John Powecerro Dovolo *vs.* The United States, and in Frank F. West *vs.* The United States, the complainants were, at the time of their alleged losses, unnaturalized foreigners, subjects of Portugal.

In William Gordon *vs.* The United States, and in William G. Lord and Alexander Munn *vs.* The United States, the complainants, at the time of their alleged losses, were subjects of Great Britain.

In all the four first-named cases the same principle is involved.

The petitions are all in due form, containing, with the other requisite averments, that of the complainants having at all times during the rebellion borne true allegiance to the United States.

The counsel for the United States in each of the cases has filed a demurrer, upon the ground that an unnaturalized foreigner cannot claim indemnity before this court for losses sustained by the depredations of the rebel cruisers.

In these cases we do not consider that the questions of paramount and divided allegiance, consequent on naturalization—which have been so elaborately argued—are in any way involved. None of these cases present a question of conflict of jurisdiction, growing out of the claim of any government to the allegiance of its native-born subjects on the one hand, and the protection of another government due its naturalized citizens or subjects of foreign birth.

Happily for the peace of the world, all these troublesome issues, growing out of native allegiance and protection to the sojourner of the *lex loci*—so long mooted by publicists, and which, in many instances, threatened serious complications between the United States and foreign nations—have been amicably adjusted by treaty stipulations.

Great Britain was, of all Christian nations, the most sensitive and exacting in her claim to the perpetual allegiance of her native-born subjects. But that great and proud nation has so far yielded to the demands of a progressive civilization as to abandon her former dogma of "*nemo potest exuere patriam.*" In the convention of 1870, between the United States and Great Britain, the latter power finally and forever yielded her long-asserted claim of perpetual allegiance, and now recognizes the right of her subjects to transfer their allegiance to the country of their adoption.

True, that convention was held since the occurrences out of which the claims now pressed before this court took place, and, of course, the convention could not have a retrospective operation.

But really none of the questions finally put to rest by that convention arise in the cases before us. And these questions, growing out of a conflict of allegiance between the country of one's birth and the country in which he is naturalized, and the correlative rights and obligations to protect such person resting on the respective nations, are thus alluded to and amplified, not because they come within the purview of these cases, but because the counsel, both for the claimants and for the United States, have argued them so elaborately in their elucidation.

In the decision of the question raised on demurrer, it seems to us that the main issues presented are:

First. Did the act of Congress creating this court—by the provisions of which our powers and duties are to to be regulated and restrained—intend to confine the benefits of its provisions to citizens of the United States, or did it design to extend those benefits to any other class of persons? And, secondly, in case it did design to extend the scope of its operations so as to embrace all those entitled to the protection of the Government, then do the complainants whose cases are now before us come within the category of that protection?

By a close and minute examination of the act of Congress under which this court is organized, it will be seen that whenever those who suffered loss by the rebel cruisers, and for whose benefit the fund paid over under the Geneva award is to be distributed, are alluded to, they are spoken of simply as "persons," "claimants," &c. The term citizen of the United States, or citizen simply, is not mentioned in the act, and the only allusions in the act tending to define the status of those entitled to its benefits are to be found in the last sentence of the 11th section, as follows:

And no claim shall be admissible or allowed by said court arising in favor of any person not entitled at the time of his loss to the protection of the United States in the premises, nor arising in favor of any person who did not at all times during the late rebellion bear true allegiance to the United States.

It will thus be seen that the provisions of the act are broad, comprehensive, and without restrictian *as to political status*, except in the two cases mentioned. The claimant must have been "at the time of his loss" entitled to the "*protection*" of the United States, and must, at all times during the rebellion, have borne true allegiance to the United States. To every one who was at the time of his loss entitled to the protection of the United States, the door was thrown wide open, and he is invited to come forward and present his claim in the distribution of this fund, unless shut out by some other provisions which have no reference to nativity or domicile.

It appears from the language of the act that it embraces, and was intended to embrace, (and as national justice and national duty required it to have done,) in its benefits all persons entitled to the "protection" of the Government, whether native-born or of foreign birth, whether naturalized or unnaturalized.

Then, do the claimants in the cases before us come within the scope of "protection of the United States?" In each and every case the claimant has made affidavit to facts which *prima facie* bring him within the protection of the Government. They all declare under oath that they enlisted in the commercial marine, or whale-fishery, under the flag of the United States, and sailed, three of them in August and September, 1862, and the others in May, 1865, in the ships Euphrates, General Williams, and Sophia Thornton, and the bark Virginia, and that said vessels were destroyed by the confederate cruisers, at the times and places therein mentioned. It is a well-recognized principle of international law—to the violation of which no nation has been more sensitive than our own—that the deck of a vessel, so far as national rights and duties are involved, is regarded in the same light as a part of the *terra firma* of that nationality whose flag floats above that deck. Consequently, the duty of protection inures to the full extent to those treading the decks of American vessels on the high seas as to those resident on any portion of American soil. Never was this principle more clearly exemplified than in the case of Mason and Slidell. Great Britain took the ground that these men were, when on the deck of a British steamer, entitled to her protection. Our own Government—important as were the results involved—was compelled to admit the justice of the British demand. Great Britain not only vindicated her own national dignity by requiring an apology from the United States Government, but she practically bestowed that protection which she owed to Mason and Slidell by requiring that they should be placed *in statu quo* by our Government, which was done.

Our Government could not in consistency and honor have refused. It was a great principle for which our Government had contended from its origin; a principle identified with the freedom of the seas, viz, that the flag protected the ship and every person and thing therein not contraband.

It was mainly in defense of this principle that our Government, sustained by public opinion, went to war with Great Britain in 1812. She took the ground that the decks of our ships must be sacred as against any claim of search, or visitation even, on the part of any earthly power, if exercised against our consent. Instead of chaffering about the question of perpetual allegiance and the right of the British government to the service of her subjects wheresoever found, we took the high and practical ground that those who were on the decks of American vessels and under our flag *were* entitled to our protection, *and should have it.*

We deem it unnecessary to say anything further to prove that the claimants, in the cases now under consideration, are entitled to our protection in the same way and to the same extent as if resident on our soil. The next question is, are they entitled to this protection, being foreigners, unnaturalized? The act of Congress creating this court, as before suggested, says nothing about citizens in providing for who may present claims here; and it says nothing about foreigners or aliens, in specifying those who may not present such claims. It would seem that the framers of the act had a view to the case of unnaturalized aliens. Naturalized aliens having the same legal rights (we do not mean the same political privileges in entirety) with native-born citizens, of course it was unnecessary to have made any allusion to *them.* The act speaks of those entitled to the protection of the United States "*in the premises.*" Those words, "in the premises," define and limit the application of the law within a narrow circle. It is not everybody entitled to the protection of the Government that can come before this court; it is not every one entitled to that protection who was a loser by depredations on the part of the so-called confederate government, by land as well as by sea; it was not every one that lost by confederate cruisers generally that can come here. But it *is* every person entitled to the protection of the United States *in the premises*, viz, every such one who sustained loss or injury, directly resulting from damage caused by the so-called insurgent cruisers Alabama, Florida, &c., and the Shenandoah, after, &c., that can come before this court, and without reference to whether such person is native-born or foreign-born, whether naturalized or unnaturalized.

We should consider it a waste of time, as well as an exhibition of judicial pedantry, to cite any long array of authorities to prove that foreigners are entitled to protection in that country in which they are domiciled, or even temporarily sojourning. This right to protection is recognized throughout all civilized countries, not only by the great authorities on international law, but by the municipal regulations and judicial decisions of different countries. Vattel, than whom Christendom recognizes no higher authority, in summarily disposing of the question as one of abstract international obligation, says: "As soon as the sovereign admits a foreigner into his state, he engages to protect him as his own subject, and to afford him perfect security, so far as depends on him; accordingly, we see that every sovereign who has given an asylum to a foreigner considers himself no less offended by an injury done to the latter than he would be by an act of violence committed on his own subject." (Vattel, book 2, chap. 8, sec. 104.)

This principle of international law is recognized as a part of the municipal law of England and of the United States. The English courts have decided, again and again, that not only is a foreigner resident in England entitled to the protection of her laws to his person and property; but even in the case of an alien enemy, if he quietly and peaceably obeys her laws and performs the duties required of him, he is not only entitled to the protection of her laws in suing for his rights in her courts, but he is entitled to protection to his person, even as against the land of his nativity. True, this protection inures only so long as he is within the pale of her jurisdiction. If he voluntarily returns to the country whose claim to his allegiance has never been divested by naturalization elsewhere, his title to protection is at an end; but, as long as he remains on the soil or the deck of a ship of the British government, he may rightfully claim British protection. (Wells *vs.* Williams, 1 Ld. Raymond, 282; Casserres *vs.* Bell, 8 Term Rep., 166; Sparenburgh *vs.* Bannatyne, 1 Bos. & Pull., 163.)

The same obligation on the part of our Government to an alien entitled to and claiming its protection has, in divers cases, been maintained in our courts and by its highest legal authorities. Chancellor Kent, of whose name every American feels proud, and whose opinions command the highest respect wherever quoted, lays it down in his Commentaries that "alien enemies resident in the country may sue and be sued as in time of peace, for protection to their persons and property is due and implied from the permission to them to remain," &c. The lawful residence does, *pro hac vice*, relieve the alien from the character of an enemy, and entitles his person and property to protection. (2 Kent's Com., 63, and the authorities there cited.)

The same learned judge, in a judicial opinion, declared that "by the law of nations (which is a part of the common law) an alien who comes to reside in a foreign country is entitled, so long as he conducts himself peaceably, to continue to reside there, under the public protection. * * * And it has now become the sense and practice of nations, and may be regarded as the *public law of Europe*, that the subjects of the enemy, so long as they are permitted to remain in the country, are to be protected in their persons and property, and to be allowed to sue, as well as be sued."

(Clarke *vs.* Morey, 10 Johnson's N. Y. Rep., 73; The Venus, 8 Cranch, 253; Dana's Wheaton's International Law, secs. 321, 322.)

If this right of the foreigner inures to him in time of war between his native and his adopted country, how much more consistently may it not seem to belong to him in time of peace? If he may rightfully claim this protection when merely residing or sojourning here, in the pursuit of his gainful callings, with how much greater confidence may he appeal to it when he has braved the perils of the deep and embarked his hopes and his fortunes under that flag which is the ensign of the nation's power and glory? Of all the nations of Christendom not one has done so much to vindicate the freedom of the seas against that proud and mighty nation that claims to be their "mistress" as the United States of America. No other nation has done so much in imparting to its flag that moral power which speaks to the nations in the still, small voice of warning, that it is the emblem of a nation's might, and that if he who trusts to its protection be harmed under it his wrongs shall not go unredressed. It has been not only the duty of our country, but its best policy, in "providing and maintaining a Navy," to foster and encourage our commercial marine and the daring enterprise of our whale-fishery as nurseries for seamen for our Navy in time of war. It cannot be denied—in fact, it may be asserted with pride—that wherever our flag is seen, in the ports of every nation and on the waters of every sea, it speaks in the language of invitation, to the oppressed of every clime, to place themselves under its ægis, with a pledge of its unfailing protection.

These men who are the complainants in the cases now before us, without waiting for the slow process of naturalization, and, as we may reasonably suppose, for the want of the means for reaching our shores, embarked under our flag, some of them in the ordinary pursuits of commercial enterprise, others in the danger and privations of whale-fishing. They fell a prey to the daring adventurers of the rebel cruisers.

In the discharge of its duty to those entitled to its protection our country and Government chose to hold responsible the mightiest power on the globe for its neglect to enforce its obligations of neutrality at a time when the integrity of the nation was in hazard.

As the result of an arbitration, involving the greatest triumph that peace ever obtained over war, the British government paid over the money which it is made the duty of this court to distribute, on certain conditions and limitations, among those who suffered wrong from the default of the British government to comply with her obligations as a neutral. According to the provisions of the law under which this court exists we have no right to discriminate among those who were entitled to our protection in the premises. The public law of Christendom, and the municipal law of the land, declare that foreigners, whether domiciled or temporarily sojourning on our soil, or whether on the decks of our ships, trusting to the security of our flag upon the high seas, are equally entitled to our protection against wrong from any foreign power, and equally entitled to sue for their rights in our courts. Therefore, on the ground of abstract justice and propriety, and upon the ground of legal right, we decide that foreigners, entitled to the protection of our flag in the premises, whether naturalized or not, have a right to share in the distribution of this fund.

In case No. 118, William Gordon *vs.* The United States, and in case No. 233, William G. Lord and Alexander Munn *vs.* The United States, we frankly admit we have not been free from some difficulty in arriving at a satisfactory conclusion. The complainants in both these cases were subjects of Great Britain, not naturalized in the United States at the time of their alleged losses.

Their cases present considerations different from those offered in Nos. 91, 92, 237, and 246, where the complainants were subjects of Portugal at the time of their alleged losses. So far as the right to the protection of our laws and of our flag is concerned, the complainants Gordon and Munn had a right to such protection, as against other nations than their own. And if the conflict had been directly between Great Britain and the United States, and there had been an intent on the part of Great Britain to harm or in any way to wrong them while under our protection, all the authorities would go to prove that our Government would be bound to defend and protect them in their rights, even against their own government. Our complaint against Great Britain was not that she had directly or intentionally wronged our Government or its citizens, but that wrong had been done through her neglect to observe her neutral obligations.

In the distribution of this fund the measure and scope of our powers must be sought for in the act of Congress creating this court. While the proceedings at Geneva, and the negotiations which led to the Geneva arbitration, are not positively of any binding force or authority for our guidance, yet, as parts of the *res gesta*, they are useful in enabling us to judge of the motives and influences which operated on the arbitrators, and of the ends and objects of their award. In cases of doubt they are valuable in aiding us to arrive at a proper construction of the act of Congress which prescribes our duties.

While Great Britain admitted that she has been negligent of her duty, she never did admit that she had committed a wrong against our Government or its citizens under the laws of nations. Those representing her interest, as appears from the British counter-case, contended that her neglect was in not rigidly enforcing her own municipal laws for securing neutrality. To the charge, among other causes of complaint on the part of those representing the United States, that she had failed to enforce her own municipal regulations, her reply was that that was a matter with which we had no concern; and that it was a question between her and her own people, with which we had nothing to do. While, as before said, these preliminary discussions and negotiations are of no binding authority upon this court, yet does not national courtesy and good faith require of us to suppose that Congress, in creating this court, never intended we should distribute this fund other than for the purposes for which Great Britain supposed she was paying it? For instance, suppose Congress had chosen to keep half the fund and cover it into the Treasury of the nation; or had directed this court to distribute it among those whose commercial interests had been injured by the terror and alarm caused by the insurgent cruisers, or among those who had suffered loss by the depredations of rebel cruisers, other than the Alabama, Florida, and Shenandoah. In such cases, would not Great Britain have had cause to complain that she had been misled, overreached, deceived? Would our Government have been acting in good faith in making such disposition of this fund?

If Great Britain supposed, as seems to have been the case, that in paying this money it was to indemnify those who had been injured by her failure to execute her own municipal laws, would she not regard any action on our own part in indemnifying her own subjects for her neglect as inconsistent with the objects and purposes for which she agreed to the arbitration in the first place, and to the payment of the money in the second place? And while we might be bound to indemnify a British subject entitled to our protection who had suffered a direct positive wrong from his own government, are we bound to indemnify him for a loss consequent upon the failure of his government to do her duty as to the conduct of her own subjects? Suppose it had been proposed at Geneva to hold the British government responsible for losses sustained by her own subjects because of failure to execute her own laws, would she not have promptly replied, "That is my own affair; I am fully competent to take care of my own subjects. Whilst you may hold me accountable for a direct injury done even to my own subjects while under your protection, you have no right to hold me accountable for a wrong done to myself or to my own subjects in a failure to execute my own municipal law."

So far as the proceedings at Geneva can throw any light on the subject, there is but one case mentioned by which we are enabled to judge as to how the claims of British subjects for damage done by the insurgent cruisers were regarded, and that case is very significant as far as it goes. We allude to the case of John Burns. This case on its first examination seems to have been summarily rejected, or rather refused consideration. John Burns was a British subject, resident in Manchester, England. His claim was on behalf of his son, who, it seems, had entered as a seaman on board the Lafayette, a United States ship captured by the rebel cruiser Alabama. Although it does not clearly appear, yet the presumption is that John Burns presented his claim as heir-at-law of his son. The record does not state whether the son had been naturalized in the United States or not. But the concise statement touching the status of the claimant, as given in the report of a British committee appointed by the British board of trade, is as follows: "As regards the claim by John Burns for his deceased son, Joseph Burns, it will be enough to observe in the first place that it is apparently advanced by a British subject." (Papers relating to the Treaty of Washington, vol. 3, page 316.)

To take the most liberal view of the case of British subjects sailing under our flag—as it is a matter of great doubt whether, in the cases alluded to, a British subject can be regarded in the same light as a foreigner of some other nation entitled to our protection "in the premises"—and as the only case reported of a British subject presenting a claim at Geneva would seem to militate against such construction; and as it is much safer for a court of limited jurisdiction to keep within the limit of its powers rather than to run the risk of exceeding them—

We therefore decide that while foreigners entitled to our protection in the premises, other than subjects of Great Britain, are entitled to participate in the distribution of this fund, and to sue in this court, we cannot see that British subjects are so entitled.

In cases Nos. 91, 92, 237, and 246 the demurrers are overruled, and in cases 118 and 233 the demurrers are sustained.

ANN ELIZA GANNETT, OF MASSACHUSETTS, administratrix of the estate of Abraham Osborn, deceased, *et al.*, *vs.* THE UNITED STATES. — No. 184.

1. All claims for damage caused by the so-called insurgent cruisers Alabama, Florida, and their tenders, and all claims for damage caused by the so-called insurgent cruiser Shenandoah, after her departure from Melbourne on the 18th day of February, A. D. 1865, must *directly result* from damage caused by said cruisers.
2. No claim for "*prospective profits*" can be admitted or allowed under the act of Congress of June 23, 1874, creating the Court of Commissioners of Alabama Claims.

The case is stated in the opinion of the court.

Messrs. Corwine and Manning for the complainant.

Mr. J A. J. Creswell for the respondents.

WELLS, presiding judge, delivered the opinion of the court:

Petition embracing alleged facts as follows:

To the honorable judges of the Court of Commissioners of Alabama Claims:

1st. Your petitioner, Ann Eliza Gannett, administratrix of the estate of Abraham Osborn, deceased, for herself and the other parties whose names are set forth in the caption and made part hereof, respectfully represents that said Abraham Osborn, together with said parties, was the owner of the whale-ship Splendid on the 11th day of August, 1862, which was fitted out and fully equipped at Edgartown, Dukes County, State of Massachusetts, to pursue the whale-fishing in the Atlantic Ocean for a voyage of thirty months, with a full complement of officers and crew; that said ship was owned at Edgartown; that she was driven out of said Atlantic Ocean by the rebel cruiser Alabama while engaged in pursuing her voyage and business on those fishing-grounds, and after obtaining supplies at the port of Saint Catherines she proceeded to the Arctic Ocean and the Anadir Sea; that while so engaged she was pursued by the rebel cruiser Alabama, with the purpose of capturing and destroying her, and was compelled to leave said fishing-ground, and then and there and thereafter prevented by said rebel cruiser from returning to said fishing-ground for a period of more than two months; that when so compelled to leave, the preparations which had been made at that time, and the work that had already been done, promised a most successful season's catch; that the unlawful act of the Alabama caused injury to the property and interests of petitioners, "directly resulting from damage caused by" said cruiser, in this, that it broke up the season's catch, destroyed the enterprise, and put an end to the voyage, to the great pecuniary damage and serious material injury of your petitioner, whereby the said owners lost their entire outfits, refits, and investment, except the ship itself, and that was greatly deteriorated in value, requiring large outlays to fit it for another season's voyage; that the master of said ship was compelled to escape with his said ship from the pursuit of said rebel cruiser, or otherwise have his said ship burned, as was the fact with many whalers at that time, being on the same cruising-ground.

And petitioner avers and states that it cost the owners of the Splendid, for the preparation of said voyage, for the outfit of said vessel, &c., the sum of $50,000.

That that season's catch, covering a period of about one year, broken up by this act of said rebel cruiser, was well worth, and would have realized the owners of said ship, the sum of $50,000; which loss wholly and directly resulted from the damage caused by said rebel cruiser, in manner and under the circumstances aforesaid.

* * * * * * *

To which the United States interposes a demurrer, as follows:

1. Because the said claim of said complainant is not admissible under the provisions of the law creating this court.

2. Because the said claim is not a claim directly resulting from damage caused by the so-called insurgent cruisers Alabama, Florida, and their tenders, or any of them, nor one directly resulting from damage caused by the so-called insurgent cruiser Shenandoah, after her departure from Melbourne on the 18th February, 1865.

3. Because the said claim is based upon unearned freights, gross freights, prospective profits, freights, gains, and advantages.

4. Because the Government of the United States is not bound to afford a convoy to every ship upon the high seas, and cannot be held responsible for unlawful acts perpetrated upon citizens of the United States by hostile and belligerent cruisers.

5. Because the said claim is not admissible under well-established principles of mercantile law.

Section 11 of the act of Congress, approved June 23, A. D. 1874, under which this court was organized, would seem to dispose of this case; in fact, two words of this section, if the exact meaning of the same could be clearly reached, would remove a difficulty which has involved lengthened discussion, and presented an amount of legal learning very interesting to the court and creditable to the gentlemen engaged in the case. The two words "directly resulting," occurring in the third line of section 11, in almost any other connection, would seem to have by themselves a significance that could not be misinterpreted; the words in their connection in this section of the law, it seems to the court, are not used loosely, as though Congress, in the hurry and confusion of its session about to close, had not been carefully critical in expressing the intent of the law-making power. Section 11 reads as follows: "That it shall be the duty of said court to receive and examine all claims admissible under this act that may be presented to it, *directly resulting* from damage caused by the so-called insurgent cruisers Alabama, Florida, and their tenders, and also all claims admissible under this act *directly resulting* from damage caused by the so-called insurgent cruiser Shenandoah," &c. Now, if Congress had intended such construction of this section as has been insisted upon by claimant in this case, why was the word "directly" used at all? The case of claimant might possibly have been covered by the language of this section if it had read, "That it shall be the duty of said court to receive and examine all claims admissible under this act that may be presented to it, *resulting* from damage caused," &c., leaving out the word "directly," for the term "resulting from" implies a direct or indirect result, a result of the hour, or a result after months or years, a result now and here, or a result hereafter; not so with the phrase "directly resulting;" this fairly implies an immediate consequence, a prompt following after an act now and here done and performed.

It is hardly possible for this court to fail to distinguish the difference in two cases, the one where a vessel is captured by one of these insurgent cruisers, the immediate announcement that she is a prize, her officers and men in irons transferred at once to the confederate vessel, the captured vessel in flames, and all this within an hour; the other case, a vessel driven from her fishing-ground, and a conclusion reached after a lapse of two months or more, which may be correct or incorrect, that her prospects or season's catch is broken up, that her voyage, intended for years, is at an end, except to return to her port of departure. In the one case, all is certainty, a "direct result;" the captured vessel in flames immediately after her surrender, and sure to be totally consumed, except so much of the same as may be beneath the ocean's surface; and in the other case, a something to occur in the future, and possibly to be qualified as to loss or no loss by the timidity or cowardice of a commanding officer, or the destruction of a vessel by fire, collision, or storm.

The construction placed by this court on the words "directly resulting" does not imply that we entertain the idea that Congress acted wisely or unwisely in the use of the word "directly" as it occurs in section 11; the court has nothing to do with the action of Congress in this respect; it is our duty to construe the law as we find it, and to give, as we may have the ability, a reasonable construction to every part of section 11, as it comes to our hands from the law-making power.

In giving an opinion as to the construction of section 11 and other portions of the act of June 23, A. D. 1874, the court has carefully examined the authorities cited from the Congressional Record, vol. 2, part 6; "The Treaty of Washington, by Cushing," pages 164, 165, and 166, and the various decisions of the courts affecting the construction of the act of June 23, 1874.

If the claimant in this case can substantiate what she alleges as fact in her petition, it may be a proper subject for congressional action in the future so to legislate as to bring such case within the purview of the law, and thus give to her and others the benefit of a portion of the fund which Great Britain, in the furtherance of justice, has paid the United States as compensation for an omitted national duty. Congressional legislation must give the relief, if any is to be had. This court is without the power, much as its sympathy might be enlisted for the claimant, to give her any relief.

In considering this case, as it is connected with section 11 of the law creating this court and defining its duties, we have not been unmindful of that provision of section 12 of the same law which prohibits the allowance of any claim based on "prospective profits," which prospective profits might be involved in the statement of claimant in her petition that the "season's catch," covering a period of about one year, broken up by the act of the rebel cruiser Alabama, was well worth, and would have realized the owners of said ship, the sum of $50,000.

In enacting this provision of the law, of course Congress had in view that part of the decision and award of the tribunal at Geneva which was cited by counsel, and reads as follows:

And whereas prospective earnings cannot properly be made the subject of compensation, inasmuch as they depend in their nature upon future and uncertain contingencies, * * * the tribunal is unanimously of opinion that there is no ground for awarding to the United States any sum by way of indemnity under this head.

Now, were there no uncertain contingencies connected with the "prospective" or expected catch of the whale-ship Splendid, "equipped to pursue the whale-fishing in the Atlantic Ocean for a voyage of thirty months"?

The dangers of the sea are topics of talk with a host of our legal brethren from the opening to the end of the year, and every year since our Government was founded. There is no end to the number of volumes on the subject of marine law, embodying elementary principles and adjudicated cases, abroad and in this country, a large proportion of which exhibit the uncertain contingencies connected with ocean-navigation.

Millions of capital are invested to guard against marine risks, and in every policy of insurance issued some of the perils of the sea are enumerated. God's providence and His wisdom can only protect against the dangers of the deep.

In view of all this, in view of the actual realities of life, we are led to the conclusion that there were many "uncertain contingencies" connected with the "season's catch" of the whale-ship Splendid, the season embracing a term, as stated in the petition, of not less than one year, and with the vessel fitted to pursue the whale-fishing for thirty months.

After full consideration of the arguments and authorities cited by counsel, the court sustains the demurrer filed in this case, and enters judgment for the respondents.

MOSES HYNEMAN
vs.
THE UNITED STATES. } No. 643.

The act creating the Court of Commissioners of Alabama Claims limits its jurisdiction to claims for losses directly resulting from damage caused by certain so-called insurgent cruisers.

The cost of an adjustment of general average on a ransom bond taken from the master of a vessel captured (but not destroyed) by the Alabama is not a loss directly resulting from damage caused by one of the said cruisers.

The case is stated in the opinion of the court.

Mr. Frank W. Hackett for the complainant.

Mr. J. A. J. Creswell for the respondents.

PORTER, J., delivered the opinion of the court:

In December, 1862, the complainant shipped from New York on the steamship Ariel certain merchandise destined to San Francisco. When the Ariel had prosecuted her voyage about as far south as Cuba she was pursued, fired upon, and stopped by the rebel cruiser Alabama. The commander of the Alabama evinced a strong desire to destroy the steamship, as he had done, and continued to do, so many other valuable vessels. But the Ariel had on board six hundred and sixty-seven passengers, including one hundred and forty United States marines and their officers, too many to be taken on board of the Alabama or to be sent adrift in small boats. Embarrassed by this circumstance he exacted from the master of the Ariel a ransom-bond, which purported to be executed by the master for himself, the owners of the ship, and of its cargo, and stipulated well and truly to pay the sum of $261,000 "unto the president of the Confederate States of America, his successor or successors in office, within thirty days after the conclusion of the present war between the said Confederate States and the United States." On the arrival of the goods at San Francisco the owners of the steamship line, regarding the case as one of general average, placed it in the charge of professional adjusters. The proceedings of the adjusters have not been very substantially proved in this court; but we assume the professional competency of the persons so employed, and the technical accuracy of their work. They apportioned the respective amounts which the vessel, the freight, and the cargo were liable to contribute if payment of the bond were finally exacted; and they also apportioned the expenses of the adjustment among these different interests. They fixed the sum which would be payable by Mr. Hyneman as his portion of the bond at $4,880.53, and his portion of the expenses of the adjustment at $78.73. He paid the last-mentioned sum in gold, and he claims to recover it from the money awarded to the United States at Geneva. Can we allow it? It is a case on which several cases are said to depend, and deserves the careful consideration which we have endeavored to give it.

It may be admitted that where a ship is seized and detained by a superior force, a sum of money paid to ransom her constitutes a case of general average. (Emerigon on Insurance, 485; 1 Parsons on Maritime Law, 299; Clarkson *vs.* Phœnix Ins. Co., 9 Johnson, 1; Girard *vs.* Ware, Peters's Circuit Court Reports, 142.)

In the present case no money was paid, but a bond was required, and we think the claimant justly entitled to the inference that if the master had refused to give the bond the ship and her cargo would have been destroyed. It is clear, also, that by long-established usage, as recognized by the best writers, (2 Phillips on Insurance, 100,) the charges of the adjuster or *despacheur* are to be borne proportionately by the owners of the property saved by the payment of a ransom. The peculiarity of this case is that payment of the bond was never demanded, and, as the facts show, never could have been enforced. It must be regarded now as an instrument utterly void in law. Can the claimant recover from this fund the sum which he was compelled to pay toward the expenses of an adjustment consequent on the giving of such a bond?

By the act of Congress of 23d June, 1874, our powers are thus limited: "It shall be the duty of said court to receive and examine all claims admissible under this act that may be presented to it directly resulting from damage caused by the so-called insurgent cruisers," &c. In the jurisprudence of most countries a distinction has been necessarily drawn between the proximate and remote causes of loss. In Livie *vs.* Janson, (12 East., 648,) Lord Ellenborough held that if a ship meet with sea-damage which checks her rate of sailing, so that she is taken by an enemy from whom she would otherwise have escaped, the loss is to be ascribed to the capture and not to the sea-damage. So, where a vessel was compelled by sea-damage to put into a foreign port for repairs, and the climate of the country rendered necessary the sale of a part of the cargo, a loss thus arising is not a consequence of the perils of the sea. (Goold *vs.* Shaw, 1 Johnson's Cases, 293.)

In Hillier *vs.* The Allegheny County Insurance Company, (3 Pa. State R., 470,) it was held that, where goods not touched by fire were removed under a reasonable apprehension that they would be consumed by a fire then raging in the immediate neighborhood, the injury sustained was not covered by a policy against the peril of fire. The books are full of such cases. They were well known to the eminent lawyers of each house of Congress who so long had this act in their charge. The losses cognizable in this court were therefore defined with severe precision. We are to consider and determine upon claims for losses arising not simply from the wrongful acts of the insurgent cruisers, nor merely growing out of the injuries really occasioned by such acts, but for losses directly resulting from damage caused by the said cruisers. An act of damage must be shown to have been committed, and the act must appear to be the direct, as distinguished from the remote cause of the loss. The loss from a probable or anticipated injury may have been greater in some cases than from a real act. The remote result of an act of damage may have been ruinous to the party suffering it. Upon the consideration of these cases we are expressly prevented from entering. In every case brought here two things must be shown to have concurred, namely, damage done by one or more of the insurgent cruisers, and a loss as its direct result. If either of these elements be wanting we are powerless to give a claimant any redress.

Has this claimant suffered any loss which is the direct result of damage caused by the Alabama? She did no damage whatever to the Ariel, or to her cargo, and did not exact from her the payment of a dollar of money. The apprehension on the part of the owners of the Ariel that they might at some time be required to pay led them to demand the money from the claimant, and he, to save the trouble of a contest over it, paid the sum required. If he has lost by the transaction he has been unfortunate; but it is plain to us that his loss is not one directly resulting from damage caused by the Alabama, as these terms are employed in the act of Congress, whence our powers are derived.

Judgment for the United States.

IN RE THE SHIPS JAMES MAURY, GENERAL Pike, Milo, and the bark Nile.

Where a vessel, captured and bonded in the Arctic Ocean, is obliged to convey to a port of refuge the crews of other vessels captured and burned, a sum is to be awarded to the owners as compensation for property and expenses incurred. Also a sum in lieu of catch in the enjoyment of which the ship's company shall have part, which sum shall include compensation for provisions consumed for the enforced use of the vessel, the compulsory service of officers and crew, and shall embrace the consideration that the vessels were left thirty days' sail at least from the point of departure, to which point they had a right to claim to be returned.

A statement of the case will be found in the opinion of the court.

——— ——— for the complainants.

Creswell & Hackett for the respondent.

JEWELL, Judge, delivered the opinion of the court:

These are all cases of whaling-vessels captured near the close of the month of June, 1865, in the Arctic Ocean, by the confederate cruiser

Shenandoah. None of them were destroyed, nor does it appear that any property was taken from them by the cruiser, but that they were severally spared from the destruction which befell a large number of whalers at that time, and bonded by the cruiser, and ordered to take on board and carry to San Francisco or to Honolulu the officers and crews of the several vessels which had been burned.

The James Maury was captured June 28, 1865, a prize crew put on board of her, the master and mate ordered on board the Shenandoah, where they were detained until the master had executed a bond to the Confederate States for the assumed value of his vessel, and until the cruiser had placed on board of her the crews of eleven of the burned ships. Then the master was returned to his vessel with a safe-conduct from the commander of the cruiser, saving him from capture by any confederate vessel on his passage to Honolulu, to which port he was directed to proceed and there land the men so placed on board.

At the same time a large number of men were placed on board the bark Nile, which, being fitted out for only one season, had not sufficient provisions for the increased number of persons, and a portion of the provisions from the Maury was transferred to the Nile for use on her passage to Honolulu with the men so placed on board. The value of these provisions is shown to have been $1,205.90.

The James Maury, with 150 men on board, was restored to her master, if that can be called restoration, June 30, 1865, and, according to the orders of the commander of the cruiser, the master made sail for Honolulu, where he arrived in safety on the 11th day of August, after a passage of 42 days, or in 44 days after his capture.

At the time of the capture of the Maury she was actively engaged in the whale-fishery, and had already taken some whales, and had all her supplies and materials on board for that purpose. On receiving this large number of men, who were in such excess over his own crew, the master was obliged to make such provision for their shelter and comfort as he could, or as humanity or their demands required. At that season, in that climate, it was necessary to furnish them a sleeping-place between decks, and all the whaling apparatus and extra rigging, and other similar articles found in the way between decks were thrown overboard; the lumber found there used for the fitting up of berths for the men, the spare sails and duck cut up for bedding, and generally such use made of everything on board as the necessities of the men required. Much property was lost, destroyed, or appropriated to the use of the men, with or without the consent of the master of the Maury, whose consent to the use of any article found on board which might subserve the comfort of his enforced passengers would not, probably, have been asked. In fact, all on board had been prisoners, and whatever was spared, whether ship or stores, was spared for the common use of all so far as was needful to the safe arrival at Honolulu. Some question was made by the counsel for the Government whether the destruction of property on the passage was not consented to by the master of the Maury, and so its value could not be claimed here; but we must consider it is one of the necessary, in fact an inevitable, result of the condition of things. Indeed, nothing is more creditable to the character of the officers and men in all these vessels than the fact that there has not been shown in any case the least wanton destruction of property, or the least insubordination on the part of any man at any time. In every case the men placed on board were at least five times the number of the officers and crew of the ship on which they were placed, and at any time they could, if they pleased, have taken the vessel under their control. The Maury arrived at Honolulu August 11, was immediately refitted, and in the very short period of seventeen days was again at sea in pursuit of her calling. But at this late date, August 28, she could not hope to reach the Arctic Ocean, from which she came, until so late a period that the season, which closed about October 1 or a little later, would be past. She therefore sailed for the winter cruising-ground.

The facts in regard to the other vessels are substantially the same, except that they were ordered to San Francisco.

The General Pike had 222 men placed on board of her, so that with her own crew she had for a time on board 252 men. Of these, urged by considerations of humanity alone, Captain Weeks, of the bark Richmond, took 52, and carried them to the Sandwich Islands, thereby incurring for himself and owners a loss from the abandonment of his season's employment for which this court has already expressed a regret that it could, under the circumstances, make no compensation.

She arrived in San Francisco August 1, after a voyage of about 32 days. Here, all the crew, being advised by counsel that they could not be longer held, left the ship, as did all the officers, and she remained in San Francisco till her owners sent out a master to take charge of her and ship a new crew. But if the same dispatch had been used in this case as in the case of the Maury at Honolulu, or of the Milo, which went to San Francisco, the time of sailing would have been too late to proceed again to the Arctic Ocean.

In this case, as in the case of the Maury, there was a considerable destruction of property by throwing it overboard and in fitting up bunks for the men.

The Milo was captured June 22, and bonded, as in the case of the Maury, and 160 men of the crews of the whalers previously captured put on board of her, making, with her own officers and crew, 194 men on board. The master informed the captain of the cruiser that he had not sufficient provisions to make the voyage to San Francisco with so many men in safety, and he was directed to take, and did take, a quantity of provisions from a vessel just captured, and not yet burned.

He sailed for San Francisco June 23, where he arrived July 20, in safety.

The narrative of the facts of the capture of the Milo, given by the master, Capt. Jonathan C. Hawes, is as follows:

18th int. Please now describe the circumstances of your capture?

Ans. About 11 o'clock on the 22d of June, 1865, I saw a steamer approaching; I was boiling at the time. Supposing her to be a Russian telegraph vessel, with later news from San Francisco, I set my colors, and awaited his approach, hoping to get further news in regard to the assassination of Mr. Lincoln, whose death I had heard of the night before. He hailed my ship and ordered me on board. I asked him what ship it was. He said, "Never mind what ship it is; come on board and bring your papers, and bear a hand about it." I went on board; was met at the gangway by an officer in uniform, who ordered me to the captain's cabin. I was then told by the captain that I was on board the confederate steamer Shenandoah, and that I and my vessel were prisoners. He put me under oath to state the value of the vessel. The value of the vessel and the oil on board was finally fixed at $46,000 in gold. He told me I must take 100 men that he had on board, and that if I would, and sign a bond, he would release my ship; otherwise he would burn her. I asked him what I should do with 100 men; he said he did not care what I did with the men, but would give an order and permit to take them to San Francisco. In order to save my vessel I then signed the bond, and he ordered me to get the 100 men out quick. I found that he had on board the officers and crews of the Euphrates, Abigail, and Wm. Thompson, all of New Bedford, which ships he had already captured and burned. I then went on board my ship and ordered my crew to go on board of him for the hundred men, and he proceeded to capture the Sophia Thornton, of New Bedford, which ship was about one-fourth mile off; after putting a prize-crew on board of her, he ordered me to lay alongside of the

Sophia Thornton, under the penalty of being blown out of water, while he went in persuit of another ship, the Jireh Swift, of New Bedford, which he captured and set on fire; he then came alongside of my ship, called me on board, told me he had two more ship's crews that he was going to put on board, to which I protested on the grounds of humanity, and I also said I had not provisions enough. He told me that he was going to put the other two crews on board, and that I must take what provisions I deemed necessary to get the men to San Francisco out of the Sophia Thornton, and that he would lay alongside of me until I did. He brought his guns to bear on me, and I went to work getting provisions out of the Sophia Thornton. While taking provisions, he went and captured and set on fire the Susan and Abigail, of San Francisco. Supposing he was coming to put another crew on board, we set sail and left, thinking it the most prudent to do so, when he sailed to the northeast, and I headed for San Francisco. This was the last I saw of him.

19th int. What flag was the Shenandoah flying?

Ans. The Russian flag.

20th int. What happened after you last saw the Shenandoah?

Ans. I gave orders to clear the ship for the reception of the men I had been compelled to take on board. We had 194 men, all told; 12 of these left at night to inform the fleet north of us of the presence of the Shenandoah. The first thing to do was to get a place for them to sleep. This we did by heaving overboard cask, 500 bbls., 30 bbls. of blubber, wood, &c., and everything that was in the way for that purpose. We used our lumber, nails, spikes, and canvas, and some sails; one suit of sails to make berths for the men, and then they could not all sleep at one time. We made our way to San Francisco as best we could, and arrived there in 28 days, without much sickness.

21st int. Under whose command was the ship on the voyage to San Francisco?

Ans. Nominally mine; but of course I had no liberty to go anywhere else.

22d int. What was the contents of the permit you received from the captain of the Shenandoah?

Ans. The Milo was bonded, and was ordered to San Francisco by Captain Waddell, and was not liable to seizure from Confederate cruisers while on that course.

23d int. Have you that permit now, or a copy of it?

Ans. I have not.

24th int. On your arrival at San Francisco what happened?

Ans. My crew left, and most of my officers, and my passengers, immediately.

25th int. In what state was the Milo left?

Ans. In very bad condition, except as to seaworthiness. The provisions were pretty well eaten up. The ship was well cleaned out every way, and very dirty. The slops, tobacco, and all small stores were all cleaned out.

26th int. What did you next do?

Ans. I entered a protest first; and then, as I could get no telegraph home, I had to determine for myself what I would do. I concluded to refit, and I raised money on the oil and by drafts on the owner, and refitted for a cruise of six or seven months down to the islands. I shipped a new crew and officers, with a few exceptions. I tried to retain my old crew, but I found I could not do so, as they claimed the voyage was broken up.

27th int. Why did you not return to the whaling-grounds in the Arctic?

Ans. I deemed it too late to get back for a season there, so I cruised along the coast and down to the islands.

28th int. When did you get away from San Francisco?

Ans. Near the middle of August, 1865.

29th int. When does the season in the Arctic usually terminate?

Ans. The 1st of October.

35th int. If you had not been captured in the Arctic, what voyage would you have made in the usual course of whaling down to the 1st of April, 1866?

(Objected to.)

Ans. I should have staid in the Arctic till October 1, and then gone to the Sandwich Islands or San Francisco to refit. If I had gone to San Francisco I should have cruised down the coast after refitting, and reached the Sandwich Islands about April 1, 1866, as I did. If I had gone from the Arctic to the Sandwich Islands, I should have refitted, then gone over on to the coast between seasons, and then back to the Sandwich Islands, arriving April 1, 1866. The between-season whaling-ground was the same, except that I had about six weeks more on the coast than I should have had if my season north had not been broken up.

The spoliation of papers and the safe-conduct given by the commander of the cruiser is shown in the case of the *General Pike*.

Deposition of Hebron M. Crowell. Copy of permit produced by Hebron M. Crowell in answer to the 12th direct interrogatory.

THOMAS J. COBB, *Commissioner*.

This is to certify that register of the bark General Pike was this day retained by the C. S. steamer Shenandoah; said bark General Pike having been released under a ransom-bond of forty-five thousand dollars.

J. I. WADDELL,
Lt. Comdg. C. S. N. C. S. steamer Shenandoah.

JUNE 26, 1865.

This is to protect Master Crowell of the bark General Pike from capture, on his way to San Francisco, Cal.

J. I. WADDELL,
Lieutenant Commanding, C. S. N.

26th JUNE, 1865.

The Nile was captured June 28, and bonded in a similar manner. No one of her officers or crew was found to be examined, but the testimony of one of the masters who was put on board of her shows that her case was substantially like the others:

His narrative is as follows:

Q. 4. What do you know of the capture of the bark Nile, of New London, by the Shenandoah?

A. I know she was captured the same day we were, and under the same circumstances.

Q. 5. What became of the Nile after her capture?

A. The captain was ordered aboard of the Shenandoah; they told him they were going to burn his ship, but afterward they bonded her.

Q. 6. Do you know the reason why she was bonded?

A. For the reason there were so many of the officers and crew of the captured vessels had been put aboard of the James Maury, which had been captured, that we sent a master on board the Shenandoah and asked them to give us another ship, as there was not sufficient room on the James Maury for us to go to port. The captain of the Shenandoah then bonded the Nile and a lot of us went on board of her.

Q. 7. What number of men went on board the Nile?

A. My memory is that there was about 170, all told.

Q. 8. What became of the Nile and her crew and passengers?

A. We made the best of our way to San Francisco. There was nothing else for us to do; we had to go either to there or to the Sandwich Islands.

Q. 9. Who had command of the vessel?

A. Asa W. Fish, the captain of the Nile, but he had to go to port. There was nothing else possible for him to do under the circumstances with all these men on board. We could not have taken a whale and got in the oil if we had had one alongside, there were so many persons on board. It was a matter of necessity for us to get to port as soon as possible.

Q. 10. What happened on the voyage to San Francisco?

A. Nothing particular, except that we made sail there as fast as we could.

Q. 11. On what did the officers and men live on their way down to San Francisco?

A. We lived on the stores of the Nile, whatever they had.

Q. 12. Where did you sleep?

A. Between decks and everywhere all over the ship, wherever they could get a chance to lie down.

Q. 13. How long were you in the vessel going down to San Francisco?

A. I don't recollect exactly, but I think it was about five weeks.

Q. 14. What, if any, damage do you remember was done to the ship Nile, her stores, and outfits?

A. I don't remember whether we threw anything overboard or not. We must have done considerable damage; we made room for ourselves, and made beds of sails or anything we could get. Many things might have been thrown overboard while I was below.

The Nile brought 121 captured officers and men, and arrived at San Francisco after a passage of thirty-five days. Her master, Captain Fish, left her in charge of the mate and came home overland, and rejoined her in the spring of 1866 in Honolulu. The vessel was taken in ballast by the mate to Honolulu, where she was refitted, and made a winter cruise in the winter of 1865–'66.

Such are the general outlines of these cases.

Certain items of loss are the same in kind in all, differing in amount. These are the property on board which was destroyed or consumed on the passage, and the expenses necessarily incurred by reason of going into port in San Francisco and Honolulu, respectively.

These items in the case of the James Maury are as follows:

Provisions taken from her to the Nile, in value	$1,205 90
Property thrown overboard or destroyed, in value	2,597 28
Provisions consumed on passage, in value	4,681 95
Provisions destroyed or wasted	762 50
	9,247 63
Expenses incurred or made necessary by the compulsory voyage (in Honolulu)	1,076 22
The owners also claimed for the amount of the advances made to the crew, which were claimed to be substantially lost, as the crew deserted at Honolulu, amounting to	1,581 68
Also, for new advances made at Honolulu, where a new crew was shipped, in all	413 80
They also proved that in shipping a new crew they were obliged to give them a larger lay than had been given to the old crew, the expense of which increase they estimated at the sum of	3,500 00
	5,495 48

These items of claim are here stated as being matters of damage, in which the crew of the vessel had no interest. The loss of them, if any, fell upon the owners alone.

The other element of damage for which claim is made is one in which the crew as such (the whole *equipage*, as the ship's company is called in the French law, including officers and men) have a part.

The shipping-articles of a whaling-vessel bind the ship to the men as much as the men to the ship. The men do not have wages; their compensation is given them in their *lay*, or aliquot part of the catch, and the owners cannot lawfully divert the vessel from the stipulated business. So, if the vessel is diverted from her ordinary business to engage in a salvage service, the whole ship's company have an equitable proportional claim upon or interest in the amount received or awarded as compensation.

In like manner, if the vessel is taken forcible possession of, and compelled to perform a service entirely different from that in which she is engaged, as in these cases, and especially when the whole ship's crew must share in the labor and peril thereby imposed, they must have an interest in the compensation awarded for such service and duty. The amount so received must be put in the place of the fund out of which their lay would have been drawn, as they receive no wages as such.

The principal question in all these cases is, what compensation shall be allowed to the owners and crews for this enforced employment of their vessels, respectively, and for this compulsory labor and peril of the men.

The claimants ask for it under the name of *demurrage*.

Demurrage, in its strict use, is the term employed in contracts of affreightment, to fix the sum to be paid for detaining a vessel in port beyond the stipulated lay-days.

It is, however, employed in a less literal sense in admiralty courts to designate the damages to be paid for the loss of and use of a vessel by the owner in case of unlawful capture or destruction, when the circumstances are such as to lead the court to award costs and damages against the captor.

In these cases, damages are assessed at so much per day for the detention or delay.

The term demurrage was used to designate this kind of loss or damage in some of the papers laid before the Geneva tribunal.

We do not, however, arrive at the result we reach by fixing the value of the daily employment of these vessels.

It was admitted by the counsel for the Government that this enforced employment of these vessels and their crews was a subject of direct loss or damage, but it was claimed that the amount to be awarded was not to be made in any way dependent upon, or to be measured by, the value of the service in which they were engaged; that the fact of their being in the Arctic Ocean, upon the whaling-ground, engaged in what was generally a most lucrative employment, the fact that they thereby lost an entire season's business, should not be taken into the account in fixing the amount of this direct damage or loss.

Evidence was offered tending to show that a fair price for the passage of men from the Aleutian Islands to San Francisco was about $85 per man, and it was claimed that this would be a fair compensation for the damage caused by this enforced service.

With this view we cannot agree.

We had occasion to consider this question in the case of the Baron de Castine.

That was a small vessel, worth from $5,800 to $8,000, engaged in the trade between Maine and Cardenas and New York. On the voyage in question she was under charter to carry a cargo of lumber from Maine to Cardenas, and bring thence to New York a cargo of sugar, for the round sum of $2,250, with demurrage at $35 per day.

When she had made about one third her voyage to Cardenas she was captured and bonded, and forty-four men put aboard of her; and she was ordered to land the men not south of New York. She did go into Boston after about a five-days' voyage, where she staid about seventeen days to get some repairs, when she sailed again to fulfill her charter. Her master thought she arrived at or near the point where she was captured within thirty days from the day of capture.

The demurrage fixed in her charter for thirty days' detention would amount to $1,050, and we were urged by the counsel for the Government to award no more than that sum.

But this demurrage was the compensation fixed between the parties for delay in port. This vessel had been forcibly turned from her course in mid-ocean. She had been compelled to perform an entirely different voyage, to encounter entirely new perils, and the court did not think the value of this compulsory service should be measured by the demurrage fixed in the charter, and awarded as damages the sum of $2,000.

What are the general facts in regard to this branch of the claim?

These vessels were all fitted out in New Bedford or New London at a large expense, and then sent to the Pacific Ocean, to cruise for whales in the Arctic Ocean during the summer, from 1st of June to the 1st of October, and to return to Honolulu between seasons to refit and ship home oil, and then make a cruise in the winter season on the western coast of North America.

During the last days of June, while engaged in their business, nearly all having already taken one or more whales, and one while engaged in cutting in a whale, they were captured. All the captured vessels except the four in question were burned, and in nearly every case of such destruction we have found quite a large quantity of oil and bone on board, the result of their labor up to the time of capture. While engaged in this very lucrative employment these vessels were captured and compelled to abandon their employment, and go to a port nearly three thousand miles away, and so distant that using all required diligence they could not return to the Arctic Ocean till the season was just closing or already closed.

What shall be held to be the rule of damage in these cases? What shall be given as compensation for this service and loss? That it was a direct damage—a loss directly incurred—is not and cannot be denied.

Here the property was taken from the possession of the owners, was forced into a service not contemplated by them, exposing their large ventures to new and unknown risks, and forcibly depriving them of its use in an employment for which it had been specially, and at great expense, prepared, and surrendered to the owners again at a point thirty or forty days' sail from the point of capture.

In the schooner Lively, (1 Gallison, 315,) damage in the nature of demurrage was allowed against the captors who had made an unlawful seizure.

Story, J., says: "I shall allow demurrage, including therein wages and expenses of the ship, from *the time of capture until she could return to the place of capture.*"

The English admiralty reports are full of cases in which vessels have been unlawfully captured or unlawfully detained after capture, and under circumstances which led the courts not only to discharge the vessels, but to award the owners costs and damages for such unlawful detention. In all these cases the measure of damages had regard to the character and employment of the ship, and has been measured by the time of the detention.

In the Corrier Maritimo (1 C. Rob., 287,) damages in the nature of demurrage were allowed for a period longer than the time of detention, and must have included a period enabling the vessel to return to the place of capture, as was allowed in the case of the schooner Lively.

In cases of collision, the courts of England always, (see the Gazelle, 2, W. Rob., 279,) and the courts of this country since the case of Williamson *vs.* Barrett, (13 How., 101,) have allowed damages in the nature of demurrage, and generally under the name of demurrage, as compensation for the loss of the use of a vessel during the period of necessary repairs.

The courts have always held to a considerable strictness of proof in such cases that but for the injury the vessel would have had employment, and as to the value of such employment.

We do not, however, consider these claims as within the doctrine of either of these two classes of cases.

In them, damages were given for a detention during a period of entire inactivity.

These vessels were not inactive; on the contrary, they were in the highest degree employed, forcibly taken from their ordinary avocations, one of them while in the act of cutting in a whale, and compelled to engage in a duty and to perform a service which, when performed, would leave them thirty or forty days' sail from the place whence they had departed.

What shall be the sum awarded for this service, for compulsory service is a damage or loss as direct as the loss of property?

It has been strenuously urged by the counsel of the United States that the fact that these vessels were engaged in a lucrative business should not, under the terms of the act giving us jurisdiction of these claims, be taken into consideration; that an inquiry into the employment of the vessels necessarily involved a consideration of prospective gains or profits, which we are forbidden to allow. But we are to give some damages, some compensation, for service rendered. In any case we must consider the character, situation, and employment of the vessel. The element of value and employment cannot but enter into the calculation as really as the question of time. What would be ample compensation to one vessel would be entirely inadequate to another.

What was intended by prospective catch, prospective gains and profits, as connected with this class of cases, is somewhat shown by the character of the claims filed before the Geneva tribunal as well as before this court. In all the cases of whalers destroyed, the owners claimed not only the value of their vessels and outfits, but for the season's catch which was lost. So vessels driven from the fishing-grounds by the presence of the cruisers presented claims for catch lost, or for prospective profits, gains, and advantages.

Acting upon the view of the counsel for the United States, the experts called by the Government have estimated the value of the service rendered by showing what is a fair and usual compensation paid for transporting passengers from the Aleutian Islands to San Francisco; and the counsel for the Government claims that a fixed sum per man transported should be awarded, using the price of passage above referred to as a basis of computation.

But with the exception of the consumption of provisions, the injury to the claimants caused by this enforced service in no way depended upon the number of men carried. One hundred men, as much as two hundred, took the vessel from its employment; indeed, fifty-two taken by Captain Weeks in the Richmond cost him his entire summer's employment as much and as truly as one hundred and fifty-one on the James Maury.

We think a sum should be awarded in each case to the owners as such simply, which sum will compensate them for the property destroyed and expenses incurred, the elements for fixing which we have already indicated in the case of the James Maury.

We think there should also be awarded to the owners, jointly, a sum to be received by them in lieu of catch, and in the enjoyment of which the ship's company shall have part, in the same manner as if the sum was the proceeds of oil and bone, which sum shall include compensation for the provisions consumed by the crew of the vessel in making the voyage, and for the enforced use of the vessel during the voyage, and the compulsory service of the officers and crew, and shall also embrace the considerations that the vessels were left at a point thirty days' sail, at least, from their point of departure, to which point they had a right to claim to be returned, or to receive compensation for the failure so to be.

Acting upon the principles and governed by the considerations before stated, we shall enter judgments in these several cases.

In the case of the James Maury, we award to the owners alone for the loss and destruction of their property the sum of $10,324.25, which sum will be divided among them according to their respective interests in the vessel and outfits, the court having deducted the amounts severally received by the several parties from insurance in entering the judgments in their favor.

And we award to all the owners, jointly, as compensation for the damage for the use of the vessel and for the compulsory service of the officers and crew, the sum of $16,925, which sum is to be received by the owners, and the same, with interest thereon at four per cent. per annum from the date of capture, is to be held by them as and for and in lieu of catch of said vessel, and such sum, with such interest, is to be distributed among the said owners and the officers and crew of said vessel in their due proportions, and in accordance with their several and respective interests in the catch of said vessel.

In the case of the General Pike, we award to the owners alone for the loss and destruction of their property, and to be divided among them according to their respective interests in the vessel and outfits, the sum of $8,921.66.

And to the owners jointly, for the use of the vessel and the compulsory service of the officers and crew, to be received by the owners in lieu of catch, the sum of $18,730.

In the case of the Milo, we award to the owners alone the sum of $9,157.84, and to the owners jointly for the use of the vessel and the compulsory service of the officers and crew, to be received by the owners in lieu of catch, the sum of $16,585.

In the case of the Nile, we award to the owners alone the sum of $8,250.65, and to the owners jointly for the use of the vessel and the compulsory service of the officers and crew, to be received by the owners in lieu of catch, the sum of $14,375.

There were several claims presented at the same time when these cases were heard, made by officers or men of these vessels, asking for compensation for loss of catch or of wages after capture.

All these claims are embraced within the equity of the judgment to be made in these cases, and each of these men will receive out of the judgments herein made, in lieu of catch, all the compensation which we believe under the law we can award them. As to loss of wages after the arrival of the vessels at Honolulu or San Francisco, it need only be said that they voluntarily abandoned the enterprise, choosing to consider the voyage ended, when they might have, if they had so chosen, remained by these ships and continued their respective voyages. These claims will therefore be dismissed.

WILLIAM PHILLIPS ET AL.
vs.
THE UNITED STATES.
} No. 1228.

In re BARK RICHMOND.

The court has no authority to make compensation for damages occasioned by taking the crews of vessels destroyed by one of the so-called insurgent cruisers from a vessel captured and bonded, and carrying them to a place of safety; the vessel for which compensation is claimed never having been captured.

The damage under these circumstances is too remote.

A statement of the case will be found in the opinion of the court.

Mr. William W. Crapo for the complainants.

Mr. J. A. J. Creswell for the respondent.

JEWELL, J., delivered the opinion of the court:

This is a claim made by the owners of the bark Richmond for compensation for the use of the said vessel, and damage for consequent loss of the catch of the same.

It appears that the bark Richmond was, in the month of June, 1865, in the Northern Pacific Ocean, near Behring's Straits, pursuing the whaling business. The confederate cruiser Shenandoah had captured a large number of whalers, and among them the bark General Pike

The others had been burned and the General Pike spared, and the officers and crews of the other vessels, to the number of 252, placed on board of her for conveyance to the nearest port, or to any port which they might be able to reach. The last of these captures was on the 28th day of June.

On the 1st day of July the master of the Richmond felt himself compelled to take on board his own vessel a portion of the officers and men from the General Pike under circumstances fully detailed by him in a "statement" annexed to the petition, which is as follows. We also add the statement of the masters, made at the request of Captain Weeks:

Statement of the master of the Richmond.

We left Honolulu in the bark Richmond, bound on a whaling-cruise to the Arctic Ocean. While in the prosecution of such, on our arrival in the vicinity of Behring Straits, we came up with a whale-ship on fire. Not knowing the cause of it, I began to save such articles as I could from the wreck, as she had drifted into the ice, and her mast falling over the side, I found I could save many articles valuable to the use of my own bark, and as the wind was against me, I was not losing much time by so doing. While doing this a ship came to me with all sail set, steering to the southward, hailing me as he passed by, telling me there was a pirate close at hand, at the same time advising me to flee, as he was doing, for probably all that remained would be destroyed. But on due consideration I determined not to leave, for I would as quick lose the ship as go without oil. I came to the conclusion I would await a southerly storm or foggy spell usual at such times of the year, and take advantage of the opportunity and get through the straits in spite of the Shenandoah, as it proved to be. My experience in those waters would enable me to do this. While waiting for a favorable opportunity to do this we raised a sail in the north coming toward us. A few hours after the wind died away and a boat was lowered from her and came in pursuit of us. Coming alongside I was surprised to see so many faces of shipmasters. They had been taken by the Shenandoah and put on board the General Pike. They stated they were crowded and suffering from want of room, &c. They all joined in begging me for the sake of humanity to relieve them. I went on board of the General Pike to see for myself, and found they had not misrepresented the matter. I next returned to my own vessel, consulted with my officers, and came to the conclusion we ought to relieve them. I then told the shipmasters and prisoners that if they still insisted on my taking a portion of them, and would give me the same in writing, with their signatures, which was agreed to and signed by all the shipmasters, I dare not do otherwise. Under such conditions I had to submit. They put on board of me 52 men; with those I sailed for Honolulu, and thereby losing my season.

W. P. WEEKS,
Master.

Statement of the masters.

AT SEA, *July* 1, 1865.

We, the undersigned, do solemnly swear that our ships were burned by the pirate Shenandoah, and we were placed with our crews on board of bark General Pike, 252 men, all told; and being afraid of sickness, on account of the crowded state of the ship, we requested Captain Weeks, of bark Richmond, to take some of our men, which he kindly consented to do out of humanity's sake.

O. G. ROBINSON, *Captain bark Gypsey.*
HUDSON WINSLOW, *Captain bark Isabella.*
WILLIAM H. PHILLIPS, *bark Catharine.*
F. S. REDFIELD, *brig Susan Abagail.*
JAMES M. CLARK, *bark Nimrod.*
P. H. COOLEY, *bark Wm. C. Nye.*
WILLIAM BENJAMIN, *ship Gen. Williams.*
HEBRON M. CROWELL, *bark General Pike.*

The conduct of the master of the Richmond, as shown in this statement, in refusing to flee from the Shenandoah, saying he would "as quick lose the ship as to go without oil," supporting his declaration by his action in remaining, and in finally yielding to considerations of humanity what he would not yield to fear, is worthy of the highest praise.

His desire of making a cargo of oil was greater than his fear of capture by the Shenandoah. What fear could not constrain him to do, feelings of humanity did.

After a careful examination of the necessities he voluntarily abandoned his own adventure to save the lives of the officers and men put in peril upon the overcrowded General Pike.

Nothing more honorable or praiseworthy has been shown in all our hearings. Can this court make compensation for the loss thereby incurred?

We are compelled to say that under no view of the act of Congress creating this court can we find authority so to do. The claims admissible before us must be such as directly result from damage caused by the so-called insurgent cruisers.

In two cases heretofore considered by us, where vessels were captured by the Alabama and the crews of other vessels put on board for transportation to a port of discharge, we have awarded compensation for such compulsory service. But both those vessels had been actually captured. Here there was no capture.

The petition must be dismissed.

HENRY W. HUBBELL *vs.* THE UNITED STATES. } No. 278.

CHAS. A. SHERMAN ET AL. *vs.* THE UNITED STATES. } No. 279.

EDW'D H. GILLILAN *vs.* THE UNITED STATES. } No. 1131.

The measure of damage for goods destroyed by the confederate cruisers is the value of the goods at the place and time of shipment, with charges, and marine insurance actually paid, with interest on the aggregate so produced from the time of shipment till the date of destruction, at six per cent.

The measure of damage for loss of freight in cases when freight has begun to be earned is the net freight, which is to be found by deducting from the gross freight the expenses of completing the voyage, and of discharging the cargo at the port of destination, including all inward port charges and disbursements, with a further deduction of a proper sum for the depreciation of the vessel while performing the remainder of her voyage, and of interest on the valuation of the vessel from the date of her destruction to the time of her probable arrival if the voyage had not been interrupted.

In fixing the value of goods purchased with coin or currency other than the legal-tender currency of the United States, the value of coin in currency at the date of purchase will be taken, when payment was actually made in coin at that time; where payment was actually so made at a subsequent time, the value of coin at that time will be taken, if the payment was made according to the usual course of trade. If not made according to the usual course of trade, the value of coin will be computed at the lowest rate, whether at the time of purchase or at the time when payment would have been made in the usual course of business, or when the payment was actually made.

STATEMENT OF THE CASE.

Henry W. Hubbell and Robert L. Taylor were the owners of $\frac{7}{24}$ths each of the ship Winged Racer, her outfits and freight—and each owned one undivided half part of the cargo. Edward H. Gillilan owned $\frac{7}{24}$ths of the vessel, outfits, and freight.

In October, 1867, Taylor failed in business and made a general assignment for the benefit of creditors to the claimants Sherman & Irvin and one John R. Gardner, since deceased.

The Winged Racer, on the 8th October, 1863, sailed from Manila for New York, and on the 16th November she, with her cargo, was destroyed by the Alabama, near the coast of Sumatra, in the Java Sea. The value of the vessel was claimed at $60,000. Her cargo consisted of 5,810 bales of Manila hemp, 9,607 bags of Manila sugars, 100 bales Manila hide-cuttings, 100 boxes China camphor. Its value was claimed. Indemnity was also claimed for loss of freight, stores, outfits, port-dues, &c.

Mr. Wm. Peet for the complainants Hubbell and Gillilan:

1. Under the act this question is to be determined—

a. According to the principles of law.

b. By the provisions of the act.

c. By the merits of each case.

2. The principles of law applicable to the question are—

a. Damages are more liberally awarded in cases "*ex delicto*" than in those "*ex contractu.*" (Sedgwick on Dam., pp. 79, 563, n. (1); Addison on Torts, (3 ed.,) 984; Shearman & R. on Negligence, sec. 894; Sharper *v.* Brice, 2 W. Bl., 942; Heard *v.* Holman, 19 C. B., N. S. 1.)

b. Future profits are often expressly allowed, and if the amount of the damage sustained cannot be accurately determined, the wrong-doer must bear the burden of such difficulty, and in cases of doubt pay enough to insure full compensation. (Shearman and R. on Neg., sec. 395; Leeds *v.* Amherst, 20 Bea., 239; Williamson *v.* Barrett, 13 How., 101; The Rhode Island, 2 Blatch., 113; The Narragansett, Olcott, 388; The Lake, 2 Wall. jr., p. 52.)

c. Profits directly resulting from a wrong are often awarded as an element of damage when not remote, and not dependent upon some future event so as to be uncertain or contingent. (Shearman & Red. on Neg., sec. 599; Walker *v.* Post, 6 Duer, 363–373; Griffin *v.* Colver, 16 N. Y., 489; St. John *v.* N. Y., 6 Duer, 315; Lacour *v.* N. Y., 3 Duer, 406; Sewall's Fall Bridge *v.* Fish, 3 Foster, 171; Shelbyville R. Co. *v.* Sewark, 3 Ind., 471; New Haven, &c., *v.* Vanderbilt, 16 Conn., 420.)

3. The claim now made is not excluded by any provision of the act.

4. The measure of damages in accordance with these principles—

a. For the loss of the ship is her value at the outset of her voyage. (Arnauld on Insurance, 315; Stevens on Average, 190; Snell *v.* Delaware Insurance Co., 4 Dall., 430.)

b. For loss of freight is the amount of freight which would have been earned but for the capture. (The Gazelle, 2 W. Rob., 229; Williamson *v.* Barrett, 13 How., 101; The Ann Caroline, 2 Wall., 536; Ralston *v.* The State Rights, Crabbe, 22; The Rebecca, Blatch. & H., 347; The New Jersey, Olcott, 444; Abbott on Shipping, pp. 601, 527, quoting the Copenhagen, 1 Rob. Ad., 28: The Der Mohr, 4 Rob. Ad., 314; The Prosper, Edw. Ad., 72–'6; The Fortuna, Edw. Ad., 56, 57; The Lively, 1 Gall., 315; The Narragansett, 1 Blatch., 211.)

c. The loss of outfit is the cost of the outfit at the outset of the voyage. If full freight is allowed, the measure of damages will be the value of the outfit on board at the time of destruction. Under this head premiums of insurance had should be allowed as damages. (Maly *v.* Shattuck, 3 Cranch, 458.)

d. For loss of the cargo is the market-value at the port of destination, either on the day of destruction or on the day when it would have arrived but for the capture. (Dusan *v.* Murgatroyd, 1 Wash. C. C., 13; The Joshua Barker, 1 Abb. Adm., 215; The Gold Hunter, 1 Blatch. & H., 300, 308; The Rebecca, 1 Blatch. & H., 347, 356; The Colonel Ledyard, Sprague, 530; Brown *v.* Ashley, 1 Lowell, 27; Bartlett *v.* Rudd, 1 Lowell, 223.)

e. If the value of the goods at the port of shipment (Manila) is the measure of damage, the damages would be, pursuing the usual course of trade, the value in New York at maturity of a sterling bill on London payable six months after acceptance, and bought at Manila at the time of the purchase of the cargo with the silver dollars by which the purchase was made.

Mr. Joseph H. Choate for the complainants C. A. Sherman *et al.*

1. The claimants are entitled to actual and complete indemnity; *i. e.*, to the amount they could have realized for their property as it stood when destroyed, if such destruction had not taken place.

2. The measure of damages under this principle is—

a. For the loss of the ship, her value at the time of her destruction.

b. For the loss of freight, an amount equal to the gross freight less the estimated cost of earning that amount had the voyage been completed.

c. For stores, provisions, and outfit, the actual value of what was on board at the time of capture.

d. For the cargo, its value at the port of destination at the time when, in the ordinary course of navigation, it would, but for the capture, have arrived at that port. (Abbott on Shipping, 8 ed., p. 504; 3 Kent's Com., 5 ed., 242; Tudor *vs.* Macombe, 14 Pick., 34; Stevens & Benecké on Insurance, p. 208; Sedgwick on Dam., 6 ed., p. 424; Sturgis *vs.* Bissell, 46 N. Y., 462; Sherman *vs.* Wells, 28 Barb., 403; Spring *vs.* Haskell, 4 Allen, 112; McGregor *vs.* Kilgor, 6 Ohio, 352; Medbury *vs.* N. Y. & E. R. R., 26 Barb., 564; Sedgwick, pp. 313, 372, 409, 576, 577, 76 *et seq.*, chap. xiii; Williams *vs.* Reynolds, 22 Q. B., 221; Bell *vs.* Cunningham, 3 Peters, 59; Smith *vs.* Condry, 1 How., (U. S.,) 28; Heard *vs.* Holman, 19 C. B. Rep., (N. S.,) 1; Williamson *vs.* Barrett, 13 How., (U. S.,) 101; The M. M. Caleb, 10 Blatch. C. C. Rep., 467; The Rhode Island, 2 Blatch. C. C., 113; The Amiable Nancy, 3 Wheaton, 546; Masterton *vs.* The Mayor of Brooklyn, 7 Hill, 62. Papers relating to the Treaty of Washington, vol. III, pp. 212–214.)

e. If the value of the goods at the port of shipment is the measure of damages, the importer, "on the merits of the case," should be allowed what it actually cost him in New York, in currency, to provide the means in the East Indies to purchase and pay for the goods there, with a further allowance of the advance in that market between the date of purchase and the date of destruction.* (The Vaughan and The Telegraph, 14 Wall., 258.)

Mr. J. A. J. Creswell for the respondent.

The measure of damages which shall be settled here will be the measure by which we must abide in the case of like claims brought against the United States in the future. (Papers relating to the Treaty of Washington, vol. iii, pp. 223, 224.)

---

* Messrs. Field, Lowe, Beaman, Tenney, Cole, and other counsel filed briefs on the questions involved in these cases, or participated in the argument.

The court must be governed by the act of Congress creating it, which expressly forbids the allowance of compensation for prospective damage.

The damage occasioned by the loss of a ship is to be determined by ascertaining her market-value at the time of destruction.

The measure of damage for the cargo destroyed should be found by reverting to the time and place of shipment, taking the original cost and adding reasonable expenses and interest. The rule contended for by the complainants would involve an allowance for prospective profits.

Claims pending before this court are in the nature of cases arising from marine torts, where the rule adopted is to compute the value of the cargo at the port of departure.

The cases cited by counsel for claimants are cases of breach of contract, or involve the law of common carriers, where special considerations apply.

Where suit is brought on an open policy, the value at the time and port of departure has been taken as a basis for the computation of damages. (Kent's Comm., vol. 3, pp. 335, 336; Mayne on the Law of Damages, marginal pages 186, 188; 12 East., Usher *vs.* Noble, p. 639; Warren *vs.* Franklin Insurance Company, 104, Mass. Repts., 518.)

In cases of jettison and general average the rule is different, but there nothing is contingent; the other goods have arrived in safety and actually brought the advanced price. If, in case of jettison, the remainder of the cargo does not arrive, the owner of the jettisoned goods is thrown back for his compensation to the value at the time and place of departure. (3 Kent, 243; Tudor *vs.* Macombe, 14 Pick., 34; Mutual Safety Insurance Company *vs.* The Ship George, Olcott's Reports, 157; Gray *et al.* vs. Waln., 2 Sergeant and Rawle, 229.)

The same rule prevails in cases of capture as in cases arising on an open policy of insurance. (The Charming Betsey, 2 Cranch, 126; Amley *vs.* Shattuck, 3 Cranch, 491; The Anna Maria, 2 Wheaton, 334, 335; The Amiable Nancy, 3 Wheaton, 546; L, Amistad de Rues, 5 Wheaton, 385; The Apollon, 9 Wheaton, 362; Taber *et al. vs.* Jenny *et al.*, 1 Sprague, 315; 1 Lowell, 27, 223.)

The true rule in estimating the value of the cargo is the *restitutio in integram.* The actual loss sustained by the party at the time and place of injury is the measure of damage. The rule in case of collision is to award as damages the value of the goods at the time and place of departure, with expenses, although in cases of breach of contract to deliver, it may be otherwise. (Smith *et al. vs.* Condry, 1 Howard, 28; The Ocean Queen, 5 Blatch., 493; Schooner Lively, 1 Gallison, 315; The Vaughan and Telegraph, Benedict 1, p. 49; 14 Wallace, 258; Sedgwick, marginal p. 469, note; The Glaucus, 1 Lowell, 371.)

No freights can be allowed by this court except those absolutely earned. (Act of 23d June, 1874.)

The words "unearned freights" refer to freight to be earned after her destruction on the voyage, during the prosecution of which the vessel was lost. Freight should be allowed *pro rata* from the commencement of the voyage to the date of destruction.

In entering judgment the value of the goods at Manila, in the currency of that place, should be taken, and this amount converted into the currency of the United States or its equivalent, taking gold at its present value.

JEWELL, J., delivered the opinion of the court:

These claims were for the loss of the ship Winged Racer, and for the cargo, and for the freight of the vessel, on a voyage partly performed from Manila to New York.

The claimants first named were each owners of $\frac{7}{24}$ths of the vessel and freight, and joint owners of the cargo which they had bought in Manila and China.

The third claimant owned $\frac{7}{24}$ths of the vessel and freight.

The owners of the cargo showed that the cargo could have been sold in New York at the time of the probable arrival of the vessel for a large profit over the cost in Manila and China. They also contended that the goods might have been sold in New York, to arrive, at the day of the destruction, for a large profit.

Before the hearing in the above-named causes, it was arranged that, in connection with the argument upon the questions of law proposed to be presented by the counsel in the principal cases, counsel in various other cases pending before the court in which questions were raised as to the measure of damages in regard to ship, outfits, provisions, cargo, or freight, should be heard with briefs and arguments, so that, if possible, all questions of this class should be at the same time presented to the court.

In pursuance of this arrangement, briefs were filed by several gentlemen of the bar, and the questions have been presented to the court by briefs and oral arguments of exhaustive ability, and the counsel of the United States has with equal ability and exhaustive research presented his views.

The court acknowledge their obligations to the various counsel for the claimants as well as to the counsel for the United States for the valuable assistance thus rendered.

For the authority of this court to award any sum either as loss or damage, or as indemnity or compensation for loss or damage on ship, cargo, or freight, we must look to the law under which we act.

The act, section 11, directs us to examine all claims admissible under it, *directly resulting from damage* caused by the so-called insurgent cruisers, &c., and "to decide upon the amount and validity of such claims *in conformity with the provisions hereinafter contained*, and *according to the principles of law* and *the merits* of the several cases."

By this, we understand that each claim is to be decided upon according to the principles of law and the merits of the several cases, and such a sum awarded to each claimant as the principles of law and the merits of his case entitle him to receive, unless the allowance of such amount is specifically forbidden by some provision of the act "thereinafter contained."

What the provisions of law are upon or according to which we are to make up these claims we are not told in the act; we are to seek them in general principles acted on by the courts, or to be found in the decisions to which we look for the authoritative declaration of the law of the land.

We ought, as it seems to us, to look for these principles especially in the decisions of the Supreme Court of the United States, which are of paramount authority, certainly in cases to which the United States is in any sense a party. We may look for them in the decisions of the circuit courts of the United States to the practice and procedure in which we are specially referred in the act. And we may also look to the decisions of the courts of the several States, not as conclusive upon us, but as worthy of examination by reason of the weight of reasoning and broad application of principles exhibited by those very high tribunals. And as these questions, the fund to which they have reference, and this court itself, each and all, are but the fruit of a great settlement between the two leading commercial and maritime powers of the world, we may and ought to draw from the law of nations, and the decisions of the courts of Great Britain, and especially from those tribunals before which questions of the law of the seas, of the rights and duties of neutral nations, are brought and tried, such rules as will best accord with that enlightened sense of justice by which this nation will be willing hereafter to be measured, and to which she will hereafter, without hesitation, appeal.

It was not improper for the counsel of the United States, in his very able argument, to call to our attention, and the attention of the claimants here, that we must bear in mind that, in making a standard according to which damages are to be awarded to the claimants before us, we at the same time supply a standard according to which hereafter, in all time perhaps, damages will be claimed and enforced against our own Government.

This consideration itself increases in our view the gravity and importance of the questions to be decided; it imposes upon us the greater obligation to consider with the strictest care the matters under deliberation.

That Congress had this consideration in view in framing the act is evident from the act itself; and section twelve comprises the "provisions hereinafter contained," which limit and restrain us in applying what otherwise we might apply to the fullest extent, namely, the allowance of damages in each case according to the principles of law.

The primary purpose of the act we conceive to be to discover what the *loss or damage* directly suffered by each claimant is according to the principles of law, and to award him that sum, with the limited interest provided in the act; and that amount we are to determine and award, unless we are prevented from allowing the whole of said sum by the restraining clauses before referred to.

There are some preliminary considerations which we will dispose of before proceeding to an examination of the chief questions at issue.

It is urged upon us most earnestly by all the counsel for claimants that the allowance for damage should be of the most liberal nature, inasmuch as these claims arose out of the acts of a wrong-doer; that the capture and destruction of these vessels was attended by wanton outrage and violence, presenting, as is urged, the cases in which courts have uniformly permitted the largest liberality in the assessment of damage. We do not think these considerations apply.

These captures were made in war; there was no violence greater than is allowed by the laws of war. To be sure, usually captured ships are not destroyed; they are commonly taken as prize before the courts for condemnation; but as the confederacy had no prize-courts, they exercised an undoubted, although extreme, right, and burned their prizes. Every merchant who made an adventure upon the seas was fully aware of the dangers to which his vessel or cargo was exposed. He "met but what he looked for should oppose."

Besides, this fund is the result of a liability of Great Britain for an act of negligence. This is not a suit against the actual wrong-doer. To be sure, by the law of nations we held England liable for these losses, and by the treaty she agreed to be treated as liable, but from first to last she protested that her liability was that which arose from oversight and omission, from a want of vigilance, an inadequacy of exertion in particular cases, a mistake of her duties, and not a wanton or willful act. And, as we understand it, our own Government finally acceded to that view.

In our own highest court, where the owners of a privateer were held liable for the unlawful act of the master and crew, a claim for vindictive damages was rejected, though Mr. Justice Story, in giving the opinion of the court, says, "upon the facts disclosed this must be pronounced a case of gross and wanton outrage, without any just provocation and excuse." (The Amiable Nancy, 3 Wheaton, 546.)

We are, therefore, of opinion that this consideration cannot enter into our judgment in estimating the amount of damage in these cases.

The various claims for damage arising under this act are:

First. For the vessel.

Second. For those outfits or supplies which are put on board prior to the commencement of the voyage and needful or pertaining to the navigation. As to those, it is in every case a question whether they are or not included in the valuation of the vessel itself.

Third. For those supplies which are in the nature of provisions to be consumed on the voyage.

Embraced in these second and third classes are the outfits and supplies put on board vessels fitted for whaling or similar voyages, differing in details from the outfits and supplies of ordinary vessels, but presenting no differences of principle.

Fourth. For the loss of the freight, either as due for the carriage of goods in a general cargo or the amount to become due or agreed to be paid under a contract of affreightment or charter-party, either for a voyage actually entered upon, the goods being already on board, or for a voyage agreed to be made from a port not yet reached, but for which the vessel has sailed, or on a voyage agreed to be made, but for the performance of which no steps have been taken or progress made, except to bind the ship and owners, if the ship or vessel survives accidents, so as to be able so to do.

All these claims have reference to the owners of the vessel, and can be made by them only, or by their representatives.

Fifth. For the loss of goods on board, whether specifically as cargo entered on the manifest and paying freight, or as the property and personal effects of officers or men or of passengers.

As to the ship:

There has been no difference of opinion in the discussions before us as to the measure of damage to the ship or vessel. The decisions of the courts all agree in giving the owner of the vessel its value at the time of its loss or destruction. In the law of insurance, its value at the commencement of the risk is taken to be its value through the voyage, although in fact the ship is continually deteriorating; but this slight deterioration is compensated for as an element of the freight.

There is nothing in the act limiting the right to give the value of the ship if destroyed. (The Baltimore, 8 Wall., 386, and cases in note; Lowndes on Collisions, 141 *et seq.*)

As to outfits:

As to that class of outfits which pertain to the navigation, such as spare spars, sails, extra canvas, and the like, and materials for the temporary repair of the ship, it has been contended by the counsel for the United States that they properly belong to and are included in the valuation of the ship itself. There is no difference of opinion that when the value of the vessel is clearly proved, exclusive of this class of outfits, and the value of the outfits as a separate item of value is clearly shown, their value, if destroyed, is to be given.

There is nothing in the act restraining us from giving the value of outfits if thus shown; but we shall in each case, according to the proofs, estimate the value of the ship and outfits, either collectively or separately, as justice shall require.

As to the provisions:

There has been no difference of opinion in the discussions before us as to the allowance for the provisions on board, unconsumed at the time of loss. Their value must be given either as a separate item of valuation, or as a component part of freight, according as we shall decide to give judgment for the loss of freight. Provisions are a fluctuating quantity, at its maximum at the beginning, and constantly diminishing as the voyage proceeds, till the minimum is reached at its termination.

In the case of vessels fitted out for whaling or similar voyages occupying long periods, some of the outfits pertaining to navigation, as well as the provisions put on board and the paraphernalia and machinery and the vessels for containing the product of the catch, are substantially cargo on board and must be governed by the rules applicable to cargo.

As to the measure of damage for the loss of goods:

This question has been argued before us with great ability upon both sides. It is claimed by the owners of goods destroyed that the act intended and expressly directed us to award to each claimant such a sum as would give him an "*indemnity* for losses," (§ 5,) such as would be a "*compensation* for the actual loss or damage," (§ 12;) that the claims were for "*damage directly resulting* from the acts of the insurgent cruisers," &c., (§ 11;) that the words "compensation" and "indemnity" (§ 12) are used to indicate the extent of the claimant's rights; that nothing can be indemnity or compensation for this loss or damage which does not put the claimant in the same situation in which he would have been if the capture and destruction in the particular case had not occurred. It is, therefore, claimed that the value of the goods destroyed must be the sum which they would have brought at the place of destination at the probable time of their arrival, and that the average length of passages between the ports of departure and destination should be taken to ascertain the time of probable arrival in each case.

That this was the market for which the goods were intended, that anything less than the value at the port of destination would not give "indemnity" or "compensation" for the "damage or loss."

It is further claimed that if this measure of value cannot be allowed, at least the value of the goods at the port of destination at the date of the loss should be given.

All of the numerous authorities cited in support of these positions were of cases arising *ex contractu*. They were chiefly actions brought against carriers, either by land or sea, for non-performance of the contract of carriage. They were actions between the parties to the contract. There is no doubt that in an action against a common carrier by the owner of the goods for non-delivery, the measure of damage universally given is the value of the goods at the time and place when and where the carrier has contracted to deliver them. (Angell on Carriers, § 482; Sedgwick on Damages, c. xiii. See the very numerous cases cited by these authorities.)

The basis of the doctrine in all these cases is, that it is the policy of the law to hold the carrier liable for the full value at the time and place of destination, to remove from him all temptation to fraud. (Gillingham *vs.* Dempsey, 12 Serg. and R., 188.)

In this case, which was the first case where the question arose in Pennsylvania, and in which all the English and American authorities up to that time were most exhaustively examined, C. J. Tilghman says: "If we consider the policy which should regulate these contracts, it is best to remove from the carrier all temptation to fraud, which will be best done by making him answerable for the value at the place of *delivery*. If the goods should be of increased value at the place of delivery, as they generally are, and the liability extends no further than the value at the place of shipment, there is very great temptation to fraud." * * * "And it would require very strong authority to satisfy me that where the carrier fraudulently disposed of the goods at the place of delivery, and made great profit thereby, he or his principal should be responsible for no more than the value at the place where he received them." (Watkinson *vs.* Laughlin, 8 Johns., 213; Emory *vs.* McGregor, 15 Johns., 24.)

Another class of cases cited by the counsel for the claimants grows out of the contract of insurance.

When jettison is made of goods for the relief of the ship in case of peril, the owner of the goods so jettisoned, *if the ship arrives*, is entitled to be paid for them the price they would have brought at the time of the arrival and at the place of destination. This value is given on the obvious equity that the owner of the goods whose destruction has enabled the others to arrive shall be in no worse condition than are those whose property has been saved by his sacrifice.

But if the *ship does not arrive*, if the rest are not carried forward, the goods jettisoned are to be paid for at their value at the place of shipment, with charges, insurance, and interest. (Tudor *vs.* Macomber, 14 Pick., 34.)

So if the ship is compelled to put into port in distress, and to make repairs or procure supplies, where the master has no funds and no credit, he may sell a part of the cargo to procure funds; and *if the ship afterwards arrives*, the owner of the goods sold shall have for them the price which they would have brought if they had remained on board, namely, their value at the time and place of destination.

But if she *does not arrive*, the value to be paid for them is their value at the port of departure, with charges, insurance, and interest. (Abbott on Shipping, 372; Mayne on Damages, 223; Richardson *vs.* Nourse, 3 B. & Ald., 237.)

Both these classes of cases are exceptions to the general rule followed in actions upon policies of insurance, and both stand upon the same ground, that the owner of the goods sacrificed in jettison, or sold for the exigencies of the voyage, shall be in the same condition as are the other owners whose goods have been insured a safe arrival by his sacrifice. If they gain a profit, so shall he, but if the ship fails to arrive then the goods of all parties are to be valued at the same standard, namely, that of the place of shipment.

But the act creating this tribunal, it seems to us, has expressly taken away from us the power to estimate the damage upon the principle contended for. Section 12 expressly provides that in no case shall any claim be admitted or allowed for or in respect to * * * *prospective profits*, freights, *gains*, or *advantages*.

Prospective profits means that profit or advance in price which the owner of goods expects will take place between the place of shipment and the place of destination.

This is sometimes called *profits*, sometimes *probable* profits, and sometimes *expected* profits. (Phillips on Ins., § 1209; Benecké, pp. 26, 27, 28, 29, 30, 119, 125; Stevens and Benecké, 14.)

Prospective profits, as applied to goods, can refer only to the difference in price between the port of lading and the port of discharge.

Profits expected after the time of discharge have never been given as damage in any case.

Profits in this sense—expected profits, prospective profits—are the constant subject of insurance, and are certainly as insurable as any other interest; but an insurance to cover them must be of profits *eo nomine;* they cannot be issued under the name of goods or cargo unless in a valued policy. Of course, such expected profits may be included in the valuation of goods in a valued policy on goods, but valued policies rest upon principles peculiar to themselves, by force of which the assured may value as high as he pleases, and the insurer is bound thereby. Valuation in the policy binds both parties in the absence of gross fraud.

The act enjoins upon us to decide upon the amount and validity of these claims "in conformity with the provisions of the act, and according to the principles of law and the merits of the several cases," (§ 11.) We are to find some rule of valuation which will accord with the provisions of the act *and* with the principles of law at the same time. Both injunctions are to be obeyed if they can be, and the act assumes that they may; and if in examining these claims we can find a course of decisions which will enable us to follow settled principles, and at the same time to give effect to the restrictive clauses in the act, those decisions we must follow.

The rule of damages followed by the courts of this country and of England in actions upon the contract, and between the parties to the contract of carriage or affreightment, as we have seen, cannot be followed by us. They include a valuation which we are expressly forbidden to allow.

But there are two classes of cases, either of which we may follow, keeping within the principles of law, and at the same time not contravening the provisions of this act. One of these arises in actions of tort, and the other in actions of contract.

From the earliest period in our judicial history actions have been brought by the owners of goods against persons other than the parties to the contract of affreightment, growing out of torts committed against the goods while in transit on their way from the port of lading to an intended port of discharge.

The earliest of these which reached the Supreme Court of the United States was in 1794. (Del. Col. *vs.* Arnold, 3 Dallas, 333.)

This was a case of a vessel wrongfully captured by the commander of the Constellation, an American vessel of war, and brought into the port of Philadelphia, where the captain instituted proceedings for her condemnation. Pending these proceedings the cargo was sold, and the consul of Denmark intervened in the cause, claiming the vessel and cargo as the property of a Danish subject. The cause was heard by the Supreme Court upon appeal, and Chief-Justice Marshall gave the opinion of the court, wherein they fixed the standard of damages by directing in their decree "that the cause be remanded to the circuit court, with directions to refer it to commissioners, to ascertain the damages sustained by the claimants, * * and that the commissioners be instructed to take the actual prime cost of the cargo and vessel, with interest thereon, including the insurance actually paid, and such expenses as were necessarily sustained in consequence of bringing the vessel into the United States, as the standard by which damages ought to be measured."

A large sum was awarded against Captain Murray in pursuance of this decree, which he was obliged to pay, and which was afterwards reimbursed to him by act of Congress from the Treasury of the United States. (Act January 31, 1805.)

The rule of damages thus established has been followed from that day to the present, through a series of decisions entirely unbroken and unchanged. (The Charming Betsey, 2 Cranch, 64; Maley *vs.* Shattuck, 3 Cranch, 458, (1806;) The Schooner Lively and Cargo, 1 Gallison, 315, (1812;) The Anna Maria, 2 Wheat., 327, (1817;) The Amiable Nancy, 3 Wheat., 546, (1818;) L'Amistad de Rues, 5 Wheat., 385, (1820.)

The same rule was applied in the case of an unlawful and unjustifiable seizure of a vessel by the officers of the revenue in 1824. (The Apollon, 9 Wheaton, 362.)

Story, J., says, p. 376: "This court on various occasions has expressed its decided opinion that the probable profits of a voyage, either upon ship or cargo, cannot furnish any just basis for the computation of damages in cases of marine tort." * * "When the vessel and cargo are lost or destroyed, the just measure has been deemed to be their actual value, together with interest upon the amount from the time of the trespass. * * * And it may be truly said that if these rules do not furnish a complete indemnification in all cases, they have so much certainty in their application, and such a tendency to suppress expensive litigation, that they are entitled to some commendation upon principles of public policy."

The rule established in these cases was followed in the first case of damage arising from collision which came before that court. (Smith *vs.* Condrey, 1 Howard, 28, (1843.)

This rule has been followed by the district and circuit courts in all succeeding cases, and has been affirmed in a very recent case by the Supreme Court. (The Vaughan and Telegraph, 14 Wallace, 258; The Ocean Queen, 5 Blatchf., 493.)

The other class of cases are those actions brought upon an unvalued or open policy of insurance.

It is claimed in the argument before us that the rule in these cases does not make good the *damage* or *loss*, does not *indemnify* or *compensate* the parties.

But it does give that indemnity which, by the custom of merchants ever since insurance was practised in England or in this country, has been given in actions upon policies of insurance not valued; that is, under open policies. And in fixing the standard of indemnity to be given in a case of collision the Supreme Court expressly followed the practice adopted in cases of insurance from the earliest times. (Smith *vs.* Condrey, 1 Howard, 28.)

The injured ship in this case was at anchor, ready to sail, in the harbor of Liverpool, laden with salt, intended for sale in the port of Alexandria, where she expected to arrive in season to dispose of her cargo at a large profit. The plaintiffs claimed to recover the value of the salt at the place of her destination.

Taney, C. J., in giving the opinion of the court, says: "The plaintiffs offered to prove that if the ship had not been prevented from sailing by the injury complained of she would have arrived at Georgetown in season to have made a large profit on her cargo."

But, it will be observed, he makes no allusion whatever to the long course of decisions in the cases of illegal captures already referred to, but adopts the rule of law in cases of insurance as furnishing the proper standard of damages. He says, (p. 35,) "It has been repeatedly decided in cases of insurance that the insured cannot recover for the loss of probable profits at the port of destination, and that the value of the goods at the place of shipment is the measure of compensation. There can be no good reason for establishing a different rule in cases of loss by collision. It is the actual damage sustained by the party at the time and place of the injury that is the measure of damage." He expressly calls the damage thus measured the *actual damage* suffered by the party.

The text writers on insurance are uniform in their definitions of the words *loss* or *damage*, and of the corresponding words, *indemnity* and *compensation.*

Indemnity is the compensation for loss or damage.

Mr. Phillips says:

"The principle of insurance is indemnity."

"The indemnity proposed in marine insurance is to restore the assured as nearly as may be to the condition he was in at the outset.

"It is not intended by the contract of insurance to put the assured in the same situation in case of loss that he would have been in had the adventure terminated successfully. He must take the chances of his speculation on the state of the markets. The indemnity refers to the beginning of the risk." (2 Phillips on Insurance, § 1220.)

Ibid., § 1219.—"The value of the interest is to be estimated at the time of the commencement of the risk."

Emerigon, (Am. Ed., 1850,) c. 1, § iv, p. 13, states the principle upon which insurance is based.

"It is plain that insurance is not a source of gain to the assured."

"*Assecuratus non quærit lucrum, sed agit ne in damno sit,*" says Straccha.

"In a word," he continues, "one may have insured only what one runs the risk of losing, and by no means advantages which one may fail to realize."

Ibid., p. 213.—"As soon as the assured is indemnified for this value [the value at the time and place of lading] his lawful interest is satisfied." (1 Arnould on Ins., 301, 302; *Ibid.*, 324, 325, 329; Benecké, ch. 4; Stevens & Benecké, 13.)

That this is the rule that the *loss* or *damage* to be *compensated* for or *indemnified* against in cases of insurance in policies not valued, is the value at the commencement of the voyage, hardly needs a citation of authorities.

The leading authorities in England are: Usher *vs.* Noble, 12 East., 639; Lewis *vs.* Rucker, 2 Burr., 1167.

The case of Winter *vs.* Haldemand, 2 B. & Ad., 649, is interesting, because it was a case of loss by capture under an open policy.

Sir James Scarlett, in argument, stated the rule (pp. 652, 653) in accordance with which the case was decided. He says: "The rule, invariably adopted in case of an open policy, is to estimate a total loss, not by any supposed price which the goods might have been deemed worth at the time of the loss, or for which they might have been sold had they reached the market for which they were destined, but according to the cost, viz, the invoice-price and all expenses incurred till they are put on board."

The leading American cases are: Snell *vs.* Delaware Ins. Co., 1 Wash. C. C., 509; Carson *vs.* Marine Ins. Co., 2 Wash. C. C., 468; LeRoy *vs.* United Ins. Co., 7 Johns., 343; Coffin *vs.* Newburyport Ins. Co., 9 Mass., 436.

The latest case on this subject is Warren *vs.* Franklin Ins. Co., 104 Mass., 518.

It is needless to cite authorities further. The rule of damage, or of value in case of damage, is perfectly clear in all cases of marine torts, and the same rule is also universally adopted in that great branch or class of contracts known as insurance, and equally well settled in this country where we distribute this fund, as in Great Britain, whose government has paid the sum out of which arises our jurisdiction.

Were these claimants prosecuting their claims in a court from which an appeal might be taken to the Supreme Court of the United States, can there be a doubt what would be the standard of damage and indemnity which would be there applied?

In some aspects the rule of law applicable to insurance seems peculiarly applicable here, inasmuch as England may in some sense be considered in the light of an underwriter upon an open policy, against any loss by capture at the hands of the cruisers for whose depredations she was held responsible.

We ought also to say that in coming to this conclusion we have not been constrained in our judgment by the restriction clauses of the act, but that without them we should have felt bound to adopt the same standard of value as being "according to the principles of law." It seems to us that the restrictive clauses of the act were, so far as they apply to goods, intended and most carefully adapted to *declare* the law upon this branch of the subject, and not to make any new rule.

We therefore are of opinion that the measure of value of goods destroyed by the depredations of the cruisers for whose acts this fund is created, is to take the value of the goods at the time and place of shipment, with charges upon them till put on board, with the marine insurance actually paid, and interest on the aggregate so made from the date of purchase or shipment till the time of the destruction at the rate of six per cent. For that sum judgment will be entered, and by the terms of the act interest thereafter will run at four per cent.

In every case, therefore, we must look to the time of payment for the goods in cash, as shown by the evidence, to obtain the basis for the calculation.

We believe this measure of value to be that universally adopted in all cases of marine torts by the Supreme Court of the United States, which that court would certainly apply if an appeal lay from our decision to that court.

It is also the measure of value given by the tribunals of all countries in fixing the indemnity required upon contracts of marine insurance.

Further, any other measure of value we are forbidden to give by the language of the law under which we act, which expressly excludes *prospective profits* from our estimate of the loss.

As to the freight:

Having now considered the question of the measure of value of the cargo, we will proceed to the consideration of the question of freight.

As between the owners of the ship and cargo, the parties to the contract of affreightment, freight is not earned until the goods are discharged at the port of destination, unless the owner sees fit to receive them at an intermediate port.

As between the parties, no freight is earned until that port is reached; but as between parties other than the parties to the contract, freight is property in every sense of the law from the moment when the charter-party is executed and the vessel has commenced to take in her cargo, or has left any port for the purpose of performing the voyage to which the contract of affreightment refers.

As against the charterer, the owner of the ship has a right to earn freight from the moment of the signature of the contract.

As against a wrong-doer, freight is earned from the moment of the inception of the voyage.

Freight is property which may be insured. It is property for which contribution must be made in cases of general average, and in case the vessel is destroyed or injured by any act or negligence of a stranger to the contract, damages in all cases may be recovered for its loss.

It is none the less property because intangible, or because it is a *chose in action*. The rules of law applicable to tangible property are equally applicable to this, and are applied daily in all the courts.

In cases of insurance upon an open policy on freight, the owner recovers the gross freight without deduction. (2 Phillips on Ins., § 1238; Arnold on Ins., ed. 1872, p. 304.)

In cases of general average the owner of the vessel is bound to contribute not only on the value of his vessel, but on the amount of the net freight made up to the time of the injury or sacrifice. (Dixon on Average, 187; Lowndes on Average, 107.)

In cases of loss of freight which is to be contributed for in general average, gross freight is contributed for. (See authorities last cited.)

In cases of collision and other marine torts, net freights are allowed against the wrong-doer. (Williamson *vs.* Barrett, 13 How., 101, 111; The Gazelle, 2 Wm. Rob., 279; The Baltimore, 8 Wallace, 386; The Glaucus, Lowell, 371; The bark Heroine, 1 Benedict, 226; Egbert *vs.* Balt. & Ohio R. R., 2 Benedict, 225; The Galatea, 6 Benedict, 259; Allen *vs.* Mackay, Sprague, 219; The Rebecca, Blatch. & H., 147.)

In cases of illegal capture, or of destruction of a vessel by illegal capture, the owner has been throughout the whole history of prize courts held to be entitled to his freight, not net freight merely, but full or gross freight. (See authorities below.)

If a neutral vessel having enemy's goods on board is taken, the captor pays the whole freight, because he represents the enemy by possessing himself of the enemy's goods *jure belli;* and, although the whole freight has not been earned by the completion of the voyage, yet, as the captor by this act of seizure has prevented its completion, his seizure shall operate to the same effect as an actual delivery of the goods to the consignee, and shall subject them to the payment of the freight. (The Copenhagen, 1 C. Rob., 289, 291; The Hoop, 1 C. Rob., 196, 219; The Bremen Flugge, 4 C. Rob., 90; The Vrow Henrica, 4 C. Rob., 343; The Anna Catarina, 6 C. Rob., 10; The Catherine Elizabeth, 1 Acton, 309; The Fortuna, Edwards Ad., 56.)

The allowance is of *full freight.* (The Fortuna, *ubi sup.*, 57.)

The neutral's vessel's right to freight has priority over even the expenses of the captors. (The Vrow Henrica, 4 C. Rob., 343.)

A neutral vessel was lost by the negligence of the captor while being taken into port, to which she was being taken in order to unliver her hostile cargo. The captor in this case, a naval officer of Great Britain, was held liable to payment of the entire freight, in addition to the value of the vessel and cargo. (Der Mohr, 4 C. Rob., 314.)

The English government paid the amount.

The doctrine of these cases is well established in this country. (The Commercen, 2 Gallison, 261.)

Story, J., "The general rule that the neutral carrier is entitled to his freight is now too firmly established to admit of discussion." (p. 264.)

Same case on appeal, (1 Wheaton, 382,) Story, J., in giving the opinion of the Supreme Court, affirmed this doctrine.

C. J. Marshall and Livingston & Johnston, J. J., who dissented from the judgment, affirmed the same doctrine, and would have allowed freight, which the majority of the court in the particular case denied.

When neutral property was found on board of an enemy's ship, and the captors substantially delivered the property to the owners at the place ultimately intended as its destination, the captors were held entitled to freight upon the property. (The Ship Anna Green and Cargo, 1 Gallison, 274.)

Having seen how freight is treated in the prize-courts and in actions against trespassers, we proceed to see how freight is considered in the law of insurance. When is freight recoverable under a policy of insurance? When does it become cognizable in insurance law as a value, as a property, which may be lost or damaged or destroyed?

Where cargo is on board of either a general ship, sailed by the owners, or where the vessel is actually carrying her cargo under a charter-party for a particular voyage, there is no doubt that the pending freight is an existing value, the right to which is protected by all courts, and for the loss of which, if insured, the owner may recover.

And where the ship is under a contract to carry freight by a charter-party executed, the freight reserved or agreed to be paid is an existing value, may be the subject of insurance, and may be recovered from the underwriters in case of the loss of the ship.

"Where the freight is the price of the hire of the ship under a charter-party, the cases show that the inchoate right to freight vests in the ship-owner directly the ship has broken ground on the voyage described in the charter-party." (1 Arnould Ins., 237, § 106.)

"Inchoate rights to freights founded on subsisting titles, unless prohibited by positive law, are insurable." (Lucena *vs.* Crawford, 2 Bos. and Pull., 95.)

"Where there is an expectancy coupled with a present existing title, there is an insurable interest." (*Ibid.*, p. 293.)

The test of insurable interest is "an expectancy coupled with a present existing title."

In Robinson *vs.* Manf. Ins. Co., 1 Met., 146, Chief-Justice Shaw says:

"In general the inception of a voyage even in ballast from one port to another pursuant to a charter-party is an inception of the voyage on which freight is to be earned, and if the vessel is lost before arriving at the first port to take in cargo, it is a loss on freight." (See also 3 Kent, 5 ed., 311; Riley *vs.* Hartford Ins. Co., 2 Conn., 373; Hart *vs.* Delaware Ins. Co., 2 Wash. C. C., 346; De Longuemere *vs.* The Phœnix Ins. Co., 10 Johns., 127; The same *vs.* The New York Ins. Co., 10 Johns., 201.)

In McGaw *vs.* Ocean Ins. Co., (23 Pick., 409,) C. J. Shaw said: "In general terms it may be said that the insurance on freight will attach when the ship-owner is in such a situation in regard to his vessel and voyage that nothing but the intervention of one of the perils insured against can prevent him from completing his voyage and earning his freight." (Adams *vs.* Warren Ins. Co., 22 Pick., 165.)

Mr. Justice Chambre, in the case already cited, of Lucena *vs.* Crawford, says: "It would be very extraordinary if freight could not be made the subject of protection by an instrument which had its origin in commerce, and was introduced for the very purpose of giving security to mercantile transactions; *it is a solid, substantial interest ascertained by contract,* arising out of labor and capital employed for the purposes of commerce."

Mr. Phillips summarizes the doctrine of all these cases.

1 Phillips on Ins., § 334, p. 192.—"A charter party being made for successive passages at an entire freight, the interest in the whole

freight commences on the first passage, though the ship may sail in ballast merely on that passage, provided it is let by the assured or he has a cargo at the intermediate port."

And § 335.—"A vessel being chartered from A to B, the interest in the freight commences under the charter-party on the vessels sailing for A either in ballast or with a small quantity only of goods for B."

And he supports these positions by Livingston *vs.* Col. Ins. Co., 3 Johns., 49; Hart *vs.* Del. Ins. Co., Condy's Marshall, 281 *n*, 2 Wash. C. C., 346; Adams *vs.* Warren Ins. Co., 22 Pick., 165; Robinson *vs.* Manf. Ins. Co., 1 Met., 143.

Freight, as between the owner of the vessel and any other person than the owner of the goods, is property or value the moment the goods are on board or a valid contract is made by the owner of the vessel therefor.

What would be the measure of damage in a suit by the owner of the vessel against the charterer for a breach of his contract to furnish a cargo may be seen in the following cases, and is substantially the same as net freight: Hunter *vs.* Fry, 2 Barn. & Ald., 421; Fuller *vs.* Staniford, 11 East., 232; Smith *vs.* McGuire, 3 Hurls. & N., 554; Ashburn *vs.* Baldwin, 7 N. Y., 262; Fox *vs.* Harding, 7 Cushing, 516; Bailey *vs.* Damon, 3 Gray, 92.

Freight, therefore, being recognized in all courts as property, which may be destroyed, damaged, or lost by the acts of wrong-doers, is clearly an element of value, for which the claimants now before us are entitled to receive some sum as indemnity for the loss and damage which they have sustained.

In the cases above cited from the admiralty courts of England, the doctrine of which is approved by our own courts, (The Ship Anna Green and Cargo, 1 Gallison, 274,) where neutral vessels were arrested and carried into port in order that the entire cargo which they contained might be condemned, it was held that the owner of the neutral vessel not being in fault, was entitled to the full freight which he would have earned if his voyage had not been interrupted.

The cases before us present closely analogous situations, looking at the cargoes and vessels separately. The owner of the vessel destroyed, but for the destruction of his vessel, would have proceeded on his voyage and earned the freight which was agreed to be paid for the carriage of the goods on board. The wanton destruction of the cargo did not, as against him, the owner of the vessel, destroy or take away his property in the freight which the law everywhere recognizes.

If the confederate cruiser had captured one of these vessels, and had been allowed to take her with her cargo into an English prize-court for condemnation, and had there failed to make good his right to condemnation, on the ground that inasmuch as he had fitted out his vessel in England he could make no lawful prize, those courts would have restored the vessel and cargo, so that the vessel might proceed on her voyage and earn her freight; or, in case the property had been burned in port by the negligence of the captors, would have awarded to the claimant the value of the ship, cargo, and freight. (Der Mohr, *ubi sup.*)

Freight, gross freight, net freight, prospective freights, or expected freight, are terms often used in the books.

Freight is the generic term which includes all.

Gross freight needs no definition; it is the entire sum to become due to the owner of the vessel on the complete discharge of her cargo at the port of destination.

Net freight is a term never used as between the owner of the vessel and the charterer. It is a term whose use is made necessary by some occasion to apportion the gross freight by reason of an act or thing which has occurred pending the voyage, causing either a temporary or permanent interruption of the voyage, in which case it is needful to look at the freight to be earned if the whole voyage should be completed, as an existing value either in whole or in part, in connection with or in comparison with the other values engaged in the enterprise, namely, with the vessel and the cargo on board.

This comparison of values is perhaps never made between the owner of the vessel and the charterer. As between them the question is almost universally of the whole freight or of no freight. If the vessel arrives at an intermediate port, and the owner then receives his goods, he pays freight *pro rata itineris peracti.*

But this comparison of values often takes place from necessities growing out of some forcible or providential interruption of the voyage.

Forcible, as by capture or seizure of vessel or cargo, or of both.

Vessel and cargo may be seized as being both hostile property.

The vessel may be hostile while the cargo is neutral.

The vessel may be neutral while the cargo is hostile.

Both may be neutral and yet seized unlawfully.

If the vessel is neutral, yet she must be carried in to unliver the hostile cargo.

If the vessel is hostile, she must be taken in to discharge and deliver up her neutral cargo to the owner.

So there may be damage done to vessel or cargo, or both, by collision. The voyage is interrupted or destroyed, and the various values of ship, cargo, and freight must be examined into at a point between the port of lading and discharge.

And then there are losses by the perils of the seas, in which the vessel, cargo, and freight may be either partially or totally lost, and these values must be adjusted and compared as between the owners and underwriters of the several subjects.

In all these cases there is an estimation of freight as the property of the owner.

The losses which we are called upon to consider took place by capture, unlawful capture as against England, at a point between the ports of departure and destination, and are entirely analogous to the cases of unlawful capture and seizure administered under the law of prize.

The voyage is interrupted in its midst, and we are to fix the values of the several elements constituting the loss, at the time and place of the destruction.

"According to the principles of law," as administered in all the courts, these claimants are entitled to recover for the loss of freights destroyed by the acts of these cruisers.

What shall be the freight allowed?

It cannot be the gross freight, because the allowance of that is expressly prohibited by the act.

The disallowance of gross freights is an implied permission or direction to allow net freights.

It is clear we are to allow some freight; if not gross freight it must be net freight.

On this subject we derive instruction from the proceedings at Geneva. The arbitrators rejected the claim for gross freights, and did allow a large sum as net freights, as their proceedings show.

There are two terms used in the act descriptive of freights which remain to be considered.

What are "prospective" freights? Prospective we conceive to be synonymous with "expected" freight, which is a term very often used in the books. We have already defined the term prospective as applied to profits as being the profits which the owner of goods hopes to gain from the difference in price between the port of shipment and the port of discharge, sometimes called profits and sometimes, also, expected profits.

Prospective, as applied to freights, we conceive to mean that expectation of obtaining a cargo, and so of having a freight upon a voyage projected but not yet entered upon, as to which the owner has no certainty, no contract, no charter-party, but which in the law of insurance may or may not be held to give an interest on which insurance would attach.

It is called an "expectancy," as when a ship is going in ballast to a place where the ship-owner owns goods, which she shall there take on board and carry to another port. (Hart *vs.* Del. Ins. Co., 2 Wash. C. C., 346.)

Or where he does not own the goods, but has contracted to purchase them, and has prepared funds to pay for them, and the goods are ready to be delivered to him to put on board. (1 Parsons on Ins., 177.)

What are prospective freights may be further illustrated by Forbes *vs.* Aspinwall, 13 East., 323; Forbes *vs.* Cowie, 1 Camp., 520.

In these cases the owner had no charter-party or other contract for freight, but goods were on board sufficient to purchase the remainder of the homeward cargo that were saved and afterward bartered for goods which would have completed her homeward cargo. She had discharged part of her outward cargo and taken in fifty-five bales of cotton, part of her homeward cargo, and was lost in this condition. It was decided that she should recover only the freight on the fifty-five bales of cotton. (So in Riley *vs.* Hartford Ins. Co., 2 Conn. Rep., 368.)

Freight was insured on goods laden or to be laden, and a part of a cargo was taken on board at Gibraltar, and the ship was proceeding toward the Cape de Verde Islands with funds on board to purchase salt there to make up the cargo, when she was lost.

It was held that the insurable interest had commenced only in respect of the goods shipped at Gibraltar.

Another example of prospective freight may be found in Adams *vs.* The Penn. Ins. Co., 1 Rawle, 97.

To apply a phrase before quoted, we should say "expectancy," not "coupled with an existing title," is "prospective." (1 Arnould on Ins., 293.)

Congress seems to have had in view the probability that claims might be made not only for the freight actually on board or actually contracted for, but for the freight which the vessel, if not destroyed, might have subsequently earned, either with or without any definite grounds of expectation, and to have declared that all these should be excluded. They may have thought insurable interest on freight would be sought as a test of loss of freight, and intended to have excluded that test in these cases.

Such freights or compensation for the loss of the use of the vessel during repairs after collision have been demanded, and in some cases allowed. (Williamson *vs.* Barrett, *ubi sup.*)

What meaning shall we give to the term "unearned freights?"

The counsel for the Government insists that under the use of the words unearned freights, net freights for the entire voyage cannot be allowed, but only net freights *pro rata itineris peracti.*

Having shown that freight is property, as clearly recognized in law, as the ship or the cargo, or bullion, or coin; that although intangible and resting in action, it nevertheless is protected everywhere by the courts, and that it may be lost or destroyed or damaged, we feel constrained to award a sum sufficient in law to indemnify the claimants for this loss or damage, unless prohibited therefrom by the express provisions of this act.

We will not presume, except upon clear proof derived from the consideration of this statute, that Congress intended to take away from any of these claimants that which the courts of all nations under like circumstances protect.

We shall not, in the decision of the case now before us, which is the case of a vessel with her cargo actually on board, go further than is necessary for the decision of this and cases exactly similar. We only propose here to show that the term "unearned" does not apply to this principal case and to others similar to it. And in stating to what cases we conceive the word "unearned" does apply, we must not be understood as limiting it to precisely the cases we name. It is sufficient for the decision of this case to show that it may apply to other cases and does not apply to this.

The term unearned can have no application as between the owner of the vessel and of the cargo in an action upon the contract of affreightment, as between them freight is never earned till complete delivery.

But as against underwriters on freight, freight is not unearned when anything has been done toward earning it under a contract or charter-party therefor. So soon as the ship is bound to the goods and the goods to the ship by a valid contract, and any forward step has been taken by the ship toward the performance of the contract having connection with no other thing, the underwriter is liable for a loss of freight.

Still more, when, as in the present case, the cargo was on board and the ship was actually engaged in carrying the goods, the vessel as against wrong-doers had begun to earn, as against them freight was not unearned.

As against the owner of the goods under the contract it was not earned, but as to him even it was not unearned—it was partly earned.

To what does the term apply?

Without deciding that it may not apply to other cases, we think it was intended to apply to cases where charter-parties had been made, binding both the ship and the charterer, where under the law of insurance the owner of the ship may have had an insurable interest in the amount of the freight to become due under the contract, but where no forward step had been taken by the vessel toward the execution of the charter; where nothing has been done under the contract, where nothing has been done which would not have been done if there had been no contract.

For example, a vessel being upon a passage from New York to San Francisco with a cargo, during this passage the owners charter her for a voyage from San Francisco to any other port. This charter-party executed would give the owners an insurable interest in the entire freight, not only upon the voyage to San Francisco not yet finished, but also in the second voyage to commence at San Francisco, but till she reaches San Francisco, and has discharged her cargo there, she has taken no step, done no act, toward earning the freight upon the second voyage. The freight in this voyage, though insurable, is in no part earned.

We think that the word unearned as used here was not intended to exclude us from allowing freight on the voyage actually pending at the time of destruction, but was intended to exclude us from making the time when insurance on freight attaches the test of the right to freight; to exclude us from allowing freight in that class of cases where as against the underwriter the assured might recover for loss of freight, but in which the freight, though contracted for in a valid charter-party, was in no part earned, where the ship had not commenced the series of acts the performance of the whole of which would entitle her to the entire freight.

In allowing net freight in the particular case under consideration, and in similar cases, we shall feel bound to charge the gross freight in cases where we think justice shall require it, with interest on the value of the vessel, and also a sum to cover the probable depreciation of the vessel, in addition to the other items usually mentioned as needing to be deducted from the gross freight. The act gives interest on the value of the ship from the date of her destruction at 4 per cent. We cannot give to the owner without charge the use of the same ship the value of which in contemplation of law the Government pays for on the day of its destruction.

The questions raised by the difference in currencies present great difficulties and embarrassments. If these claims were being considered by a board of assessors, as might have been under the treaty, and if the amount of the claims were to be paid directly from the exchequer of Great Britain, which has but one currency, it is extremely probable that every claim would have been reduced to the standard of gold, and that value which is the coin equivalent of these claims would have been awarded. It is quite possible, indeed quite probable, that this consideration induced the arbitrators to award a sum in gross, thus remitting all questions of value represented by or dependent upon the fluctuations of our currency to a tribunal to be established by the United States. These difficulties must now be met by us.

In the argument of the eminent counsel for the United States, we were urged to fix for the value of all goods purchased in coin or in any other currency than the legal-tender currency of the United States, such a sum in currency as would be equivalent to the value of coin at the present time. But we see no principle upon which such a standard can be adopted. It would still be entirely uncertain how near or how far the sum so fixed would be from the value of gold as compared with currency at the time when the amounts awarded by us will be in fact paid. It would make two standards of value, for which we see no necessity, and no warrant in the law.

We are left to adopt some rule. It cannot be contended that in the case of goods bought during the war for currency we should reduce their nominal cost to the standard of coin at the day of purchase, and then reduce the coin-value to the value of currency of to-day, which it would be necessary to do if we would have only one standard of value.

We are entirely clear that such a course would be unjust to a large class of the claimants. It will give more equal justice to all to reduce the coin-prices actually paid in cases where purchases were made in coin to currency at the rate of the day of purchase, and enter the judgment for the currency cost so ascertained. We see no way in which we can justly adopt two standards.

To be sure, the rule last suggested will give judgment for a sum in currency, which, received in the prices of gold of to-day, will, if exchanged into gold, give the claimant a sum in coin in excess of what he would otherwise be entitled to claim.

But the fact that this consequence would follow was not deemed by the Supreme Court a sufficient reason for changing the standard of currency adopted in the circuit court in the case of The Vaughan and Telegraph, 14 Wallace, 258; Cushing *vs.* Wells, Fargo & Co., 98 Mass., 550.

But the rule first suggested would give to the other claimants a sum much less than they ought to receive.

The inequality in both these cases arises from the fact of the appreciation of the legal-tender currency as compared with gold. If we adopt gold as the original standard of value, we give to the Government the benefit of this appreciation and fail to indemnify the claimants. If we adopt the other standard, we give the benefit of this appreciation to the several claimants. The claimant in this case obtains an incidental advantage. But as between the claimant and the Government, we think this incidental benefit belongs to him. He was compelled by force of law to purchase in legal tender; it was not optional with him whether to do so or not. The value of this enforced currency did not depend upon him. The disadvantage of its use ought not therefore to fall upon him, but rather upon the Government, which compelled him to make use of it. No rule which we can adopt will give exact justice in every case; and as we can have but one rule, and must enter our judgments in currency, we must make our valuations according to that standard. This, if not exactly right in every case, has the advantage of simplicity and uniformity, and will more nearly give a just indemnity in every case than any other course.

Applying these principles to the determination of the present case, after having given due consideration to each portion of the large mass of testimony presented to us, we award—

In No. 278, to Henry Wilson Hubbell, the sum of........ $114,283 41
In 279, to Charles A. Sherman *et al*..................... 114,283 41
In No. 1131, to Edward H. Gillilan, the sum of 23,450 00
with interest on each of the above-mentioned sums, to be computed at 4 per cent., from November 10, 1863.

The several judgments to be entered by the clerk in the usual form.

RAYNER, J, dissenting as to the principle upon which net freight is allowed.

BUCK AND SPOFFORD AND SUNDRY OTHER claimants *vs.* THE UNITED STATES. } Nos. 406, 407, 408, 409, 410, 411, 412, 597, 598, 599, 600, 601, and 656.

IN THE MATTER OF THE DESTRUCTION OF THE SHIPS HIGHLANDER AND JABEZ SNOW.

Where a vessel has sailed under a charter-party with cargo aboard she is entitled, under the act of Congress of 23d June, 1874, to net freight for the whole voyage, in accordance with the terms of the charter, though destroyed by an insurgent cruiser, when but one day out.

Where destroyed while sailing in ballast, under charter, to take in cargo at her port of first destination, to be carried thence to a port of final destination, she is entitled to net freight on the cargo which she was thus to have taken on board.

Where destroyed while sailing under one charter to deliver, at a designated port, cargo on board, and to bring other cargo home, she is entitled to net freight for the round trip.

Where destroyed while sailing under two distinct and independent charters, to carry under the first cargo to an intermediate port, and under the second to carry other cargo to a port more distant, she is entitled to net freight under each charter, though destroyed before the fulfillment of the first, if she has made it satisfactorily to appear by proper proof or necessary legal presumption that she entered fairly at the same time on the commencement and prosecution of both voyages.

STATEMENT OF THE CASE.

As to the Highlander:

On the 7th March, 1863, a charter-party was entered into between the captain, and Messrs. Hyde & Jones of London, that the Highlander should sail to Akyab, Rangoon, or Bassein, (with liberty to make an intermediate voyage,) for a cargo of rice, and after loading should proceed to Cork or Falmouth for orders. The Highlander, after making the intermediate voyage allowed by the charter-party, was proceeding to Akyab to load, when on the 16th December, 1863, she was captured and burned by the Alabama. The owners claimed net freight under the Akyab or rice charter, viz, gross freight less all expenses which would have been incurred by the owners if the vessel had continued her voyage and delivered the cargo of rice in accordance with the charter-party.

As to the Jabez Snow:

On the 25th February, 1863, the captain signed a charter-party providing that the vessel should sail from Liverpool on or before the 31st March, 1863, to Montevideo. That as soon as discharged at that port she should proceed to Callao, there report to the agents of the government of Peru, and after fulfilling certain provisions of the charter-party, and loading her cargo, should sail from Callao to Havre direct.

On the same day the captain entered into another charter with different parties, providing that the ship should with "all convenient speed" proceed to Cardiff, there load a cargo of coal, and deliver the same in Montevideo.

At the time these charter-parties were signed the vessel was lying in the port of Liverpool. From Liverpool she proceeded to Cardiff, loaded the cargo of coal and sailed for Montevideo. On the 29th May, 1863, before reaching that port, the vessel and cargo were destroyed.

The owners of the vessel claimed the net freight under both charters, viz, the gross freight under the two charters less all expenses that would have been incurred if the two cargoes had been delivered.

*As to the Sonora:**

The complainants, owners of the vessel, entered into a charter-party while the ship was on a voyage from New York to Melbourne. By this charter-party the ship was bound, upon the discharge of her cargo at Melbourne, to proceed from that place to Akyab, in British India, for a cargo, either directly or after an intermediate voyage to another port in Australia or the China seas, and in case of such intermediate voyage to leave her last port for Akyab on or before December 1, 1863. She made an intermediate voyage to Hong Kong, left that port for Akyab before December 1, 1863, and was burned by the Alabama in the straits of Malacca on the 26th day of December, 1863.

Besides the loss of vessel, outfits, &c., the owners claimed the net freight on the Akyab charter.

Mr. C. C. Beaman, jr., for the complainant.

---

* The argument of counsel for the complainants in Cushing *et al. vs.* The United States, (case of the Sonora,) No. 288, having been extensively referred to by counsel for the complainants and for the respondent, has also been reported, although the case did not come on for trial with the cases of Buck *et al.*

The freight claimed does not come under the definition of "prospective" or "unearned" as given by the court in the case of Hubbell *vs.* The United States.

The court allowed in that case net freight for the whole voyage when the cargo was on board. The net freight now claimed does not differ from that then allowed in being prospective or unearned.

The word "prospective" as applied to freights does not relate to the fact of its being on board but to its dependence upon an expected usual course of business or upon an absolute contract.

According to the "principles of law" an award can be made for net freight in these cases:

a. In cases of insurance upon a policy on freight the owner can insure and recover the gross freight on a voyage upon which the ship has entered even though the cargo is not on board. (Arnold on Insurance, edition of 1872, pp. 30, 31, and 304.)

b. In cases of general average the owner of the vessel is bound to contribute on the value of his vessel and the amount of his net freight, under the charter on which he has cargo on board, and under the charter upon which he has entered, although he has not yet received the cargo. (The brig Mary, 1 Sprague, p. 17; Dixon on Average, p. 187.)

c. Freight has been allowed a neutral vessel with cargo on board, but when she had not sailed from the port where she received her cargo. (The Catharina Elizabeth, 1810; 1 Acton English Admiralty Rep., 309.)

There is nothing to show that net freight as now claimed would not be allowed a neutral vessel captured under the circumstances in which the Highlander and Jabez Snow were destroyed.

d. In cases of collisions and other marine torts, freights are allowed against a wrong-doer to the extent claimed in the cases now under consideration. (Statute 53 George III, A. D. 1813, p. 792; 17 and 18 Victoria, A. D. 1854, p. 595; 25 and 26 Victoria, A. D. 1862, p. 305; 9 U. S. Statutes at Large, p. 635; Allen *vs.* McKay, Sprague, p. 219; The South Sea, 1856, (Swabey's Reports, p. 141;) Case of the Orpheus, 1871, 3 Law Reports, (Admiralty,) p. 308; The Canada, 1861, (1 Lushington, p. 586.)

Messrs. Paine and Grafton for the complainants, (owners of the Sonora.)

I. According to the statute creating the court, it is to decide upon the amount and validity of claims presented in conformity with the provisions of the act, according to the principles of law, and the merits of the several cases.

Causes within the jurisdiction of the court must have originated in a marine tort, therefore the court should look to cases of collision and capture for the establishment of the "*principles of law*" which are to control this case.

1. In cases of collision, as against the owner of the offending ship, the owner of the injured ship, if without fault, is entitled to her net freight, whether she is or not totally lost; provided, the performance of the charter-party is defeated by the collision.

As against the captain of the offending ship, the rule is the same, unless his misconduct is such as to warrant an award of exemplary or vindictive damages.

As between the owner of the injured ship and the owner of her cargo, the question of liability depends wholly upon the relative responsibility of these parties for the failure of their contract. (The Gazelle, 2 W. Rob., 279; Williamson *vs.* Barrett, 13 How., 101; The Canada, 1 Lushington, 586; The Ann Caroline, 2 Wall., 550; The Rebecca, 1 Blatch. &

H., 347; The Cayuga, 14 Wall., 270; The Heroine, 1 Benedict, 226; Egbert *vs.* The Baltimore and Ohio R. R. Co., 2 Benedict, 225; The Favorita, 18 Wall., 598.)

2. In cases of capture of neutral ships the following are the rules of damages applicable to freights, both in England and the United States:

As against the captor the owner of the captured ship, if without fault, is entitled to her full freight, whether she is or is not totally lost, provided the performance of the charter-party is defeated by the capture.

As against the owner of neutral cargo, in case of total loss of both ship and cargo, without the fault of either, there is no liability for freight in favor of the owner of the ship, because if the cargo fails the ship, so also does the ship fail the cargo.

As against the owner of neutral cargo, in case of total loss of ship alone, without fault of ship or cargo, there is no liability for freight in favor of the owner of the ship, because the cargo waits in vain for the ship to perform the charter-party.

In case of detention or partial loss the liability, as between owners of ship and cargo, will embrace full freight, *pro-rata* freight, or no freight at all, according to the relative responsibility of the parties for the failure of their contract. (The Pearl, (1804,) 5 C. Rob., 199, Am. ed.; The Copenhagen, 1 C. Rob. Adm., 289; The Race-Horse, 3 C. Rob. Adm., 101; The Lucy, 3 C. Rob. Adm., 208; Der. Mohr, 4 C. Rob. Adm., 314; The Anna Catharine, 6 C. Rob. Adm., 10; The Lively, 1 Gall., 315; The Commercen, 1 Wheat., 382; The Nuestra Señora de Regla, 17 Wall., 30.)

3. The reason for including the net freight of the charter-party in the award of damages in the case now before the court is vastly stronger than in the case of a collison, or in the case of a capture of a neutral ship by a belligerent.

II. The statute forbids allowances for—

1. Gross freights.
2. Unearned freights.
3. Prospective freights, gains, or advantages.

Gross freight is the entire amount of freight-money to be received. (The Heroine, 1 Benedict, 226.)

The expression, "unearned freight," applies to cases where a chartered ship, not having begun to work under her charter-party, has not begun to earn her freight, and to an unchartered ship which has not commenced the projected voyage; but it does not apply to a case where a ship has begun to earn her freight—has partly earned it. Unearned freight, in the sense of the statute, is not freight partly unearned, but it is freight wholly unearned. (The Hamilton, 3 C. Rob., 107; The Martha, 3 C. Rob., 107.)

The clause as to "prospective profits, freights, gains, or advantages" refers to matters purely speculative, and means the profits, freights, gains, or advantages of a prospective, not of an actual, voyage; of a voyage projected but not commenced.

III. The claimants are entitled to the entire net freight under the charter-party, for at the time of capture the vessel was working under it. There was no element of adventure or speculation in the voyage.

A ship is earning freight from the hour she starts after her cargo. (The Canada, 1 Lushington, 586; The Argo, 1 Spink, 375; the Mary, 1 Sprague, 17.)

Mr. J. A. J. Creswell and Mr. Frank W. Hackett for the respondent:

In the case of the Jabez Snow nothing had been done toward earning the Callao charter that would not have been done had there been no such charter. The vessel was destroyed while prosecuting the Montevideo charter, therefore the claimants are entitled to no indemnity on account of the Callao charter. (Opinion of the court in Hubbell *vs.* the United States.)

Collision cases afford no analogy for the estimate of the court in cases like the one at bar.

The court keeps within the limit of the direct result of the damage caused by the cruisers. (Hubbell *et al. vs.* the United States, *ante.*) The attitude of a claimant in this court is not that of an injured person suing a wrong doer.

In cases of capture of vessels under charter, but without cargo, net freights would not be allowed. (Abbott on Shipping, 470; The Copenhagen, 1 C. Rob., Adm., 289; The Frances, 8 Cranch, 418; Blakey *vs.* Dixon, 2 Bos. & Pull., 321; The Nathaniel Hooper, 3 Sumn., 542; The Société, 9 Cranch, 209.)

The decisions of the court must be made in accordance with the statute creating it, and the single question for this tribunal under that act is, admitting the claim to be a valid one, how much loss or damage did the claimant actually suffer for which this statute gives power to award indemnity? This court has not the full and peculiar powers of a court of prize, and the express prohibitions of the act creating it exclude any claim for freight made under charter-parties where the cargo is not on board.

The freight claimed in the case at bar is "unearned" and "prospective," for a vessel does not really enter upon the work of earning freight until the cargo is actually or constructively in her possession, and freight *to be* earned is an uncertain profit. (Code de Commerce, article 347; Emerigon on Insurance, pp. 181, 713; Meredith's translation of Emerigon, ed. 1850, p. 713, note; 13 East., 300; Bouvier's Law Dict.; Smith's Mercantile Law, 283; Abbott on Shipping, 405; Emerigon, p. 178; papers relating to the Treaty of Washington, iv, 53.

PORTER, J., delivered the opinion of the court:

In the case of the ship Winged Racer, we were called to consider, among other subjects, a claim for the loss of freight. After a protracted argument by eminent counsel, we reached in that case conclusions which were and are satisfactory to the minds of a majority of the court. In the cases above mentioned, some new phases of the question, growing out of a different state of facts, were presented. This led the counsel of the Government to insist on re-arguing the original questions decided in the Winged Racer; and, specially desiring to be right on a point involving so large a part of the money paid by Great Britain, we accorded this privilege both to them and to the counsel of various claimants. I am now to state the views entertained by the court, after listening to these elaborate and learned arguments, and then to apply the principles we have adopted, to the solution of the questions presented in the cases of the Highlander and the Jabez Snow.

The Government of the United States presented at Geneva a large claim for the loss of freights. The British experts launched pointed and severe criticisms at the claim made for gross freights, but they could not deny the soundness of the claim for net freights, if the conduct of Great Britain had rendered her liable for the acts complained of by the United States. In the award made in our favor, this principle was set forth as one of the conclusions of the tribunal, that, "in order to arrive at an equitable compensation for the damages which have been sustained, it is necessary to set aside all double claims for the same losses and all claims for gross freights, so far as they exceed net freights."

When the act of 23d June, 1874, was framed, Congress, following out this principle, gave to this court the following direction, (section 12:) "And in no case shall any claim be admitted or allowed for, or in respect to, unearned freights, gross freights, prospective profits, freights, gains, or advantages." The term "prospective," it will be observed, is predicated here, not only of *profits*, to which it stands in juxtaposition, but also of *freights*, *gains*, or *advantages*. We are not to allow a claim for unearned freights, gross freights, or prospective freights; thus, by excluding all other kinds of freight, permitting, and indeed requiring us to allow claims for net freight. That is, from the freight which a vessel, when destroyed, was engaged in earning, must be deducted the expenses which she would thereafter have incurred if the voyage had been successfully accomplished. By the immediately preceding section of the act, we are required to decide upon the amount and validity of such claims, not only in conformity to the provisions of the statute, but according to the principles of law. We are to exclude profits, freights, and gains which were prospective, and freights which were unearned, and we are to do this, not in some arbitrary way dictated by our own sense of justice, but according to the principles of jurisprudence as established by courts of law and adopted by the maritime nations of the world. We know, and we have known from the beginning, the importance of reaching a sound conclusion on the question thus arising both out of the treaty and the statute. During the argument we have been properly reminded of the influence which our decision may hereafter exercise on the public interests. It is said that the United States expects to carry out in the future, as she has in the past, the doctrine of neutrality. It is reasonable that the principles adopted in the distribution of the money awarded at Geneva should be applied to her, if she should ever be held responsible for violating those important rules established by the 6th article of the treaty, defining the duties of a neutral government in preventing the fitting out, within its jurisdiction, of vessels intended to carry on war against a power with which it is at peace.

What, then, is "prospective freight," as employed in the award and in the statute? A plain illustration may supply the answer. The owner of a ship at Philadelphia, finding her out of employment, concludes that if he were at the Chincha Islands he would be sure of a profitable cargo to Liverpool or New York. He proceeds, without any contract, written or verbal, equips his ship, sets sail, is captured by the Alabama, and sees his own ship sent to the bottom. He files his claim in this court, shows the loss of the vessel, proves her tonnage and the customary freight, and offers the testimony of shippers in Callao, who state that if she had arrived there they would have supplied a cargo equal to the carrying capacity of the ship. He exhibits his calculation showing the necessary deductions from the gross freight and asks the payment of his claim. We decline to allow it, and tell him this was what the award meant when it declared that "prospective earnings cannot properly be made the subject of compensation;" and this is what the act of Congress meant when it provided that a claim should not be allowed for or in respect to "prospective profits, freights, gains, or advantages." Having thus found a distinct subject-matter to which this portion of the statute is applicable, we ought, by well-settled rules of interpretation, to rest content that we have ascertained the kind of profits which Congress meant to define by the term "prospective."

What are "unearned freights," as employed in the act? What do these terms, so unusual in the language of judges, shippers, carriers, and underwriters, require us to exclude? By forbidding the allowance of unearned freights, it was certainly not intended to allow only freights fully earned. Freight is fully earned in the judicial, as well as popular sense, when the vessel has reached her port of destination and the cargo has been delivered; a place in which she would not be in much danger of destruction at the hands of an insurgent cruiser. If so destroyed, the question of freight could not have arisen at all, for her charterers would then have been her debtors, and the value of the vessel only would have been lost to her owners. It is impossible to suppose that Congress could have put so frivolous a thing into a serious statute. It is just as clear that freights wholly unearned could not have been intended; that is, where no expenses had been incurred, no stores supplied, no cargo taken on board, nothing done by shipper or owner toward the commencement of a voyage. Here, again, the vessel would have been found in her dock and out of the reach of the losses of which the statute treats. Even if she were not, her case is effectually provided for by forbidding any allowance for prospective freights. The provision respecting "unearned freights" was evidently intended to embrace something different from that of the inhibition of prospective gains, and to have some practical effect on the distribution of the money in hand. Let it be observed, then, that between these extremes—of freight wholly earned and freight wholly unearned—there is an ample territory, in which judicial investigation has gone on from the dawn of commerce to the present hour, and the results are found along the whole track of the commercial law. A ship is made ready for sea, a charter-party more or less formal is executed, her cargo is shipped, and she starts on her voyage. She has not then earned her freight, and on the shipper or charterer she has no legal claim until after the lapse of many months and the endurance of many perils. But her owner has spent time and labor in fitting her out, has supplied the necessary stores, advanced the wages of the crew, and subjected her to the largest risk to which property is ever subjected, or paid to others the required compensation for assuming such risk. Can it be maintained that her freight is unearned, in the large and general sense in which this term is used in the statute—unearned, without qualification—wholly unearned? Can it be denied that some part of it has been earned? Not as against the shipper, if he has done nothing to change the contract, but even as against him, if he has interrupted the voyage, and certainly as against every one who willfully or carelessly stops her progress. Here the decisions, European and American, have a uniformity scarcely to be met with in any other department of the law.

The ship Cambodia sailed under charter from Bombay in ballast for Howland's Island, intending to call at a port in New Zealand for water, and, having got on shore on the coast of New Zealand, was so damaged that she was obliged to abandon her voyage. Lord C. J. Cockburn (afterward one of the arbitrators at Geneva) held that, as the ship had sailed with the sole object of going to Howland's Island to earn freight thence to the United Kingdom, the interest in the freight had commenced, although not a pound of the cargo was on board when she struck. (Barber *vs.* Flemming, 5 Law Reports 59, Queen's Bench Cases.) True, this was an action on a contract of marine insurance, created by parties who could make their own terms, and we ought to look for precedents arising outside of the law of contracts altogether. Take, then, the case of a general average arising from the jettison of goods for the common safety of ship and cargo. Here Mr. Lowndes, citing Williams against The London Assurance Company, (1 M. and S., 318,) states the rule in these terms: "When a ship is chartered to fetch or carry a cargo belonging to the charterer, the freight under the charter must contribute to the general average, whether or not the cargo is on board the ship at the time of the general-average act; since the loss of the chartered ship, whether laden or not, would deprive the ship-owner of his expected freight." (Lowndes on General Average, 236.) In the case of the brig Mary, Judge Sprague carried out the doctrine, by holding that where, by a charter-party, a gross sum, not divisible, was to be paid as freight for a voyage out and home, the principal object of the voyage being to obtain a return cargo, and a general average occurred on the outward passage when the ship was sailing in ballast, the whole freight for the round voyage must contribute. (1 Sprague's Decisions, 17.) Turning to cases of salvage, we find the same rule to prevail. (The Nathaniel Hooper, 3 Sumner, 542.) It is true that Mr. Benecke differs from Sir William Scott in the view taken by the latter in the case of The Progress, (Edwards, 210,) that where a ship goes out under a charter, to proceed to her point of destination, in ballast, and to receive her freight only upon her return cargo, the court is not in the habit of dividing the salvage, (in which he is sustained by the case of The Dorothy Foster, 6 C. Robinson, 88;) but it is sufficient to observe, respecting this difference of opinion, that no man of his age was of higher authority on maritime law than the judge who pronounced the judgment in that case. In the cases of collision of vessels the same doctrine prevails. Even the case of the South Sea *vs.* The Clara Symes (Swabey's Reports, 141) is really in harmony with the other cases, for although the claim for freight was there rejected, and the owner of the injured vessel was directed to pay the costs attending the claim which he had made for freight, yet this was because of the doubt that arose, from the character of the vessel, whether the master could have carried out the charter-party, even had the collision not occurred. The decision of Dr. Lushington in the Gazelle, (2 W. Robinson, 279,) and in the Argo, (1 Spink, 375;) The Report of the Registrar and Merchants in the Canada, (1 Lushington, 586,) made under Dr. Lushington's own eye; the decision of Dr. Phillimore in the Orpheus, (3 Law Reports, 308, Admiralty,) where the cargo was not on board at the time of the collision; the opinions of several of our eminent admiralty judges in America—Bark Heroine, (1 Benedict, 226;) Egbert against the B. & O. R. R. Co., (2 Benedict, 225,) and the decisions of the Supreme Court of the United States in Williamson against Barrett, (13 Howard, 101,) the Cayuga, (14 Wallace, 270,) The Favorita, (18 Wallace, 598)—have placed on a foundation too solid to be shaken the doctrine that the owner of a ship injured by a collision, if not in fault, is entitled to recover her net freight from the owner of the offending ship, if the performance of the charter-party be prevented by the collision.

Undoubtedly the closest analogies to the cases in hand are found in those of the capture of vessels as prize of war. It is true that Great Britain did not admit her liability as a wrong-doer for the acts of the insurgent cruisers, and, indeed, by the first article of the treaty disclaimed it, but having negligently permitted the equipment in her own ports of vessels which could have had no other object than the destruction of our ships, she was placed by the award in the legal attitude of having wrongfully captured them. There are in the books few cases of the destruction of vessels taken as prize of war, for the reason chiefly that they are too valuable to the captor to be destroyed. One of the few is the case of Der Mohr, (4 C. Rob., 315,) which was lost by the negligence of the prize-master, an officer of the British navy, while being taken into port, and the captors were held liable both for the ship and the freight, but relieved from liability by act of Parliament. In the Copenhagen, (1 C. Rob., 289,) seized in a British port which she had entered in distress to make repairs, Sir William Scott, in treating of the question whether freight was due from the owner of the cargo to the owners of the ship for the whole voyage or only *pro rata itineris*, thus speaks: "With respect to the freight, some is admitted to be due, as the ship has brought her cargo from Smyrna through much the most considerable part of the voyage. But it is said that in matters of prize the whole freight is always given, and for this reason, because capture is considered as delivery, and a captured vessel earns her whole freight. I have already said that this is not merely or originally a matter of prize; the ship was not brought in as such; she came in first from distress, and was afterward put upon the proof of her character. It is a case of a mixed nature, and the maxim that capture is delivery is not to be taken in the general way in which it is laid down. It is by no means true, except when the captor succeeds fully to the rights of the enemy, and represents him as to those rights. If a neutral vessel having enemy's goods is taken, the captor pays the whole freight, because he represents the enemy by possessing himself of the enemy's goods *jure belli*, and although the whole freight has not been earned by the completion of the voyage, yet as the captor, by his act of seizure has prevented its completion, his seizure shall operate to the same effect as an actual delivery of the goods to the consignee, and shall subject him to the payment of the full freight." The cases of the Martha, (3 C. Rob., 107,) the Hamilton, (3 C. Rob., 107,) and the Anna Catherine, (6 C. Rob., 10,) recognize the same doctrine. In the argument before us, it was assumed that in no case of capture had freight been allowed where the cargo was not on board at the time of the capture; but The Progress (Edwards's Admiralty Reports, 210) seems to present such a case. That vessel having sailed from England to Oporto, in ballast, under a charter-party for an entire voyage out and home, and having performed the outward voyage, was captured by the French in that port and recaptured by the British and Portuguese army under Wellington before she had commenced her homeward voyage. After the capture she had been unladen; on the recapture her cargo was in warehouse on shore. Salvage was allowed on the whole freight out and home. By the decision in the Catharina Elizabeth, (1 Acton's Admiralty Reports, 309,) freight was allowed to a neutral vessel, which had not actually sailed, though her cargo was on board. It must be admitted that the American decisions have not yet satisfactorily established here the English rule, and some of them are adverse to it. The Amiable Nancy, (3 Wheaton, 546;) the Anna Maria, (2 Wheaton, 327;) the Charming Betsy, (2 Cranch, 64.) The Société (9 Cranch, 209,) was the case of a neutral vessel sailing under charter-party to Amelia Island with cargo freight free, where she was to take on board such cargo as might be tendered to her, and while thus carrying British goods was captured by a naval vessel of the United States, then at war with Great Britain, and brought into the district of Georgia, where the cargo was condemned as enemy's property. Chief-Justice Marshall certainly held the two voyages to be distinct, probably much influenced by the division made of the freight, which, as to one voyage, was to be free, but payable as to the other. In the comparatively recent case of the Nuestra Señora de Regla, (17 Wall., 30,) a Spanish steamer seized in 1861 as prize of war at Port Royal, in which a huge sum was allowed to the owner for the use of the vessel, there is some recognition of the English rule, which must seem to every one who carefully examines the subject much more consonant to the whole system of the law of marine torts.

It certainly follows from this discussion that in the cases before us the allowance of freight *pro rata itineris peracti*, so strongly insisted on by the counsel for the Government, is out of the question.

1. There is nothing in the act of Congress to justify it. We are not required to decide a case where the freight was wholly earned, or one in which it was wholly unearned, for neither the one case or the other, as we have seen, could have arisen out of the depredations of the insurgent cruisers. Such acts came too soon for the one and too late for the other. We are called upon to decide cases occupying ground intermediate between these extremes. The statute, therefore, wisely said nothing about apportioning the freight..

2. We could not undertake to determine upon and allow freight *pro rata itineris* where it had been partly earned and partly unearned, without violating those principles of law which Congress specially cautioned us to observe. Left thus untrammeled by the statute in respect to the measure of freight due, we had either to take ground in opposition to what the most enlightened publicists have written on this subject, and the most distinguished jurists have approved, or to adopt principles which have thus acquired the sanction of the jurisprudence of the maritime world. It required little sagacity and less courage to do the latter.

3. If we had undertaken to split the freight into fractions, and to parcel it out, we should have failed in everything except doing injustice. A practical eye will readily see this. Suppose the ordinary voyage of a sailing-vessel to be thirty days. In ten days from the time of commencing to put cargo on board, she has completed, it may be, four-fifths of her entire earnings. Why? The cost of loading and payment of wages to officers and men, the supply of stores, and the other smaller and incidental but inevitable expenses, are the bulk of the cost of earning the entire freight. All she then requires are those propitious influences of the elements for which she is dependent, not on the power of man, but on the favor of Heaven. Divide the whole freight thus begun to be earned, according to the number of days out, or by any other rule, and not in one case out of a thousand would justice be done. Deduct that which one of these vessels, if not destroyed, must have expended between the point of her actual destruction and the port of destination, (generally only the expenses of maintaining the crew, paying the port charges, and delivering the cargo,) and you leave her owner just where every innocent man, whose person or property is attacked in violation of law, ought by the law to be left; that is, as nearly sound and whole as if he had not been struck.

What, then, is the practical result of these doctrines in the cases before us? Where a vessel has sailed under a charter-party with cargo on board she is entitled to net freight for the whole voyage in accordance with the terms of the charter, though destroyed when but one day out. Where she was destroyed while sailing in ballast under charter to take in cargo at her port of first destination, to be carried thence to a port of final destination, she is entitled to net freight on the cargo which she was thus to have taken on board. Where destroyed while sailing under one charter to deliver, at a designated port, cargo on board, and to bring other cargo home, she is entitled to net freight for the round trip. Where destroyed while sailing under two distinct and independent charters to carry, under the first, cargo to an intermediate port, and under the second, to carry other cargo to a port more distant, she is entitled to net freight under each charter, though destroyed before the fulfillment of the first, if she has made it satisfactorily to appear by proper proof or necessary legal presumption, that she entered fairly at the same time on the commencement and prosecution of both voyages.

On these principles we decided, in June last, the case of the Sonora. She sailed from New York to Melbourne, and she was thence to sail to Akyab, in British India, to take on a cargo of rice and proceed to one of several designated European ports. The charter permitted an intermediate voyage in the China seas. Having made such an intermediate voyage to Hong Kong, she left that port for Akyab, and was destroyed by the Alabama in the straits of Malacca. In the judgment entered in favor of her owners, we allowed net freight for the cargo not on board at the time of her destruction. So, also, in the case of the Emma Jane, decided during the same month. The case of the Commonwealth, argued during the present month, affords an illustration of the application of the same principle. She sailed from New York to San Francisco with a large freight-list, and when about twenty-eight days out was destroyed by the Florida. After she had sailed, and before receiving information of her destruction, her owners executed a charter binding her to proceed from San Francisco to the Chincha Islands to take on guano deliverable at Hamburg. She had not sailed under the charter for the Chincha Islands. She had done nothing whatever under it. Her officers did not even hear of it until after her destruction. As to that charter, her gains were prospective, which the award declares "cannot properly be made the subject of compensation, inasmuch as they depend in their nature upon future and uncertain contingencies." We accordingly disallowed to her freight under that charter, but admitted her right to net freight on the voyage to San Francisco. We could not have done otherwise.

In the cases of the Highlander and the Jabez Snow, now before us, we have as little difficulty in allowing the freight. The Highlander was to proceed under charter to Akyab, Rangoon, or Bassein, (with the privilege of an intermediate voyage to a port in India or China,) to take on, at one of those ports, rice deliverable at Cork or Falmouth. She had performed the intermediate voyage, and was proceeding in ballast to Akyab for cargo when she was destroyed by the Alabama. The Jabez Snow carried with her two charters, under one of which she sailed from Cardiff with coal for Montevideo, and by the other she was to proceed thence to Callao to take on guano deliverable at Havre. She was destroyed by the Alabama, with the coal on board, before reaching Montevideo. So far as we can judge, after a careful scrutiny of all the testimony before us, each of these vessels, at the time of her destruction, was proceeding in good faith in the actual execution of the contracts which she had thus lawfully assumed. We know of nothing more which either of them could have done in the prosecution of the respective voyages thus commenced and suddenly terminated by the act of the most successful of the insurgent cruisers. We accordingly allow to each of them net freight on the cargo which she was thus proceeding to take on board when destroyed. While we do not agree with the claimants respecting the amounts which they are entitled to claim, these are the principles of law on which we have reached the conclusions embodied in the judgments about to be entered.

RAYNER, J., dissenting.

ELIZA A. PIKE, ADMINISTRATRIX, &C., *vs.* THE UNITED STATES. } No. 736.

SAMUEL STEVENS ET AL. *vs.* THE UNITED STATES. } No. 737.

SAMUEL STEVENS ET AL. *vs.* THE UNITED STATES. } No. 775.

IN RE TEXAN STAR, OR MARTABAN.

The simulated transfer of a ship by American owners to a British subject, and the hoisting the British flag over said ship, when understood and intended by both parties to be done merely as a cover to prevent capture, and for the purpose of misleading and escaping a confederate cruiser during the late civil war, was not such a conveyance as divested the title of the owners. Such pretended transfer was null and void as against the right of the owners to sue for compensation before this court; and the ship having been destroyed by a confederate cruiser, her original owners are not deprived of the protection of the United States in the premises, and the consequent right to sue for relief before this court.

If the transfer of the ship had been valid and binding, the mortgage of the ship to the vendors, (the original owners,) with absolute control and authority over her, invested such mortgagees in possession with the rights and privileges of the mortgagors—preserved to them the protection of the United States in the premises—and secures to them their status as complainants before this court.

The forfeiture of a vessel to the United States, as provided for in the act of Congress of 1792 (sec. 4171 Rev. Stat.,) attaches not to the act of change of name and flag, and sale to a foreigner, but it is the failure to report the same to the collector of the proper collection-district, and to obtain a new American register, that works the forfeiture. Therefore, where a vessel in such case is destroyed before she can possibly return to such district, the owners do not, in consequence, lose any of their rights to redress, or forfeit the protection of the United States.

A statement of the case will be found in the opinion of the court.

Mr. C. C. Beaman, jr., for the complainants:

The complainants were directly injured by the destruction of the vessel.

a. The transfer to Currie was merely colorable and was not a sale.

b. The bark would have been condemned had she been brought before a prize court. (1 Kent Com., p. 87; Sir Wm. Scott in the Sechs Geschwistern, 4 C. Rob., p. 100; The Jemmy, 4 C. Rob. Rep., p. 31; The Omnibus, 6 C. Rob., p. 71; The Packet de Bilboa, 2 C. Rob., p. 133; The Andromeda, 2 Wallace, 481; The Cheshire, 3 Wallace, 231; The Baigorry, 2 Wallace, 474; The Bermuda, 3 Wallace, 514; The Jenny, 5 Wallace, 183.)

c. The sale was void as to third parties. (2 Kent Com., p. 521; Hamilton *vs.* Russell, 1 Cranch, 310; The Princess Charlotte, Browning & Lushington Rep., p. 75.)

d. The complainants are not estopped from asserting their ownership—

1. As against Currie. (Bigelow on Estoppel, p. 268; Van Rennselaer *vs.* Kearney, 11 Howard, 297; Ormsby *et al. vs.* Ihmsen, 34 Penn. State, 462; Gray *vs.* Bartlett, 20 Pick., 186; McCune *vs.* McMichael, 29 Georg., 312; Jewett *vs.* Miller, 10 N. Y., (Selden,) 402; Hill *vs.* Epply, 31 Penn., 331; Ferris *vs.* Coover, 10 Cal., 589; Tilton *vs.* Nelson, 24 Barb., 595; Storrs *vs.* Barker, 6 Johns. Ch., 166–170; Whitfield *vs.* Parfitt, 4 De Gex & Smale, 240; Myers *vs.* Willis, 17 C. B., 77; Langton *vs.* Horton, 5 Beav., 9; Ring *vs.* Franklin, 2 Hall, 1; Mark *vs.* Pell, 1 Johns. Ch., 594; Strong *vs.* Stewart, 4 Johns. Ch., 167; Steere *vs.* Steere, 5 Johns. Ch., 1;

3 Phillips Ev., Cowen & Hill's notes, 1431, *et seq.*; Jones *vs.* Blum, 2 Rich., (S. C.,) 475; Hayworth *vs.* Worthington, 5 Blackford, 361; Chapman *vs.* Tunier, 1 Call., 244; Dabney *vs.* Green, 4 Hen. & Mumf., 101; European, &c., Co. *vs.* Royal Mail, &c., Co., 4 Kay & Johnson, 676; Gardner *vs.* Cazenove *et al.*, 1 H. & N., 423.)

2. As against the United States. (La Flora, 6 C. Rob., 3, and note in index, p. 2; Dodson's Reports, p. 175, case of the Bennet, Reusse *vs.* Myers, 3 Campbell, (N. P.,) 475.)

e. The complainants were the legal owners of the vessel under the mortgage, accompanied by absolute power of attorney and possession. (6 Opinions Attorneys-General, 647; DeMattos *vs.* Gibson, 1 Johns. and Hemming's Reports, 79; Weston *vs.* Penniman, 1 Mason, 306; Lincoln *vs.* Wright, 23 Penn. State Reports, 76; Deane *vs.* McGhie, 4 Bing., 45; Kerswill *vs.* Bishop, 2 C. & Jer., 529; Dickinson *vs.* Kitchen, 8 El. & Bl., 789; Brobst *vs.* Brock, 10 Wallace, 519; Powell on Mortgages, 9, 10; 2 Black. Com., 158; Littleton, 332; 4 Kent Com., (12th ed.,) pp. 162–165; 1 Washburne Real Property, 562, 567, 568, 569, 570; Lowell *vs.* Shaw, 15 Maine, 242; Hotchkiss *vs.* Hunt, 49 Maine, 213; Ely *vs.* McGuire, 2 Ohio, 372, (ed. of 1833;) Wright *vs.* Ross, 36 Cal., 414; Mowry *vs.* Wood, 12 Wis., 413; Harding *vs.* Coburn, 12 Met., 333; Esson *vs.* Tarbell, 9 Cushing, 407; Veazie *vs.* Somerby, 5 Allen, 281; Woodruff *vs.* Halsley, 8 Pick., 333; Pratt *vs.* Harlow, 16 Gray, 379; Gellston *vs.* Hoyt, 13 Johns., (N. Y.,) 561; Philips *vs.* Ledley, 1 Wash., p. 226.)

f. Or the complainants were owners of the vessel, by a parol sale and delivery by Currie. (The Amelia, 6 Wall., 18; Wardover *vs.* Hogeboom, 7 Johnson, 308; Sharp *vs.* U. S. Ins. Co., 14 Johnson, 201; Lamb *vs.* Durant, 12 Mass., 34.)

Currie was not the owner. A bill of sale does not necessarily change the ownership of property. (Horn *vs.* Ketaltas, 46 N. Y., 605; Ross *vs.* Norvell, 1 Wash., (Va.,) 14; Brogden *vs.* Walker, 2 Hen. & J., (Md.,) 285; Reed *vs.* Jewett, 5 Me., 96; Caswell *vs.* Keith, 12 Gray., 351; Fuller *vs.* Parrish, 3 Mich., 211; Carter *vs.* Burris, 10 Smede & Mar., (Miss.,) 527; Despart *vs.* Walbridge, 15 N. Y., 374; Tyler *vs.* Strang, 21 Barb., 198; Picard *vs.* McCormick, 11 Mich., 68; Fowler *vs.* Stoneum, 11 Tex., 478; Howard *vs.* Odell, 1 Allen, 85; Blanchard *vs.* Fearing, 4 Allen, 118; Clarke *vs.* Washington Ins. Co., 100 Mass., 309; Ward *vs.* Beck, 13 Com. Bench, N. S., p. 688; Collins *vs.* Blanteen, 2 Wilson, (K. B.,) 347.)

The claimants were entitled to the protection of the United States in the premises. (Vattel, book 2, chap. c.; President's Message, Dec. 6, 1875; U. S. Statutes at Large, vol. 14, 212; Abbott on Shipping, p. 58; 6 Opinions of the Attorneys-General, pp. 648, 649; The Margaret, 9 Wheaton, 421; Smith's Mercantile Law, pp. 143–144; Parsons's Maritime Law, vol. 1, p. 39; Bixby *vs.* Franklin Insurance Co., 8 Pick., 86; Ocean Ins. Co. *vs.* Pollocks, 13 Peters, 157; Coolidge *vs.* Ingles, 13 Mass., 26; 3 Kent Com., 139, 146, and 149; Long *vs.* Duff, 2 Bos. & Pull., 209; Hatch *vs.* Smith and Trustee, 5 Mass., 42; Consular Regulations of the U. S., Art. xvii.)

The complainants, at all times during the late rebellion, bore true allegiance to the United States. Their act in transferring the vessel is not evidence to the contrary. (Vattel, book 3, chap. 10, sec. 178; The Bennet, Dodson's Reports, p. 179; English Statute of 1854.)

This claim has been examined by the Department of State, the Tribunal of Arbitration, and the British board of trade, and not criticised. It was included in all presentations and estimates, and undoubtedly included in the award of the Tribunal.

Mr. J. A. J. Creswell, for the respondent—

Cited statutory provisions in relation to vessels of the United States. (Customs Regulations Treasury Department, 1874, p. 1; Rev. Stats., § 4132, § 4311, § 4312, § 4136, § 4180, § 4165, § 4177, § 4178, § 4189, § 4190, § 4308; 6 Opinions Attorneys-General, p. 652; Consular Regulations, secs. 219, 220, 221, 225; Rev. Stats., § 4172;) and contended—

1. That the bill of sale executed and delivered by the owners, through their agent, the master, to Currie, did in law convey a good and valid title to Currie. The fact that no purchase-money was paid would not impair the validity of the transfer. (14 Johns. 210; 20 *id.*, 338; 3 Har. & McHen., 433; 4 Serg. & R., 564; 17 Mass., 249; 4 N. H., 397; The Ariel, Moore's P. C. Reports, vol. xi, p. 131; 1 J. J. Marsh, 388; 16 Wend., 460; 9 Cowen, 266; 1 Bland Ch., 249; 2 Ham., 182. Disapproving 1 B. & Cres., 704; 2 Taunt., 154; 5 B. & Ald., 606; 1 Greenl., 1; 2 McLean, 543.)

The pretext that the transfer was merely colorable will not avail. (16 sec. act Dec. 31, 1792; The Margaret, 9 Wheat., 421.)

The owners of vessel and cargo are now precluded from denying that she was a British ship. (Phil. Int. Law, 2d ed., 1873, vol. iii, pp. 734–5; Halleck's Int. Law, chap. 20, sec. 17, p. 486; The Fortuna, 1st Dods, Adm. R., 87; The Success, *ibid*, 131; The William Bagaley, 5 Wall., 410.)

The complainants therefore have no standing in this court, for if they claim as owners they must claim as owners of a British ship. There is no justification for a demand by the complainants as mortgagees in possession, or as owners by sale and delivery without paper title. The Virginius, 14 Opinions Att'ys Genl., 340.

The complainants voluntarily expatriated the vessel and placed her beyond the protection of the United States.

RAYNER, J., delivered the opinion of the court:

From the evidence in these cases it appears that the bark The Texan Star was built in Boston in 1858, and measured $798\frac{47}{95}$ tons. In 1863 she was successfully engaged in the East India trade, her managing owners being Samuel Stevens & Co., of Boston, and her commander or master being Samuel B. Pike, who owned one-sixth of the vessel. On July 3, 1863, Stevens & Co. wrote to Captain Pike, warning him that one of the confederate cruisers was on her way to the East Indies, and saying to him:

> We advise that you place your ship under the British flag immediately, (or any other flag.) You have probably been advised by Atkinson, Tilton & Co., of the process, which is as follows: You are to sell her and receive notes in payment, and as soon as the transfer is made you to take a mortgage and give the notes in payment; then receive an irrevocable power of attorney in your favor to sell or to manage the ship as you please, receive all moneys, &c., which will place you in the same position as at present. If you find it difficult to do this, and a good price can be obtained, you had better *sell*. * * * In regard to ship's employment, in case you do not sell, we can only advise as heretofore, that you act according to the best of your judgment.

On the 11th of November, 1863, Captain Pike arrived at Maulmain, where he received the foregoing letter from Stevens & Co. At Maulmain Captain Pike took on a cargo of rice for Singapore. On the 13th of November he wrote to Stevens & Co. doubtfully about his change of flag, saying he "would not like to make such arrangement, unless he was satisfied with the parties to whom the transfer would be made." On December 9 Captain Pike again wrote to the same parties, saying "Since I last wrote you, matters in this vicinity have undergone a great change." He went on to state that after completing his loading, and being about ready to clear from the custom-house, the mail-steamer from Singapore had arrived, bringing news of the destruction of American shipping in the Straits of Sunda, and that in consequence of this he deemed it necessary, for the interest of all concerned, to change the flag, in accordance with the advice he had received.

Accordingly it was arranged that Captain Pike should make a temporary transfer of the ship to Mark R. Currie, of the house of M. R. Currie & Co., and that her name should be changed to The Martaban; that Currie should give in return a mortgage to the nominal vendors for the nominal consideration of 80,000 rupees, with the understanding that Captain Pike should, as master, continue to exercise the same absolute control and management of said vessel as before.

It was further agreed that Currie was to receive one per cent. for his services in the matter. All this was accordingly done, and the paper-writings passed. The cargo was already on board, 12,556 bags of rice of 164 pounds each, with freight agreed upon at one rupee four annas per bag. Captain Pike paid the cost of the proceedings. On the 12th December, 1863, Captain Pike sailed from Maulmain, and on the 24th of the same month the Martaban, as then called, was captured and, with her cargo, burnt by the Alabama, when within only a few hours' sail of Singapore.

These claims of the parties complainant against the United States for the value of the said ship, freight, and master's private property, are preferred upon the grounds, first, that there was in fact no sale at all, and that the right of property in the ship by the owners, Stevens and others, was never divested; secondly, that even if this be not so, and the sale must be regarded as valid and binding, yet, as mortgagees retaining possession, they must be regarded as virtual owners of the property, and are entitled to remuneration before this court.

To the allowance of these claims the counsel for the United States objects. He takes the position that the claimants are excluded under the operation of the restriction imposed on this court by the twelfth section of the act of Congress establishing this court, as follows: "No claim shall be admissible or allowed by this court arising in favor of any person not entitled at the time of his loss to the protection of the United States in the premises." That the complainants having sold their vessel to a British subject, and put her under a British flag, the said vessel was British property; and, therefore, not being entitled to the protection of the United States *in the premises*, they can have no showing before this court.

The act of Congress under which this court derives its jurisdiction provides that all claims are admissible before it directly resulting from damages caused by the so-called insurgent cruisers Alabama, &c., and claims admissible must be those "arising in favor of persons entitled at the time of loss to the protection of the United States in the premises."

It is proven that the claimants are American citizens, whose status as to loyalty, non-compensation from other quarters, &c., brings them within the category of rightful claimants, so far as that status is concerned. It is proven that they suffered loss and damage directly resulting from the acts of the confederate cruiser, either as owners of the ship or as mortgagees in possession. Is there any other consideration in the premises, by which they have forfeited this protection? All the facts, the circumstances, and the evidence, go to prove that the conveyance of the ship to Currie was never intended or regarded by any of the parties to have any validity. It was designed and carried out in collusion and pretense. It was not done in the way of trade or of commercial enterprise. It was not to secure gain, but to avoid loss. There does not appear to have been any attempt at secrecy or deception, or misrepresentation, except as against the common public enemy.

Stevens & Co. advised Captain Pike to place the ship under the flag, as a precaution against threatened danger; and instructed him as to the manner of proceeding, empowering him to reserve to himself in the mortgage full control and management of the ship, "according to the best of his judgment." The evidence shows that about that time there was a sort of panic with the American shipping in the East Indian seas. Captain Pike seems to have been reluctant to put the ship under another flag, and so far from attempting anything clandestinely, he first consulted Mr. Brooke, the American consul at Maulmain, and applied to him to aid him in the matter. M. R. Currie & Co. wrote to Atkinson, Tilton & Co.:

> We have had the vessel transferred to our Mr. Currie, in order that he (Captain Pike) may sail in safety from Southorn privateers.

E. J. Stanley, an assistant in the firm of Currie & Co., testified that Captain Pike was brought to the office of Currie & Co., and introduced to them by Brooke, the American consul, to—

> Consider the question of danger to the vessel and her cargo, in consequence of the presence of the confederate cruiser Alabama, and to make arrangements to avoid the same.

Captain Pike wrote to Stevens & Co. that he deemed it necessary, "for the interest of all concerned, to change the flag." Currie did not *pay* a rupee for the ship, but received a commission of one per cent. for his services, and even executed a mortgage for ten thousand rupees more than the nominal consideration of the collusive sale. Currie never claimed any ownership in the vessel, but admitted the pretended sale was in order to be safe against danger from the Alabama. Captain Pike, in the terms of the mortgage, retained the absolute power of attorney to manage and control the vessel as he pleased. Captain Semmes, in his journal, speaking of the capture of the Texan Star, says he asked Captain Pike if he did not know that the transfer was intended merely as a cover to prevent capture, and that Captain Pike replied, "Yes, I do know it." Semmes burned the ship, because he was shrewd enough to discover that the pretended transfer of the ship was a sham to escape him. He burnt her *as* an American ship. Currie has never interposed any claim to the ship. Great Britain did not, through her representatives at Geneva, take the position that she was an English ship, or attempt to evade her responsibility for the destruction by the Alabama.

Looking at the matter, therefore, with all its circumstances and surroundings, the pretended transfer from Pike to Currie must be regarded as no sale at all, but as utterly null and void—intended as such by all the parties at the time, and so regarded since—and that when the vessel was destroyed, she was the property of Stevens and others. There are, however, other questions that present themselves, touching the right of the parties to remuneration by this court, even admitting the conveyance of the ship to have been null and void. Although the transfer was collusive and designed to work no change in the ownership of the property, still, the question arises, are the applicants *estopped* from pleading collusion and deception? Although such sale was void, as against the rights and interests of third parties, was it binding and operative on the parties themselves? Can they be allowed to ignore and nullify their own deliberate acts with a view to their own benefit?

The first point to be considered here is, what was the nature of the act done (seeking the protection of a foreign flag)—was it wrongful in its character? Did it contravene public or private rights? It is a well-settled principle of law that contracts involving *wrong* are not to be favored. Chancellor Kent, in his Commentaries, (vol. 2, page 366,) says, in treating of contracts:

> The consideration must not only be valuable, but it must be a lawful consideration, and not repugnant to law or sound policy, or good morals. *Ex turpi contractu, actio non oritur.* The reports, in every period of the English jurisprudence, contain striking illustrations of the general rule that contracts are illegal when founded on a consideration *contra bonos mores*, or one against the principles of sound policy, or founded in fraud, or in contravention of the positive provisions of some statute law.

The "consideration" here mentioned by Chancellor Kent, as is evident from the context, is to be understood in its largest and most comprehensive sense. It means something more than the simple *quid pro quo;* something more than the mere reward or expected benefit moving the parties to the contract. It looks specially to the results and consequences as they may involve the rights and interests of others. It keeps in view the fundamental principle of the "social contract;" that every man may do what he pleases with his own, so far only as that he does not thereby encroach on the privileges of others. Did the pretended sale of the ship in the cases now under consideration come within the category of either of the objections presented by Chancellor Kent? It cannot be said to have been "*against good morals* or against the principles of sound policy." I think the position may be assumed that it is a common practice, recognized by the commercial nations of the world, to seek protection to private property on the ocean by a transfer of the ship to a foreign flag. Sir William Scott said, (see the case of the Bennet, 1 Dodson, 182:)

> It has been the practice of all times to assume disguise for the purpose of imposing upon enemies. States in declared hostility frequently stand in need of the commodities of each other's country, and ships have in all times been permitted to assume disguise, for the purpose of supplying such necessaries. *Semble* that such disguises, assumed for the purpose of deceiving the enemy, are not a ground for condemnation.

Such change of flag is a safe precaution, recognized by the courts of admiralty; and such courts are rigid in requiring that such transfers shall be *bona fide* and absolute, in order to escape condemnation before a prize-court. The reason of this is, that in cases of lawful *prize* the rights of third parties (the captors) are involved, and prize-courts will not allow legal captures to fail and enemy's property to escape condemnation by any collusions and deceptive transfers. (See the cases of The Jemmy, 4 Rob. Adm. Rep., p. 31; The Omnibus, 6 Rob. Adm. Rep., 71; The Andromeda, 2 Wallace, 481; The Baigorry, 2 Wallace, 474; The Jenny, 5 Wallace, 183.)

Such transfers cannot be said to be against "sound policy." The commercial marine of its citizens, although private property, constitutes a material portion of the power, wealth, and efficiency of every nation. Its commercial tonnage is regarded with pride by every country as an element of its strength. Therefore, any honestly-entertained purpose to secure this great element of national power and wealth by misleading the public enemy, where no wrong to third parties is involved, and where, owing to the peculiar circumstances of the case, the nation cannot afford protection, is rather favored than discouraged by national policy. It certainly is tolerated.

Was the transfer to the British flag of the Texan Star "founded in fraud?" This depends upon the *animus* of the parties in the transaction. All the testimony goes to show that Captain Pike reluctantly resorted to the transfer of the ship to the British flag as the only safe method of saving her from destruction. The thing was not done in a corner. No secrecy was attempted, except as against the public enemy. Mr. Brooke, the official representative of the American Government, was consulted, and sanctioned the proceeding. No private gain or profit was the object in view; it even entailed expense on Captain Pike and the other owners of the vessel.

Was the transfer "in contravention of the positive provisions of some statute law?" We are not aware of the existence of any such law. So far from it, prize-courts recognize such transfers, where they are *bona fide*, as being valid and binding. On the other hand, they are very vigilant in examining and exposing such transfers, when they are fictitious and intended to do wrong to others. In many cases, such pretended transfers to another flag are either to invade the rights of others or to violate the law, either of the power whose flag is abandoned or of that whose flag is assumed, or to deprive legal captors of rightful prize. In all such cases prize-courts treat such transfers as null and void. It is readily admitted that if a war had existed between the United States and Great Britain at the time, and the Texan Star, or Martaban, had been captured by a British cruiser, she would properly have been condemned as lawful prize; or if the Confederate States had had any port to which the vessel could have been taken, she would have been condemned—and why? Because, being truly an American vessel, notwithstanding the pretended sale, she would have been regarded as enemy's property, therefore making such capture lawful according to the law of nations, and because the captors would have had a just claim to the captured property.

Because the law regulating the action of prize-courts will not listen to the plea of change of flag, where the object is to deceive and defraud—and where the consequences are to impinge upon the rights of others, either nations or individuals—does it necessarily follow that a party directly concerned may not himself insist upon the nullity of such change of flag, where there is no purpose to interfere with the rights of others, or to violate any law?

In deciding upon the application of the parties in these cases, the same *reason* does not apply that applies in prize-courts. Here there are no third parties whose rights are to be injuriously affected. Here there was no disposition to violate any law, or to contravene any principle of public policy. Here the maxim of Lord Coke seems to be in point, "*Mutata legis ratione, mutatur et lex.*"

There is no law making the assumption of the flag of another nation a crime *as such*, with any special punishment annexed thereto.

True, the policy of commercial nations induces them to foster and protect their shipping interests. In the United States and in Great Britain especially this policy encourages the citizen to name and to register and to navigate his vessel as of his own country. But, so far as our country is concerned, it is not compulsory. There is a law of the United States that American vessels, unless duly enrolled and having a license in force, shall not be entitled to the privilege of vessels employed in the coasting trade or fisheries, (see Rev. Stat., sec. 4311.) But there is no law *compelling* or requiring registration, enrollment, or license; the law only denies to vessels certain privileges, if they are not so registered, enrolled, and licensed. A citizen of the United

States may own a vessel not having such registration, enrollment, or license, and may employ her in foreign commerce. The act of 10th February, 1866, chap. 8, provides:

That no ship or vessel which has been recorded or registered as an American vessel, pursuant to law, and which shall have been licensed or otherwise authorized to sail under a foreign flag, and to have the protection of any foreign government during the existence of the rebellion, shall be deemed or registered as an American vessel, or shall have the rights and privileges of American vessels, except under the provisions of an act of Congress authorizing such registry.

But it does not provide that no such vessel shall be owned by a citizen of the United States, nor that the Government will not protect him in the ownership of such vessel. The act of 1792 also provides, (see Rev. Stat., sec. 4172:)

That if any ship or vessel heretofore registered, or which shall hereafter be registered, as a ship or vessel of the United States, shall be sold or transferred, in whole or in part, by way of trust, confidence, or otherwise, to a subject or citizen of any foreign prince or state, and such sale or transfer shall not be made known in manner hereinbefore directed, such ship or vessel, together with her tackle, apparel, and furniture, shall be forfeited.

"The manner hereinbefore directed," that is alluded to, is that, (see sec. 4171:)

When the master or person having the charge or command of a registered vessel is changed, the owner, or one of the owners, or the new master of such vessel, shall report such change to the collector of the district where the same has happened, or where the vessel shall first be after the same has happened, and shall produce to him the certificate of registry of such vessel, and shall make oath, &c.

Here it will be seen that the penalty of "forfeiture" attaches, not to the transfer of the vessel to a foreign flag, (which is made entirely lawful when the prescribed conditions are complied with,) but it is the failure to report the facts to the collector of the district that works the forfeiture. In the case of Captain Pike and the other owners of the vessel, it was impossible to report the facts to the collector, in order to save the vessel from forfeiture. The vessel was destroyed. The law does not require impossibilities. *Lex non cogit vana seu impossibilia.* So far as the consequences to the vessel, the cargo and the crew, were involved, the destruction of the ship by the Alabama was as if done by the act of God.

If the captain of the ship had returned with her, and had not made known the transfer, change of name, &c., he would have been liable to the penalty of the statute; but the penalty is imposed, not for making the sale or changing the name, but for not making the fact known as required. He never did return with the ship, and consequently did not violate the statute, and the question of forfeiture is out of the case altogether.

Supposing the conveyance of the ship to Currie to have been null and void, yet can the complainants be allowed to urge the invalidity and designed collusion of their own acts? Are they estopped from denying the force and virtue of their own deed? They certainly would be, if thereby the rights and interests of third parties were to be affected. If the transfer of the ship to the British flag had been a wrongful and illegal act, it might be the safer course to leave the parties to reap the consequences of their folly or their crime. But looking to all the consequences, and the *animus* as we are able to judge of it by the testimony, we do not think the law of *estoppel* applies in this case. There are no third parties whose rights are to be affected by the denial by the complainants of the validity of the transfer to Currie. There is not estoppel as against Currie. Currie is not here to plead such estoppel, and we are not called on to go out of our way to protect the rights of him, a British subject. Bouvier, in his Law Dictionary, defines estoppel:

Where a fact has been admitted or asserted for the purpose of influencing the conduct or deriving a benefit from another, so that it cannot be denied without a breach of good faith, the law enforces the rule of good morals as a rule of policy, and precludes the party from repudiating his representations or denying the truth of his admissions. * * * The principle has come to be applied in all cases where one, by words or conduct, willfully causes another to believe in the existence of a certain state of things, and induces him to act on that belief, or to alter his own private position.

The same doctrine of *estoppel* as laid down by the Supreme Court of the United States, in Van Rennselaer *vs.* Kearney, (11 Howard, 297,) seems to be specially applicable in the cases before us. Mr. Justice Nelson then said:

Estoppel bars the truth only in the case where its utterance would convict the party of a previous falsehood; would be the denial of a previous affirmation upon the faith of which persons had dealt and pledged their credit or expended their money. It is a doctrine, therefore, when properly understood and applied, that concludes the truth in order to prevent fraud and falsehood, and imposes silence on a party only when, in conscience and honesty, he should not be allowed to speak.

The doctrine as to estoppel declares the truth only in the case where its utterance would convict the party of a previous falsehood, upon the faith of which persons had dealt, pledged their credit, or expended their money.

Currie is not within the category of this doctrine, even if he were a party contestant here, which he is not. So far from being misled by falsehood or breach of faith, he was a willing party to the transaction. There is a concurrence of decisions in many of the States of the Union in favor of the doctrine that no one can plead the acts or declarations of another by way of *estoppel*, except where he has *himself* been misled or deceived thereby.

The complainants are not estopped as against the United States. In the first place they have not misled or deceived the United States. In the second place the United States does not occupy the position of a party litigant, with rival interests to defend, but rather the position of a "respondent" to an appeal to its protection in a transaction where the complainants suffered loss, in an effort to protect its commercial marine against a public enemy.

The cases cited to prove that a colorable transfer to a foreign flag cannot be relied upon to save a vessel from condemnation by a prize-court do not, as it seems to me, apply in the cases before us. In the case of the Margaret, (9 Wheat., 421,) the transfer was to the Spanish flag, for the avowed purpose of evading the Spanish revenue-laws, which involved a loss of money to the Government of Spain. Mr. Justice Story said well in that case:

There is certainly nothing in this record that shows that the intention might not also have been to evade the American revenue-laws; for the obvious purpose of keeping the Spanish master and papers on board was to assume the American character in our ports, and to re-assume the Spanish character on the next voyage, so that the parties might obtain the fullest benefit of the double papers.

The question was, whether the vessel was forfeited to the Government under the act of 1792. The rights of third parties were involved. The proceeding was "against the principles of sound policy—founded in fraud—and in contravention of a positive provision of law." In such a case, of course, the parties defendant were not allowed to plead the invalidity of their own acts.

In the case of The Fortuna, (1 Dods. Adm. Rep., 87,) the sale was by an American owner to a Portuguese, with a view to fitting her out as a slave-ship. She was confiscated on the ground that Great Britain and the United States having declared the slave-trade to be beyond the pale of national protection, the sham sale of the vessel was void, because of the criminality of the purpose intended.

In the case of the William Bagalley, (5 Wallace, 410,) the vessel was captured in an attempt to run the blockade at Mobile. She was sailing under the confederate flag, and the court simply refused to recognize the intervention of a part-owner of the vessel, who had remained loyal during the war.

In the case of the Success, (1 Dods. Adm. Rep., 131,) the vessel was condemned for a violation of the British orders in council of January, 1810, which prohibited intercourse between all ports from which British ships were excluded. She was captured while prosecuting a voyage from Gottenburg to Malmo, under the Swedish flag; and the evidence showed that the cargo and a moiety of the ship was Swedish property, and the other moiety was British property.

In these cases mentioned, all of which were prize-cases, the condemnation was not by way of punishment or forfeiture for the desertion of one flag and the seeking the protection of another. The courts simply declared that they could not, by a fictitious transfer of the property and change of flag, avoid the responsibility that would attach to them in their original character; that when engaged in or preparing to commit any unlawful act, or to impinge upon the rights of others, all such collusive and deceptive transfers for the objects mentioned should avail nothing before prize-courts.

Even admitting the sale of the ship from Captain Pike to Currie was valid and binding, and that the complainants are *estopped* from pleading the nullity of the sale and the invalidity of the transfer, still it seems that the complainants, in virtue of the mortgage, accompanied by unqualified power of attorney and possession, must be regarded as the legal owners of the ship.

The well-recognized policy of the law, resting on an uninterrupted series of decisions, is peculiarly favorable to mortgagees in possession. If the deed from Pike to Currie was valid, the mortgage from Currie to Pike must also have been valid. Mr. Justice Strong, in the case of Brobst *vs.* Brock, (10 Wallace, 519,) in the United States Supreme Court, thus expounds the doctrine of the effect of mortgage:

> As between the parties to the instrument or their privies, it is a grant which operates to transmit the legal title to the mortgagee, and leaves to the mortgagor only a right to redeem. * * * * Courts of equity as fully as courts of law have always regarded the legal title to be in the mortgagee until redemption.

True, this case involved the title to real property, but the law leans still more favorably to mortgagees in possession of personal property. The books abound with cases that recognize a mortgagee in possession as the legal owner of the property, and as entitled to the rights and privileges, and liable to the duties and responsibilities, of ownership. The mortgagee of a ship may take out a register in his own name, and even before delivery, and may exercise the rights of ownership. A mortgagee of a ship may maintain an action of replevin against an attaching creditor, and also against one claiming to have purchased from the mortgagor. A mortgagee of personal property may maintain trespass against a stranger who takes it from the possession of the mortgagor, even in cases where the debt is not yet due, and has not come into the mortgagee's possession, and even where the mortgage is not recorded. (See the following cases: De Mattos *vs.* Gibson, 1 Johnson and Hemming, 79 Eng. Chanc. Rep.; Weston *vs.* Penniman, 1 Mason U. S. Circuit Rep., 306; Ring *vs.* Franklin, 2 Hall N. Y. Rep., 1; Esson *vs.* Tarbell, 9 Cushing's Mass. Rep., 407; Harding *vs.* Coburn, 12 Metcalf's Mass. Rep., 333.)

The above decisions clearly show that even if the deed to Currie was binding, still the legal title was in the complainants, as mortgagees in possession, and that as such they possess all the rights and remedies recognized as pertaining to absolute ownership. In a late case decided in England it was held where a ship was mortgaged to secure a loan from the mortgagee to the owner, that by reason of the mortgage the mortgagee became the rightful owner of the ship. (See Dickerson *vs.* Kitchen, 8 Ellis & Blackburn, 789.) This was in conformity with the settled doctrine in such cases. In the case of Westerdell *vs.* Dale, (see 7 Term Rep., 312,) Lord Kenyon held that—

> As to the cases respecting a mortgagee of a ship, whether in or out of possession, he is the legal owner, and must be so considered in a court of law, notwithstanding his title is subject to equitable interests.

The fact that Captain Pike, in his own right, and as the agent of others, with full powers, was in the actual and peaceable possession of the vessel when she was destroyed, gives him a status as complainant before this court—as it would have given him the right to maintain an action for any tort against the ship. (See Gelston *vs.* Hoyt, 13 Johnson, N. York Rep., 561.)

As to the effect of a mortgage upon freight, the principle is well recognized in the English courts, that a mortgage of a ship carries with it the freight, and the mortgagee intervening by taking possession before the freight becomes payable, is entitled as against the mortgagor or his assignee in bankruptcy. (See Rusden *vs.* Pope, 3 Law Register Exchequer Rep., 269, 37 ditto, 137.)

The counsel for the United States in his forcible argument, and also in his very able brief filed in these cases, takes the ground that the entire proceeding, first of a pretended sale from Pike to Currie, and then of a mortgage from Currie to the complainants, was irregular, illegal according to British law, and an attempted fraud upon the British government, and therefore should not receive relief or countenance from this court. He earnestly urges the points that ships belonging to British subjects must be registered under the merchant shipping-act in order to be recognized as British ships; that in order to obtain such registration the person applying must subscribe a declaration, denying that any alien holds any legal or beneficial interest in such vessel; that no notice of any trust, express, implied, or constructive, shall be recorded or entered by the registrar; that the movement to procure fraudulent documents and get the ship registered as a British ship, when there was no intention, in fact, of changing her American character, involved conspiracy and combination to override the law and impose a simulated British ship upon the government of Great Britain; and that if the whole facts of the case should be exposed upon a proceeding to enforce such a mortgage in a British court, the mortgage would be at once declared a fraud on British law. Admitting all this to be true, yet, with all deference to the learned counsel for the United States, I do not see how that should affect the status of the applicants before this court. They may have blundered, they may have acted illegally, judging from a British standpoint, but are we called on to take judicial cognizance of these facts? Conspiracy and combination to defraud is a judical fact, the result of investigation and trial. No such stigma as that supposed has been put on the acts of the complainants by any court—no such annulment of the mortgage. Was their loss of the ship owing to the facts of the sale and mortgage? Was it not owing to other causes altogether extraneous to the negotiations between Pike and Currie?

The counsel for the United States admits that the sale of the ship to Currie by Pike was a valid sale, as against the vendors, and that it transferred the right of property in the ship to a British subject. He also admits that "as against Currie the mortgage might be maintained upon the doctrine of estoppel." Although the mortgage was not registered, that was not material as against Currie, and it has not been set aside in any British court for illegality. Although the mortgage may not have been recorded according to the requirements of the British statute, that could not affect its validity as between Pike and Currie, or enable any one but subsequent mortgagees, purchasers, or creditors to contest the force of the mortgage, although it may not have been recorded. (See Kent's Com., vol. 4, p. 168, 12th edition.)

Although the British shipping-act required that the registration of the ship, as a British ship, should have been done with all due forms and conditions, still the neglect of such registration, while it might deprive the ship of certain rights, privileges, and advantages appertaining to lawfully-registered ships, could not affect the question of the right of property under the sale and mortgage. Shall we summarily dismiss the complainants because they may have blundered into a neglect or violation of British law, while endeavoring to avoid the misfortune that has brought them as petitioners to our bar?

Stress has been laid by the United States counsel upon the fact that prize-courts look with disfavor on mortgages and other beneficial interests, set up to captured property; and he cites the cases of The Hampton, (5 Wall., 372,) The Aina, (Spink's Eccles. and Adm. Rep., 315,) The Ida, (Spink's do., 331,) The Maria, (11 Moore's Privy Council Rep., 271,) The Amy Warwick, (2 Sprague, 150,) to sustain the position. That is all very true, and for the reason that prize-courts cannot stop to investigate all the niceties and details of beneficial interests in captured property. They interfere with and impinge upon the rights of others, captors in prize-cases.

Chancellor Kent (vol. 1, page 87) says: "If prize-courts were to open the door to equitable claims, there would be no end to discussion and imposition." In the case of Hampton, (5 Wall., 372,) Mr. Justice Miller says:

> If the claim of a mortgagee were once admitted in these courts, there would be an end of all prize condemnations. As soon as a war was threatened, the owners of vessels and cargoes which might be so situated as to be subject to a capture would only have to raise a sufficient sum of money on them by *bona fide* mortgages to idemnify them in cases of such capture.

It is not because the admiralty courts have any special spite against mortgagees *per se*, but because it would be impossible to preserve the old landmarks of the prize-court system, and to preserve and enforce the laws regulating capture, if the prize-courts had to take cognizance of and settle vexed questions of equitable interests constantly arising. But the same reason does not apply in this court. Because prize-courts eschew discrimination between absolute ownership and mortgages and equitable interests, is no reason why this court should look on them with disfavor or impatience. There is no reason why this court should adopt, as the standard of its duty or the measure of its generosity, the principles by which prize-courts regulate their action on the subject of mortgage.

We do not think we could do strict justice to those persons whom it was the purpose of Congress to relieve, by adhering technically to the principles governing the admiralty courts, whether by "instance" jurisdiction in time of peace, or "prize" jurisdiction in time of war. While keeping within the limits of "the principles of law" in admiralty, wherever applicable, we are constantly in danger of insensibly falling into the rigid technicality, which is inevitable for their guidance in courts of admiralty. In cases arising before such courts there are individual parties litigant, whose conflicting rights have to be protected and adjudicated. In prize-courts the rights of captors have to be protected; and behind all personal rights involved there are certain great elementary principles of sectional policy and sectional interests that every maritime and commercial country must scrupulously guard and maintain.

In this court our duties are somewhat peculiar. After discharging a great and important trust, our task will be ended, and we shall become *functi officio.* Here there are no individual parties litigant, whose conflicting rights have to be weighed with so much exactitude. The Government allows itself to be sued as an act of grace. It invites the citizen to its protecting generosity. To be sure, it demands that the great landmarks of the law must be kept in sight; otherwise we would not be a court, and our decisions would lack uniformity and system. But within the purview of the "principles of law," we are to decide according to "the merits of the several cases." These last quoted words are not unmeaning. They are not put there as a mere platitude.

There are many cases in the admiralty reports which are so variant in their *conclusions* (although based on concurrent principles of law) that if we were to attempt to conform our decisions to those in prize-cases, we should find ourselves in endless confusion. In many cases, (viz, The Vigilantia, 1 C. Rob., 13; The Vrow Elizabeth, 5 C. Rob., 2; The Vrow Anna Catherina, 5 C. Rob., 167; The Fortuna, 1 Dodson, 87; The Success, 1 Dodson, 130,) the courts of admiralty have decided that a ship captured, sailing under the flag and papers of an alien enemy, shall abide the consequences of its own act; that it shall not be allowed to disclaim and ignore the nationality of its own selection; that the party who takes the benefit of the flag and pass of another country is bound by them, when they turn to his disadvantage. On the other hand there are many cases reported, (viz, The Bemon, 1 C. Rob., 1; The Embden, 1 C. Rob., 17; The Endraught, 1 C. Rob., 20; The Omnibus, 6 C. Rob., 71,) where ships ostensibly transferred to neutrals, and sailing under neutral flags, with neutral documents, yet really belonging to alien enemies, have been condemned as belonging to the real and not the assumed nationality. In such cases the court not only allowed, but favored and encouraged, evidence to show that the transfer was fraudulent and simulated, and therefore not to be regarded.

Now, which rule shall this court follow in deciding cases before us? Shall we say, that inasmuch as Captain Pike changed his flag of his own accord, at the hazard of consequences, he shall not now be allowed to repudiate his own act, and prove to us the sale was a simulated one, and that his ship continued in fact to be an American ship, notwithstanding the collusive sale? Or shall we decide in conformity with the other class of cases, that the pretended sale being a sham and disguise for temporary security, was no sale at all, and the ship continued to be an American ship? We think we should not be governed by either class of decisions, so far as awarding judgment is concerned. We fully admit the soundness of these decisions, most of which were by that great judge, Sir William Scott, as applicable in the cases as presented before him. We also admit there is really no inconsistency in the decisions upon these two classes of cases, although variant in their results. They were both right, viewed from the stand-point of the established principles governing prize-court adjudications. But we are not sitting as a prize-court. Let us suppose a case by way of illustration. The Confederate States were recognized as entitled to belligerent rights by the European powers. Suppose the Confederate States had been at war with Great Britain, instead of the United States, and had captured the Martaban as a British ship; suppose she had had the benefit of a prize-court before which to carry her prizes, and suppose we had composed that court. According to the principles of law applicable in such cases, we would have had to condemn her as lawful prize. We should have had to say to Captain Pike, "You selected your nationality, and your flag; it has got you into trouble; we cannot allow you to repudiate your own deliberate act, and therefore we shall not entertain the question, as to whether the vessel was transferred to the British flag collusively or in good faith."

On the other hand, suppose the Martaban, captured as she was, as an American ship, notwithstanding her British flag and her British register. I suppose we would, without doubt, have condemned her as a lawful prize to the Confederate States steamer, the Alabama, and have admitted testimony to prove that she was in fact an American ship, and that the transfer to the British flag was a mere pretense and attempted deceit.

But, I repeat, we are not sitting as a prize-court. We have no crowd of captors clamoring for their shares of the prize-money, and reminding us of the decisions in cases of capture. The warning and admonition we hear, is that of a beneficent and paternal government, saying to us, "Don't disregard the great principles of law, on which our free institutions rely for safety, but within that condition, we confide in your sound discretion and your sense of justice to distribute this fund, with a view to the merits of the several cases."

This court will not lay down any standard of moral delinquency or shortcoming, which may affect the capacity of any one to appear before us as complainant. Whether Stevens and others, in their eager effort to avoid danger, may have complicated their affairs and jeopardized their interests, whether a British court might have pronounced the simulated sale and subsequent mortgage as an attempt to defraud and swindle British law and British interests, are questions with which this court has nothing to do.

The argument that prize-courts will not recognize the distinction between legal and equitable interests, or allow any such rival claims to interfere with their action in proceeding to condemnation of the vessel or cargo of an enemy, proves too much for the purpose for which it is introduced. It shows that prize-courts make no distinction between mortgagees and original owners, in fact that mortgagees are to be regarded as the owners.

If mortgagees are liable to the same responsibilities and dangers involved in capture as the original owners, they certainly should be entitled to the same measure of remuneration and redress from any party bound to afford such remuneration and redress. Was not Great Britain as much bound to make redress to an American mortgagee that suffered from the depredations of the Alabama upon the mortgaged property as to an American mortgagor? The question is, who suffered loss? If the effort of Stevens & Co. to save their property by means of transfer and mortgage resulted in failure, and the loss was occasioned by the default or connivance of Great Britain, was not Great Britain bound to make remuneration to them in common with other sufferers?

This claim of Stevens and others was, in due form, transmitted to the Department of State; was by that Department laid before the arbitrators at Geneva; was, in common with other claims, subjected to the rigid scrutiny of the representatives of Great Britain, and never was objected to, as was the claim of John Burns, on the ground of his being a British subject. They interposed no objection on the score of the vessel having been sold to Currie, and was therefore the property of a British subject. (See 4th volume Claims of the United States against Great Britain, and Report of the Committee of the Board of Trade, Schedule C, page 103 of British Counter Case.)

In the cases before us, it is not denied that the parties complainant were loyal during and through the war. It is not denied that they have never received compensation from any other quarter. It is not denied that they suffered loss directly resulting from damage caused by the insurgent cruiser the Alabama; but it is denied that they are entitled to the protection of the United States *in the premises.* It should be borne in mind that this is the only means afforded them of invoking that protection in the premises. It was because it was impossible, under the circumstances, for the United States to protect them that the loss occurred. It was *because* of this impossibility to obtain protection from their own Government that they resorted to this pretended sale and transfer to a foreign flag. The doctrine is laid down by Vattel (book 2, chapter 6) that—

Whoever uses a citizen ill indirectly offends the state, which is bound to protect this citizen; and the sovereign of the latter should avenge his wrongs, punish the aggressor, and, if possible, oblige him to make full reparation, since otherwise the citizen would not attain the great end of the civil association, which is safety.

The protection sought before this court is against the act of a public enemy, against which the United States could not afford protection at the time. Did the parties forfeit this right to protection because of the transfer to another flag under a pretended sale, or because the vessel no longer had an American register? We think not. They still preserved their characters as American citizens, and the protection of their Government still enured to them to be extended at the earliest possible time, and in the only possible way. By the usage of nations, cruisers are allowed, in war, to resort to stratagem in order to make a capture, and so a vessel pursued does not compromise her rights or her nationality by running up a false flag or using simulated papers or adopting other devices in order to escape capture. As to the effect of registration Chief-Justice Mansfield (in Cheminant *vs.* Pierson, 4 Taunt., 357) said:

The register is not a document required by the law of nations, as expressive of a ship's national character.

In Smith's Mercantile Law, (p. 143–4,) it is said that—

No ship is required to be registered, registry being only necessary to confer privileges on that particular ship.

Parsons, in his Maritime Law, (vol. 1, p. 39,) says:

The law is unwilling to recognize in the fact of registration any other efficiency than that of imparting certain privileges, or to permit the absence of that registration to have any other effect than merely to prevent these privileges from attaching to the ship.

Chancellor Kent, (see Kent's Com., vol. 3, p. 146:)

The registry is not a document required by the laws of nations. The registry acts are to be considered as forms of local or municipal institutions for purposes of public policy.

Attorney-General Cushing, in an official opinion, says, (see 6th Attorney-Generals' Opinions, p. 649:)

> The statutes do not *require* a vessel to be registered or enrolled; and that if owned by a citizen of the United States, she is American property, and possessed of all the general rights of any property of an American.

And, further, Mr. Cushing says, (page 652,) when speaking of the right of an American citizen to purchase and own a foreign ship:

> The ship so purchased becomes entitled to bear the flag and receive the protection of the United States.

And this without any reference to registration.

It thus seems that the complainants, whether continuing to be the absolute owners in consequence of the invalidity of the fictitious sale, or whether, as mortgagees in possession, with unlimited authority, whether with or without any register, owned property in the Texan Star; that that property was under the protection of the United States; that this property was lost to them from damage directly resulting from the act of the confederate cruiser; that the ship was destroyed by the Alabama *as* an American ship, and as the property of American owners; and therefore the complainants come within the provisions of the act of Congress providing for distribution under the Geneva award.

As to any shortcomings of Captain Pike and the other complainants, on the score of patriotism—as to whether they preferred to save their gallant bark, that had so often braved the hurricane and the tempest, rather than see her converted into a bonfire upon the ocean—that is a matter of *sentiment*, which, sitting as judges, we dare not entertain. While we might as individuals admire that defiant patriotism which would rush into the very jaws of danger rather than attempt by circumvention to delude a public enemy, yet, in the absence of all proof tending to show any ignoble or unworthy motive, in the exercise of charity, we might not be unable to impute to Captain Pike a praiseworthy object in trying to protect by indirection a portion of the commercial marine of his country, where he was utterly powerless to resist by force

Ever since Æsop wrote the fable of the oak and the reed, it has been regarded as the part of wisdom to bow to the storm that cannot be safely resisted. Owing to one of these peculiar contingencies that arise in the history of nations, our commercial marine was in danger of being swept from the seas; and that result was, in great measure, prevented by a resort for protection to a foreign flag. Those who navigate ships in commercial ventures are scarcely actuated by purely patriotic impulses. Private gain is the leading object. True, it is a pursuit where private gain and national power go hand in hand. May it not be that there is as much patriotism in trying to save a nation's commercial wealth by deceiving the enemy as by defying him, where personal prowess can avail nothing? We may admire the stoical firmness of a Scævola, who thrust his hand into the flames to be consumed, by way of showing to the public enemy his defiant resentment and unforgiving resolution, while prudence might suggest whether it would not have been wiser to preserve his hand, with which to strike for his country at a more auspicious day. Abraham did not forfeit the blessings under the covenant of the promise because he assumed for Sara the disguise of being his sister, that he might thereby deceive the Egyptian King, and thus secure the safety of himself and the honor of his wife. In justice to Captain Pike, it should be borne in mind that he was not acting for himself alone. He was acting in a fiduciary character for others who had intrusted to him their interests, and whose confidence he possessed. It may be that, while it wrung his heart with anguish to repudiate the flag of his country, even temporarily, yet that he felt that duty to others required he should do everything in his power to save their property from destruction.

We render judgments in favor of the complainants in each case.

Wells, P. J., and Baldwin, J., dissenting.

FRIEDRICH ALBERT SCHREIBER AND ARNOLD OTTO MEYER *vs.* THE UNITED STATES. } No. 740.

The doctrine held by the court in Worth *vs.* The United States, that claims may be sustained in favor of foreigners not naturalized, affirmed.

Foreigners who have never resided in this country, yet who have laden their property on board American vessels, are entitled, as to such property, to protection in the premises, and may recover for its value if destroyed.

The exclusion of British subjects from a right of participation in the Geneva fund extends only to subjects native-born, and not to persons who have acquired rights of naturalization in British India, but who still retain their citizenship of origin. A statement of the case will be found in the opinion of the court.

Mr. Frank W. Hackett for the complainants.

The complainants bore "true allegiance" to the United States.

The allegiance clause in the act is of a penal character, and the disability must be confined to such persons as Congress intended to exclude. Non-resident foreigners are not within the "mischief intended to be remedied." (Sedgwick on Statutory Law, 22, 28.) "True allegiance" means only that proof of disloyalty during the rebellion shall bar the claim. The "intent" must be regarded in construing the statute. (Sedgwick on Stat. Law, 255, note *a* and cases cited; Osgood *vs.* Breed, 12 Mass., 530; Wilber *vs.* Crane, 13 Pick., 284.)

The court has already refused to construe this language literally.

The complainants were entitled at the time of their loss to the protection of the United States in the premises.

That the cargo was apparently under the shelter of the British flag when destroyed does not prevent the complainants from claiming that, as a matter of fact, she was under the American flag.

Great Britain has always regarded the vessel as not under her flag. The United States have uniformly asserted their right of protecting the owners of this property. (6 Opinions Attorney-General, 638; Mountague-Bernard, Neutrality of Great Britain, 419.)

The flag of a ship protects her cargo against the enemies of that flag. (The Nereide, 9 Cranch, 388.)

The United States never conceded belligerent rights to the so-called insurgent cruisers.

A neutral owner is entitled to the protection of the United States against the acts of their own rebellious subjects. (Treaty with Hanseatic Republic, proclaimed June 2, 1828; treaty with Prussia, 1828.)

The fact that Meyer had a commercial domicile at Singapore, and had taken out a certificate of naturalization, does not bar his recovery.

Under the naturalization act he was a mere local and temporary British subject, never forfeiting his original and permanent allegiance to his native country. He does not come under the ruling in Worth's case. (U. S. Foreign Relations, 1873, part 2, No. 508; Cockburn on

Nationality, act No. XXX, 1852, government of the East India Company.)

Complainants had a special property in the cargo destroyed. (Homer & Sprague *vs.* The U. S. *ante;* Villalonga *vs.* The U. S., 10 Court of Claims, 452.)

Mr. J. A. J. Creswell, for the respondent.

JEWELL, J., delivered the opinion of the court:

The claimants in this case are both aliens, neither of whom have ever resided in this country; one of them, Schreiber, was born in Berlin, and the other, Meyer, in Hamburg; and both of them at the time of the loss for which claim is here made resided at Singapore, and were then carrying on business under the firm-name of Behn, Meyer & Co.

The facts out of which this claim arises are substantially these: The American ship Texan Star, owned by American citizens, arrived at Maulmain, in British India, about the 8th day of November, 1863, in search of a freight. By the 11th of the same month she had succeeded in contracting with one Abraham Cohen for the carriage of a cargo of rice from Maulmain to Singapore, and a charter-party therefor was executed on the 19th of the same month. Twenty-five days were allowed for the lading of the cargo.

After the cargo was on board, the master, in full accord with Cohen, the charterer, made the nominal change of title and of the name of the ship to that of Martaban, the facts in relation to which are fully stated in the opinion of the court in case No. 736, in which the owners of the vessel claimed and recovered judgment for the loss of the vessel and freight.

In that case a majority of the court held that the owners had not parted with their title in the vessel, notwithstanding their nominal transfer to Currie; that the acts done by them were lawful and proper attempts to deceive the enemy, and save their property from capture.

After the cargo was on board the master signed a bill of lading, making the cargo deliverable to the order of Cohen, who indorsed the same and forwarded it by mail-steamer to Behn, Meyer & Co., the claimants, at Singapore, and at the same time drew his draft on them, of which the following is a copy:

[No. 855.] MAULMAIN, *7th December*, 1863.

Exchange for $15,000. Thirty days after sight of this, my first of exchange, (second and third of the same tenor and date not paid,) pay to the order of self fifteen thousand dollars, only value received, and place the same, with or without further advice to account of shipment of rice per Martaban.

ABRAHAM COHEN.

To Messrs. BEHN, MEYER & CO., *Singapore.*

Accepted due, 22 | 25 January, 1863, Behn, Meyer & Co.

(Indorsed:) Abraham Cohen.

The claimants were commission-merchants in Singapore, and had been accustomed to receive consignments of goods from Cohen for sale, against which he was accustomed to draw drafts, which the claimants accepted, having the bills of lading indorsed to them, as in the present case.

The Martaban was captured and burned by the Alabama on the 24th day of December, 1863, on which day, and before the hour of the destruction of the vessel, the claimants had accepted the draft drawn on them by Cohen, and had received the bill of lading, duly indorsed by him.

This draft was by the custom of trade payable in Mexican silver dollars, and was paid in that coin.

The claimants seek to recover the value in currency of the $15,000 paid by them as acceptors of this draft.

That they were the owners of the cargo, at least that they had the legal title thereto, at the time of the loss, need not be discussed, as the law and authorities have been fully cited in an opinion filed by Rayner, J., in the case of Homer & Sprague *vs.* The United States.

The only question in the case is on the right of these claimants, being non-resident aliens, to prosecute this claim under the law organizing this court.

The case is this: The claimants were the owners of cargo lawfully on board an American ship, which cargo was destroyed with the vessel.

The owners have recovered for the loss of vessel and freight. Can the present claimants, being aliens, who have never resided within the United States, recover for the loss of the cargo?

There is no doubt that the value of this cargo, as well as of the ship and freight, was taken into consideration, and was included in the sum awarded to the United States by the Geneva tribunal. The loss of the ship, its value, as well as the value of the cargo on board, were set forth in the list of claims presented by our Government; and in the list of claims set forth by the English commissioners the value of the Martaban and of her cargo is included, without objection or comment. It is certain that the case of the Martaban and of her cargo was well known to the British government, for the owners of this cargo, the claimants in this case, had, in their capacity of British residents, made claim for compensation for this loss on both the Indian government and the British foreign office, on the ground that the Martaban at the time of destruction was carrying the British flag, and so her cargo was under British protection.

But their claim was rejected, and they were significantly reminded by the governor-general of India that their own proofs showed that at the time their rice was laden on board the Martaban she was an American ship.

The negative evidence in regard to the character attributed to these claimants, and to this claim by the British government, is very strong. The claim made by John Burns for the loss of the effects of his son, alleged by him to have been on board of a whale-ship destroyed, was instantly rejected by the English authorities, yet the claim of the owners of the cargo of the Martaban, amounting to a large sum, had been before the Indian government, and before the home government, as is shown by the memorial presented by the present claimants, in which all the facts were set forth—both the residence in Singapore of the claimants, the naturalization in India of one of them, and the British register of the vessel—and yet the representatives of Great Britain, who roused themselves against the petty claim of John Burns, were silent and made no objection to the claim of $15,000 for the cargo of the Martaban.

These considerations are of little importance, except as strongly tending to show that this claim was recognized as a valid one by both parties to the arbitration, and as affording very strong presumption that the value of this cargo composed a material element in the sum finally awarded.

It seems clear that the final claim of the United States included a demand for compensation for the value of all the private property destroyed by the rebel cruisers, and it seems equally clear that the tribunal gave what it estimated to be the value of this property.

It is not for us, however, to base our decisions upon what occurred at Geneva, even if we certainly knew what took place there. We are to look into the act of Congress, and unless the case of these claimants is embraced within its provisions, we cannot admit their claim, even if we knew the value of this cargo was paid for by Great Britain, and was now in the hands of the United States.

And this brings us to the consideration of the real questions in the case.

The Martaban has been adjudged by this court to have been an American vessel, notwithstanding the disguise she assumed; this cargo was placed on board of her before she assumed her disguise, and continued on board until her destruction, and was destroyed with her. The claimants are entitled to recover unless something in their *personal* con dition excludes them under the terms of the act.

The only exclusions of a personal character are to be found in section twelve, in the last clause, which is as follows:

And no claim shall be admissible or allowed by said court arising in favor of any person not entitled at the time of his loss to the protection of the United States in the premises, nor arising in favor of any person who did not at all times during the late rebellion bear true allegiance to the United States.

We will first consider the first of these clauses.

No claim shall be allowed in behalf of any person not entitled at the time of his loss to the protection of the United States in the premises.

This provision was inserted for some purpose. If the act had contemplated indemnity only to those persons who were citizens of the United States, and had sustained losses, it would have been easy to have said so in terms. Citizens of the United States are always and everywhere entitled to the protection of their Government, and no country has gone farther than ours in admitting the duty and asserting the right.

But this question has already been deliberately passed upon by this court.

In the case of Benjamin Worth *vs.* The United States, with other cases presented at the same time, the question was raised on demurrer by the counsel for the United States, "upon the ground that an unnaturalized foreigner cannot claim indemnity before this court for losses sustained by the depredations of the rebel cruisers." (See judgment of the court, opinion by Rayner, J.)

The various cases were fully argued, and the demurrer was overruled in an opinion which fully stated the right of an unnaturalized foreigner to protection in the premises, and to recover for any loss sustained and proved.

The syllabus of the case states the result as follows:

The twelfth section of the act under which the court is organized provides that no claim shall be admissible or allowed arising in favor of any person not entitled at the time of his loss to the protection of the United States "in the premises," &c. Held, that this provision embraced all persons whether native-born or of foreign birth, whether naturalized or unnaturalized, except the subjects of Great Britain, who are held to be excluded on other grounds.

The learned judge who prepared the opinion fully examined the question of the right of protection of persons and property as constantly held by our Government, and, among other conclusions stated, said:

It was a great principle for which our Government had contended from its origin—a principle identified with the freedom of the seas, viz, that the flag protected the ship and *every person* and *thing* thereon not contraband.

Nothing which we could now add would strengthen the statement of the law, or the force of the reasoning made use of by the author of this opinion, as by citation and argument he sums up the course of the law in regard to the duty of protection, and concludes as follows:

Therefore, on the ground of abstract justice and propriety, and upon the ground of legal right, we decide thatforeigners entitled to the protection of our flag in the premises, whether naturalized or not, have a right to share in the distribution of this fund.

What the words "in the premises" mean is also fully stated in the opinion:

The next question is, Are they entitled to this protection, being foreigners, unnaturalized? The act of Congress creating this court, as before suggested, says nothing about citizens, in providing for who may present claims here; and it says nothing about foreigners or aliens, in specifying those who may not present such claims. It would seem that the framers of the act had a view to the case of unnaturalized aliens. Naturalized aliens having the same legal rights (we do not mean the same political privileges in entirety) with native-born citizens, of course it was unnecessary to have made any allusion to *them*. The act speaks of those entitled to the protection of the United States "*in the premises*." Those words, "in the premises," define and limit the application of the law within a narrow circle. It is not everybody entitled to the protection of the Government that can come before this court; it is not every one entitled to that protection who was a loser by depredations on the part of the so-called confederate government, by land as well as by sea; it was not every one that lost by confederate cruisers generally, that can come here. But it *is* every person entitled to the protection of the United States *in the premises*, viz, every such one who sustained loss or injury, directly resulting from damage caused by the so-called insurgent cruisers, Alabama, Florida, &c., and the Shenandoah, after, &c., that can come before this court, and without reference to whether such person is native-born or foreign-born, whether naturalized or unnaturalized.

Since that decision, which was pronounced at a very early period in the sittings of the court, a large number of claims have been passed upon, in which the claimants were persons of foreign birth not naturalized, and in every case the court has entered judgment in their favor, when they showed a loss under the provisions of the act, except in the cases of native-born subjects of Great Britain. No matter what were the circumstances, or the place of residence, if the claimant, not a native-born subject of Great Britain, had goods on board of an American vessel which were destroyed by the cruisers, we have given him a judgment for the value of the goods destroyed, always provided he showed that he did no act during the late rebellion inconsistent with true allegiance.

An examination of the judgments heretofore entered will show a very large number of cases of this sort, in no one of which was the question of the domicile of the claimant at the time of the loss made a subject of discussion.

One of these cases, that of Levois *vs.* The United States, No. 158, is in all respects like the present.

He represented in his petition that he was born in Paris; that during the entire period of the rebellion he resided in Paris; that he was never naturalized in this country, and was a subject of France. It appeared from his own testimony taken in the case that he had visited this country prior to 1851, but from that year to 1867 he had constantly resided in Paris, and did not during that period visit the United States. At the time of the breaking out of the rebellion he had a house of trade in New Orleans, at first with one Vidal as partner, and afterwards with one Mathon. While in business with Mathon, this house made a shipment of goods to New Orleans, which was destroyed by one of the inculpated cruisers. Mathon being dead, Levois made claim as surviving partner for the amount of this loss. The case was heard, and, at first, dismissed on the ground that the disloyal acts of his partner, Vidal, in the conduct of their business were imputable to him; but a rehearing was granted, and on further proofs, showing that Levois personally did no disloyal act, and that he was not responsible for the conduct of Vidal, the court, acting upon the doctrine settled in the case of Worth, gave him judgment for the entire amount of his claim.

Between that case and the present there are no differences. Levois was a non-resident alien, as are the petitioners in the case now under consideration.

This court has in oft-repeated instances made awards in favor of seamen who were not citizens or residents of this country, whose only title to protection arose from the fact they were upon an American ship.

The only limitation of the right to recover in this court, which has been made, is in the case of native-born British subjects, who have been held under the peculiar circumstances of the case not entitled as against the negligence of their own government to protection in the premises.

The views of the court upon this question are found in the opinion of the court in the case of Worth before referred to.

It may not be amiss, however, to restate the view taken by the court in regard to the exclusions contained in the last clause of the twelfth section of the act.

The claimant is excluded unless he was at the time of the loss entitled to the protection of the United States *in the premises*, and unless he at all times during the rebellion bore true allegiance to the United States.

The language of the first exclusion is peculiar; the words are, "not entitled to the protection of the United States *in the premises*;" not simply not entitled to the protection of the United States, but not entitled *in the premises*.

Now no foreigner, no alien non-resident, is entitled to the protection of the United States as to his person, except under special circumstances. He may have sought the asylum of one of our legations, and, being there received, may be entitled to protection.

A foreigner may be entitled to protection either as to his person or as to his property, or both. If he is within this country, or on the deck of one of our vessels, his person and his property with him are under our protection. And if his property alone is within this country it is entitled to and everywhere receives the same protection as the property of citizens; and so of the property of an alien non-resident upon the seas in an American vessel, this Government has always extended to it the same protection as to that of citizens.

We think the language of this clause of the act exactly adapted to a state of facts like the present, and that Congress meant to say, "Whenever, under the circumstances of the case, the person or property of any claimant was so situated as to be entitled to the protection of the United States, you shall award to such claimant indemnity for loss; but you shall have regard to the power against whom protection is claimed. If a claimant who either in his person or his property might otherwise have been entitled to our protection, was a native-born subject of England, through whose negligence these losses occurred, you will not grant him redress. We did not engage to protect him as against the acts of his own government, even though as against all the rest of the world he was entitled to and would receive protection."

These considerations enable us to come readily at the meaning of the last of the exclusions above referred to, that the claimant must at all times during the late rebellion have borne true allegiance to the United States.

In a strict sense, no one but a citizen can bear true allegiance; that is, complete, perfect allegiance.

But this court has in numerous instances made awards to persons not citizens. The case of Levois, above referred to, is one. During the entire period of the rebellion he resided in Paris. He bore no personal allegiance; no duty was required of him personally, yet he showed that he did no act which a loyal citizen might not have lawfully done. He made such a use of his property in this country as was conformable to law, and so bore all the allegiance which a non-resident citizen could be required to bear.

Having done no act to aid the confederacy, either personally or by an improper use of his property here, the court awarded him his claim. The only doubt which arose in his case, which was twice argued, was whether his partner and agent, Vidal, in the conduct of the business did not aid the confederacy.

In the cases of very many sailors awards have been made to aliens who were not proved to have been on our ships but for the single voyage on which their property was destroyed.

In every case hitherto it has been considered sufficient for the claimant to show that he did no act at any time in aid of the rebellion.

It is to be observed that the allegiance is only *during the late rebellion.*

Construing this clause in connection with the part that precedes it, we think the true meaning is that no award shall be made in favor of any person who was not entitled to protection as to his property at the time of his loss as against the British government and as against the confederacy, and that even if he was entitled to such protection as against both governments at the exact time of his loss, yet if he at any time during the rebellion was guilty of any breach of true allegiance to the United States he shall not recover in this court.

This seems to us to furnish a construction of the law conformable to its terms and consistent with reason and justice, and entirely in harmony with all the preceding decisions of this court.

It gives full effect to the principle for which this court in the case of Worth assert that our Government has contended from its origin, viz, "that the flag protects the ship and every person and *thing* therein not contraband." (Worth's case.)

The only other objection to the recovery by the claimants in this case arises out of the fact that Meyer had applied for and been admitted to the privileges of a British subject in India. It is claimed that he comes within the case of the British subject excluded by former decisions of this court.

Meyer was not a native-born British subject, as has been the case of every one heretofore rejected. He was never naturalized in England. The qualified naturalization which he obtained gave him no rights of a British-born subject in England. It only entitled him to the enjoyment of certain privileges in British India. He did not renounce his allegiance to his native country, nor did he acquire the right of protection from Great Britain, except as to his person and property while within the jurisdiction of the colony which gave him the naturalization. Upon his return to his native country he might lawfully bear arms against Great Britain.

Lord Chief-Justice Cockburn, in his Treatise on Nationality, published in 1869, states the British law as to the effect of naturalization in the British dominions, as follows:

By the law of every other country, naturalization, if valid at all, carries with it a new nationality, and invests the party naturalized, not only with the status of a subject, but also with the rights, political and civil, (barring in some respects the higher political rights,) which attach to that status, including the full extent of protection to which a subject can be entitled in return for the allegiance he owes to the state. In this country, on the contrary, since 1851, the Government, with a view to prevent claims for protection being made abroad by persons naturalized in Great Britain, has taken care, by the terms of the grant, to limit the effect of naturalization to the dominions of the crown. * * * Thus restricted, it is plain that the effect of naturalization in Great Britain is only to remove the legal disabilities of the alien, and to place him as to certain minor political rights, and as to civil rights, on the same footing as the natural subject; and, further, that the oath of allegiance taken by him amounts to no more than a promise of that allegiance which every alien while residing in the realm is bound to render, and must be taken to carry with it the implied reservation, that it is to operate no longer than while the party remains within the Queen's dominions. When abroad he is no longer a subject. On his return to his own country his nationality of origin, so far as this country is concerned, would revive, and in case of war between the two countries he might legally bear arms against Her Majesty without incurring, legally or morally, the guilt of treason. (Ch. J. Cockburn on Nationality, 114, 115, 116.)

The commission appointed by Parliament, composed of the most learned publicists of the kingdom, and among them Lord Clarendon, Sir Robert Phillimore, Sir Roundell Palmer, W. Vernon Harcourt, and Montague Bernard, reported on the state of this branch of law, and said:

In the case of an alien-born, naturalization in the United Kingdom under the act of 1844 does not confer any rights of nationality within the colonies. (10 and 11 Vict., c. 83.) On the other hand colonial naturalization confers no rights of nationality beyond the limits of the colony granting naturalization. (Reprinted in Opinions of the Executive Department, and other papers relating to expatriation, naturalization, and change of allegiance, Washington, 1873, page 73; U. S. Foreign Relations, 1873, part 2, p. 1241.)

These citations seem to fully sustain the foregoing conclusions as to the legal condition of Meyer, and we do not think he comes within the principle upon which we have deemed native-born British subjects excluded from the benefits of the law under which we act.

We, therefore, are of opinion that the claimants are entitled to recover the loss which they have proved.

RAYNER, J., dissenting.

AGNES CROOK MCLEANE, administratrix of S. P. Bowen, *vs.* THE UNITED STATES. } No. 763.

WILLIAM JOHNSTON TAYLOR *vs.* THE UNITED STATES. } No. 1179.

This court has power to decide conclusively upon the amount and validity of claims, but not upon the conflicting rights of parties to the sums awarded.

This court cannot compel parties making conflicting claims to interplead, but in all such cases fixes the amount due from the United States, and awards payment thereof to the party having the better *prima-facie* right, but without prejudice to the right of other parties to contest the question of title to the amount awarded before other appropriate tribunals. A statement of the case will be found in the opinion of the court.

Mr. B. W. Throckmorton for the complainant Taylor.

Messrs. Selden & Morse for the complainant McLeane, administratrix.

JEWELL, judge, delivered the opinion of the court:

In the first of these cases, William Johnston Taylor claims compensation for the loss of two-sixteenths of the steamer Electric Spark, destroyed by the confederate steamer Florida July 10, 1864.

The fact of the loss and the value of the vessel and freight have already been adjudicated upon and determined by this court, and damages awarded to the owners of the other fourteen-sixteenths of the vessel.*

As to one-sixteenth, claimed by Mr. Taylor, it was admitted that he had a right to recover.

The right to the other sixteenth was contested, the petitioner in the second case claiming that her late husband, S. P. Bowen, was the true owner of the same.

The undisputed facts appear to be that the Electric Spark was built by Mr. Taylor; that in the original enrollment made by him he declared that S. P. Bowen was the owner of one-sixteenth of her.

The evidence taken in the case of Mr. Taylor, which consisted principally of his own testimony, tended to show that the vessel was built by him; that in taking out the original papers he declared one-sixteenth of the vessel to belong to Bowen; that Bowen had not paid for the interest declared to be in him, but that Taylor charged Bowen with the value of this interest on his books, payment to be made by Bowen out of the profits of the vessel, and that payments had been made on account, and profits passed to the credit of Bowen in part liquidation of the charge before the loss; that after the loss Bowen and Taylor arranged that this ownership in the vessel should be treated as a nullity, and that the sums passed to the credit of Bowen in part payment for the vessel should be treated as credits in favor of Bowen and due to him from Taylor; and that Bowen should be treated as not interested in the vessel; and that Bowen did subsequently use all these sums as debits from Taylor to himself. It was, therefore, claimed by the counsel for Taylor, that even if the legal title to the sixteenth in question was in Bowen, yet that the equitable interest was in Taylor.

There was no cross-examination of Mr. Taylor on behalf of Mrs. McLeane, and no notice given to her of the time of taking testimony in his case.

It was claimed by the counsel for the administratrix of Mr. Bowen that, as the record-title at the time of the loss was in him, this court could not inquire into equities existing between him and Taylor; and that, as Taylor could show no legal transfer of the interest in question to him before the loss, and no assignment of the claim after loss, the award of damages by this court must be to the representative of Bowen, leaving the question of title to the damages, when awarded or received, to be settled by litigation between the parties in other courts.

Upon full consideration, we are of opinion that we cannot and ought not to undertake to decide those conflicting questions of title.

The act of Congress under which this court is organized gives us no authority to compel those different claimants to interplead. We have no power to compel either of the claimants to submit themselves (if they are competent witnesses) or any witnesses they may see fit to examine to cross-examination by any other person than the counsel of the United States.

As against the United States, the parties are competent witnesses; as against each other, they may not be.

* The Electric Spark, the only merchant-steamship destroyed by either of the so-called insurgent cruisers, was captured when one day out from New York. Over one hundred and seventy-five claims were filed in the court for loss occasioned by her destruction. The other owners, through Mr. B. W. Throckmorton, recovered the value of vessel and freight at the rate of $164,000, with interest.

Besides, the extremely short period originally allowed by law, or ever since the extension lately granted by Congress, for the hearing and disposition of the claims before this court is of itself evidence that it was intended that we should consider only these claims as against the United States.

But the case of Comegys *vs.* Vasse, 1 Peters, 193, it seems to us, is conclusive authority upon this question.

That was the case of a claim made before the commissioners appointed under a treaty with Spain, made in 1821, to ascertain the damages suffered by citizens of the United States by reason of the acts of Spain.

The commissioners were to "*receive, examine, and decide upon the amount and validity* of all claims," &c.

The act constituting this court provides (§ 11) "that it shall be the duty of the court to *receive and examine* all claims, &c., * * * and to *decide upon the amount and validity* of such claims," &c.

The powers conferred upon this court are identical with those given to the commissioners under the Spanish treaty.

In that case the Supreme Court decided that these commissioners had power to decide upon the amount and validity of the claims as against the United States, but not upon the conflicting rights of parties to the sums awarded by them.

We believe that the doctrines of this case equally apply to the powers of this court.

In more than one case already passed upon by us there have been conflicting claims, and we have referred to Vasse's case as an authority which this court would follow, and have entered awards in favor of the claimant having the best apparent *prima-facie* case, always saying what we here declare, that our judgments are not conclusive except as against the United States, and that conflicting claims to the amount to be paid by the Treasury are to be decided upon by other appropriate tribunals.

We have, in cases heretofore made, fixed the value of the steamer Electric Spark and her freight at the sum of $164,000.

In case No. 1179, we award to Mr. Wm. Johnston Taylor the sum of $10,250, being the value of one-sixteenth of said steamer and freight, the title to which in him is undisputed.

And, inasmuch as the title to the remaining sixteenth is in dispute, the same being claimed by said Taylor and also by Agnes Crook McLeane, administratrix of the estate of S. P. Bowen, as set forth in claim No. 763, and as we find that the said Bowen was named in the enrollment of the vessel as the owner of one-sixteenth, and so the apparent legal title was in him at the time of the destruction of the vessel, we award to Agnes Crook McLeane, administratrix, the sum of $10,250, being the value of said sixteenth of said vessel and freight.

But this award is not to be taken or considered as a judgment of this court as to the mutual or conflicting claims of the parties above named, but only that the aforesaid sum is due from the United States, and is awarded to Mrs. McLeane as having the *prima-facie* right thereto, and without prejudice in any way to the right of said Taylor to demand and recover the same, if he shall, on proper proceedings, establish his right thereto.

THE COMMERCIAL MUTUAL MARINE INSURANCE Company *vs.* THE UNITED STATES. } No. 1089.

Insurance companies and insurers cannot recover in this court unless they show two things: First, that they suffered damage or paid losses by reason of destruction of property by the confederate cruisers Alabama, Florida, and the Shenandoah after she left Melbourne; and, second, that their business in insuring against war-risks during the rebellion caused them a net loss; both of which being proved, they may recover a sum equal to the amount of such net loss in their business, if their losses by said cruisers amounted to the aggregate of such loss, but in no case greater than the amount of the net loss on such war-risk business.

In determining such net loss, the amounts paid and received for re-insurance are to be taken into consideration.

Mr. W. W. Crapo for the complainants.
Mr. J. A. J. Creswell for the respondent.

JEWELL, judge, delivered the opinion of the court:

After a careful examination of the evidence in this case, we have arrived at the following conclusions:

That, by a proper construction of the law, we are to find, first, what amount was lost by this corporation by the acts of the Alabama, the Florida, and the Shenandoah after she left Melbourne. Under the law they may recover the amount of these losses; *provided*, their net losses on all their war-risks were as great, or greater, than this amount; but, if not as great, they may recover to the extent of their net loss.

The sum of the losses of this claimant by the cruisers above named we find to be $50,956.80.

Second. We are to find what was the sum by which the claimant's "losses in respect of its war-risks during the late rebellion exceeded the sum of its premiums or other gains upon or in respect to such war-risks." (§ 12.)

By this we understand we are to find what the result of its war-premium business during the late rebellion was, and if, on the whole, such business was attended with a profit, we can allow nothing to the claimant, but if such business resulted in a loss, we are to fix such a loss, and may allow to the claimant the whole or a part of the amount of his losses caused by the Alabama, the Florida, and the Shenandoah, to the extent of the net loss so found to have resulted from such business, but no more.

We think in such business is to be included the results of its payments and receipts for re-insurance, for the practice of re-insurance is lawful and of common usage among insurance companies, and made obligatory by the laws of Massachusetts upon this claimant under certain circumstances.

This construction of the law accords with the views expressed in the debates in Congress upon the passage of the bill.

Mr. Butler, one of the managers on the part of the House of Representatives, said, "the committee of conference have agreed to the Senate bill, so far as it does not allow the insurers and underwriters to be paid, except when, upon stating an account of profit and loss, it appears that the underwriters have incurred losses on the whole business." (Cong. Record, June 22, 1874, p. 5374.) As to the underwriters who have not suffered a loss in their whole business, the report simply says they cannot recover any pay before this tribunal. (*Ibid.*, p. 5375.)

In the Senate, in the discussion of the report of the committee of conference, Mr. Morton said: "The bill provides that the insurance companies shall not be paid except when their losses exceed their profits, taking their whole business into consideration, during the war. If on the whole they have lost more than they have made, then they shall be paid for that loss over and above their profits." (*Ibid.*, p. 5364.)

Mr. Thurman said: "This conference bill * * * provides that insurance companies may be paid, if upon an exhibit of their business they have sustained loss, the excess of their loss above their profits." (*Ibid.*, p. 5359.)

We do not, however, allow anything for the expense of doing the business, such as salaries, office-rent, &c., all such expenses being a part of the ordinary business of the corporation, and the means of fixing their amount being very uncertain.

The net loss of the claimant in respect to all its war-risks we fix at the sum of $45,247.12.

Although the amount of its losses by the Alabama, Florida, and Shenandoah was $50,956.40, we can only award so much of this sum as equals the amount of its net loss growing out of all its war-risks, or the sum of $45,247.12, leaving $5,709.28 balance of losses by the inculpated cruisers unprovided for.

The only remaining question is, what shall be declared to be the date of such loss, or, in other words, from what date shall such sum begin to draw the statutory interest?

The claimant presented certain calculations in regard to interest, but they were all entirely arbitrary, and to be adopted only in case the result which they produce would effect substantial justice. We prefer to ignore all of them, and to fix the date of the loss, or date from which our award shall bear interest at 4 per cent., as the 28th day of June, 1865, the day of the last depredations by the Shenandoah.

We therefore award to the claimant the sum of $45,247.12, with interest at 4 per cent. from June 28, 1865.

THE OCEAN MUTUAL INSURANCE COMPANY *vs.* THE UNITED STATES. } No. 1093.

In this case we apply the same principles which governed us in the preceding case.

We find the aggregate of the losses of this corporation caused by the acts of the Alabama, the Florida, and the Shenandoah after she left Melbourne to have been $48,850.

But an examination of the business of the corporation shows that "the sum" by which "its losses in respect to its war-risks exceeded the sum of its premiums or other gains upon or in respect to such war-risks during the late rebellion" was only $17,425.86.

That is, the net loss of the corporation, (exclusive of the expense of doing the business, which we disallow,) by reason of the war-risks it assumed during the late rebellion, amounted to that sum.

The amount of its losses by the cruisers covered by the treaty is, then, $48,850. Net loss on its war-business, $17,425.86. This last sum is the amount to which we must, under the provisions of the twelfth section of the act, limit our award, leaving the sum of $31,424.14, being the remainder of the amount of the losses by the inculpated cruisers, unprovided for.

We therefore award to the claimant the sum of $17,425.86, with interest at 4 per cent. from June 28, 1865.

THE MUTUAL MARINE INSURANCE COMPANY vs. THE UNITED STATES. } No. 1098.

Applying the same principles to this case which have been before announced, we find that the entire losses by the depredations of all the confederate cruisers sustained by this corporation was $88,019.17.

Of this sum, $2,250 was caused by one of the exculpated cruisers, leaving the amount of the losses caused by the acts of the Alabama, the Florida, and the Shenandoah after leaving Melbourne, $85,769.17.

We find the net loss, by reason of all its war-risks, was $44,199.72.

Beyond this sum we can, under the law, make no award, leaving a balance of $41,569.45 of the losses by the acts of the inculpated cruisers unprovided for.

We award to this complainant the sum of $44,199.72, with interest at 4 per cent. from June 28, 1865.

JOHN H. BUTMAN, EDWARD S. MATTHEWS, AND other claimants vs. THE UNITED STATES. } Nos. 993, 1343, 1746, 1791.

The private property of an officer of the Navy, which was destroyed on a Government vessel by the insurgent cruiser Alabama, may be made the subject of a claim in this court, under the act of Congress of 23d June, 1874. A statement of the case will be found in the opinion of the court.

Mr. B. F. Butler and Mr. James Lowndes for the complainants.

Mr. J. A. J. Creswell for the respondent.

PORTER, J., delivered the opinion of the court:

These cases have grown out of the destruction of the Hatteras by the insurgent cruiser Alabama. One of the petitions is presented by a sailing-master, another by the widow of a lieutenant, a third by an assistant surgeon, and a fourth by a lieutenant-commander. On the 11th of January, 1863, the Hatteras, a steamer belonging to the United States, was stationed off the port of Galveston, Tex., and engaged, under the orders of the Navy Department, in blockading that port. While performing this duty the Alabama came in sight, and the Hatteras, a much smaller vessel, with distinguished gallantry, bore down upon her. The Alabama opened fire, and in a few minutes the Hatteras was sent to the bottom, with all the property, public and private, which she had on board—the officers and men barely escaping with their lives and with the clothes on their persons. These petitions are presented for payment of the value of the personal property belonging to certain of her officers which they thus lost. The cases were argued more than once. They have been the subject of numerous and protracted consultations. On the eve of our last adjournment we decided for the petitioners, and entered judgments in their favor. We think it expedient now to place on the record a statement of the reasons which brought us to these results:

It has been more than once remarked in opinions heretofore delivered that the United States declined to receive the money due by Great Britain encumbered with any obligation to pay it to any class of claimants, but reserved the right to dispose of every part of it according to its own sovereign pleasure. When Congress entered upon the legislation necessary for a distribution of the money, that body was untrammeled by any agreement, express or implied, in regard to the kind and mode of distribution. By the 11th section of the act of 23d June, 1874, creating this court, we were directed to receive and examine all claims admissible under this act, directly resulting from damage caused by the insurgent cruisers, and to decide upon such claims in conformity to the provisions of the act, and according to the principles of law and the merits of the several cases. This was a large and general power, and the only limitations upon its exercise were embodied in certain exceptions set forth in the succeeding section. They relate to cases where compensation or indemnity has been received from any other source; to claims for gross freights and prospective profits; claims by insurance companies; claims in favor of persons not entitled at the time of the loss to the protection of the United States, and, finally, claims arising in favor of persons who did not, during the late rebellion, bear true allegiance to the United States. In considering the effect of these provisions, it should be borne in mind that we do not sit here to legislate. That power belongs wholly to another department. The business of a judge is to administer the law, not to create it; and there can be no safety to parties litigant, to the public, nor to the court itself, except by adhering to this well-marked distinction. The worst law which has ever afflicted the earth is judge-made law. When a judge can substitute his own notions of justice for those rules of civil conduct which the supreme power of the state alone can prescribe, his decisions can never have the force of law. We must take the provisions of this act precisely as we find them, and, interpreting their language in its plain and ordinary sense, give to them such effect as Congress intended—no more, no less. Proceeding on this principle, it is beyond question that the present claims are within the letter of the statute. The claimants were the owners in their own right of the property destroyed. The loss resulted directly from the act of one of the insurgent cruisers. The claimants bore true allegiance to the United States, for they were then actually engaged in its service. They were entitled to its protection, for if any man be entitled to the protection of his government, surely it is he who is injured while contending for its life. By the terms of the act, the loss suffered by an officer of the Navy is not included among the excepted or inadmissible claims, and as it falls within the general words provided for admissible claims, it must on plain principles be classed among the latter. The rule laid down by Chief-Justice Marshall in the Dartmouth College case (4 Wheaton, 645) finds here a fitting illustration: "The case being within the words of the rule, must be within its operation likewise, unless there be something in the literal construction so obviously absurd or mischievous, or repugnant to the general spirit of the instrument, as to justify those who expound the Constitution in making it an exception." Construing the present statute on this principle, we must allow these claims unless there be some sound general principle of law which obliges us to give to it an interpretation different from that which its language would ordinarily require.

It is true that claims of this nature are not to be found in the schedules presented to the arbitrators at Geneva; but this is of little importance. Congress did not direct us to determine what claims were presented at Geneva. If this had been the object of the act, much trouble might have been saved to the claimants and to the court. We have allowed many claims never preferred at Geneva. We have excluded some, and reduced the amount of many more, which were there presented. Congress required us to decide upon the amount and validity of the claims presented in this court, and to see to it that these were decided according to the principles of law and the merits of the cases themselves.

It is true that the arbitrators ruled out all claims of the United States for expenditures incurred in conducting the war. (Papers relating to the Treaty of Washington, vol. 4, page 43, &c., &c.) The property described in the present petitions was not in any sense the property of the United States, but the private property of the petitioners—paid for with their own money—liable for their own debts—and transmissible to their personal representatives. It was no more the property of the Government than would be a dwelling-house bought by an officer of the Government in his own right, and conveyed to him in fee-simple. In this proceeding, therefore, the Government is not, in any sense, through Congress or through us, taking the money paid by Great Britain to pay for public property destroyed during the war, but is simply paying for the private property of an officer in its employ in which the Government never had the shadow of an interest.

It is said that another mode of paying for such claims has been provided by the act of 6th April, 1866. (Revised Statutes, p. 48, sec. 290.) This act provides that "In case any officer of the Navy or Marine Corps on board a vessel in the employ of the United States, which, by any casualty or in action with the enemy at any time since the 19th day of April, 1861, has been or may be sunk or destroyed, shall thereby have lost his personal effects, without negligence or want of skill or foresight on his part, the proper accounting-officers are authorized, with the approval of the Secretary of the Navy, to allow to such officer a sum not exceeding the amount of his sea-pay for one month as compensation for such loss." It will be observed that this act refers only to payment for "personal effects," whereas these petitions include much more than personal effects, such as books, marine-glasses, charts, scientific instruments, pictures, mirrors, and other property, which could not, with any propriety, be classed under the head of personal effects. In two of the cases, partial payments were made under the authority of the provision here quoted, but so small in amount as not to equal a sixth part of the property lost, and therefore plainly inadequate as compensation. It is a matter of fair legal presumption that when the act of 1874 was passed, Congress had in view the effect of the act of 1866, and knew that it was inadequate to provide for the payment of the actual losses which had been suffered by such claimants as these. With the act of 1866 in full view, it passed the present statute, and omitted from it every exception applicable to the cases in hand. Indeed, the act of 1874 seems to have had in contemplation the case of a previous partial payment from some other source than the fund now being distributed, when it required the claimant to deduct any compensation or indemnity received from any insurance company, insurer, or *otherwise*, and to claim only for the difference. It would have been easy, by the use of very few words, particular or general, to exclude the cases of those for whose losses compensation had been provided by any previous statute. Congress does not seem to have thought proper to do so. It used general words comprehending such claims and authorizing their allowance, and introduced no provision looking to their exclusion. We must decline to interpolate into the act an exception which the law-making power left out.

Finally, is there anything in the general policy of the law which requires us to exclude from this distribution the claims of sailors for losses of private property while in the employ of the Government? There is nothing in the practice of our own Government in dealing with these subjects which tends to support such a theory. The research of Mr. Butler, the counsel of one of the claimants, has brought to light three notable instances in which the Government has given practical answers to the question. By an act approved on 3d March, 1817, (6 Statutes at Large, 188,) six months' additional pay was given to the officers and seamen of the brig Epervier. By an act approved on 19th May, 1824, (6 Statutes at Large, 310,) an owner was paid a dividend of prize-money for the services of a slave on board the Wasp. By an act approved on the 24th of April, 1830, (6 Statutes at Large, 414,) six months' additional pay was given to the representatives of the officers, seamen, and marines who were lost in the Hornet. Nor are such acts on the part of any government unreasonable. Is there anything fitted to unnerve the arm of the soldier in the day of battle, to say to him that even if his life be lost, his Government will secure to his family the value of the little property which he may have acquired? In the late rebellion it was a common thing for citizens incapacitated by age or other causes from marching as soldiers, to promise to provide for the families of those who were willing to enlist. Did this render the man who enlisted a less efficient soldier? We think not; but if mistaken, it is clear that such considerations were for the law-making power, not for us. If Congress, with this whole subject before it, deliberately chose to employ language broad enough to include the claims of persons actually in the employ of the Government, and not to exclude them by any exception, our exclusion of them would, in our best judgment, be not judicial decision, but that sort of judicial legislation from which every principle of official duty should cause us to shrink. We have, therefore, entered judgments in favor of the respective claimants for the actual value of the personal property destroyed in each case, after having deducted any allowances heretofore made under the statute of 1866.

RAYNER, J., dissenting.

GEO. M. ROBESON, SECRETARY OF THE NAVY, complainant, *vs.* THE UNITED STATES, respondent. } No. 2066.

An award to the Navy Department would be an award to the Government, which already has complete ownership of the money paid by Great Britain under the award of the Tribunal of Arbitration, and now remaining in the Treasury.

Congress did not intend to give this court power to adjudicate upon the rights of the Government with regard to this fund. A statement of the case will be found in the opinion of the court.

Mr. John A. Bolles for the complainant.
Mr. Jno. A. J. Creswell for the respondent.

JEWELL, judge, delivered the opinion of the court:

This petition is made by the Secretary of the Navy in his official capacity, setting forth that the Navy Department purchased for the naval service the steamer St. Mary's at a cost of one hundred and ten thousand dollars; that she was equipped subsequently as a vessel of war, her name changed to the Hatteras, and that afterward she was destroyed by the Alabama; that the bark Greenland was chartered by the Navy

Department as a transport, the Department taking the risk of her destruction by any insurgent cruiser; that while so under charter she was destroyed by the Florida; and that the Navy Department, under and by force of said contract, did pay her owners for her loss the sum of twenty-three thousand five hundred dollars.

He therefore asks judgment for the cost of these two vessels.

Under the original act constituting the court, several claims were filed by officers upon the Hatteras for property destroyed at the time of her loss, which claims were pending when the second act authorizing the filing of claims went into effect; and we infer that the presentation of these claims may have led the Secretary of the Navy, in his official capacity as representing the Navy Department, to think his duty required him to present this petition, lest he might at some time be thought remiss in the care of his special department, and be called to account therefor.

At the time the case was reached, the solicitor of the Navy Department and the counsel of the Government appointed to represent its interests before this court, submitted the whole matter to the consideration of the court.

We have, therefore, to consider whether a claim of this character is within the terms or the spirit of the law establishing this tribunal, and we are all clearly of opinion that Congress did not intend that we should consider any claims for property of the United States destroyed by any of the rebel cruisers.

It is well known that all claims for compensation for the loss of public property of the United States were either abandoned voluntarily by the counsel of the United States before the arbitrators at Geneva or were absolutely rejected by the tribunal itself, and the only damages awarded were for the value of private vessels and property destroyed. The fund out of which our judgments are paid represents the estimated value of private property alone, and does not include anything based upon the value of public property destroyed.

The reclamation made upon Great Britain was made by our Government in its capacity of sovereign, and not as a mere representative of private interests, and the indemnity received has been paid to the United States as a government. The fund is now in the Treasury, entirely under the control of Congress, invested as directed by Congress, and was so when the act constituting this court was passed. Congress might have refused to pass any act providing for the indemnification of citizens; it might have retained the whole fund; it did appropriate such part of the fund as it judged just and right to be distributed among certain classes of claimants therefor. After the payment of the amount of our judgments, as provided by law, it may still retain the balance remaining, or it may provide for a further distribution among other classes of claimants. But in so doing it will dispose of its own; of money held in the Treasury of the Government, free from all restraints except those which ought to influence any sovereign power under the circumstances. No judgment of this court can change the character of this fund, or any part of it, so as to make it in any higher sense the property of the Government than it now is.

If our judgment in this respect would have any effect it would be to lessen the right or power of the Government over the unused balance. The Navy Department is a part of the Government itself, and any award we should make to it would be to the Government, and the effect of such award would rather be to lead to the conclusion that the remainder of the fund not needed to satisfy our judgments was not in a just and true sense the property of the United States, over which Congress had supreme power and control. If our judgment is needed to confer upon the United States any title to a part of this fund, it would follow that the Government has not a complete title to the remainder.

We are satisfied that Congress did not intend to give us the power to adjudicate upon the rights of the Government in regard to this fund.

It is unnecessary to set forth the technical objections to the present petition. It is quite enough to say that there is nothing in the act which requires us to sustain this claim, and there is very much in the general considerations connected with the subject, a few of which we have indicated, to lead us to the conclusion we have reached, that the petition must be dismissed.

FREDERICK A. SCHREIBER ET AL. *vs.* THE UNITED STATES. } No. 740.

JOHN G. PARKER *vs.* THE UNITED STATES. } No. 985.

And numerous other cases.

The amendment of claims will be allowed: Where the court is satisfied that the original petition was filed in good faith; where the averment sought to be corrected originated in some error or want of information on the part of the claimant or his counsel; where the motion to amend is made when a reasonable time, and where the Government has not, meanwhile, been misled in some material point in the preparation of its proofs.

STATEMENT OF THE CASE.

The complainant Schreiber moved (after the time for filing claims had expired) to amend his petition by substituting the gold-value of $15,000, instead of the value in currency, as the words "fifteen thousand dollars" standing alone in the prayer would be construed.

The claimant Parker moved that another party be added as complainant, his name having been accidentally omitted in drawing the petition.

Mr. Frank W. Hackett for the complainants.

The court derives it power to grant amendments from two sources:

1. Section 3 of the act approved June 23, 1874, which refers it for mode of procedure and practice to the circuit courts of the United States.

2. The common law and admiralty, wherever the circuit court does not afford the desired authority.

The circuit courts have always adopted broad and liberal views upon the subject of amendment. (U. S. Revised Statutes, p. 180, sec. 954; Smith *vs.* Barker, 3 Day, 314; The Harmony, 1 Gallison, 124; Gregg *vs.* Geir, 4 McLean, 208; Etting *vs.* Campbell, 5 Blatchford, 103; Hilliard *vs.* Brevoort, 4 McLean, 24; Walden *vs.* Craig, 9 Wheaton, 576; Conkling's Practice in U. S. Courts, 464; 1 Gallison, 22; Kennedy *vs.* Georgia State Bank, 8 How., 610; Weaver *vs.* Thompson, 1 Wall., jr., 343; The Adèle, 9 Cranch, 244; The Edward, 1 Wheaton, 261; Tiernan *vs.* Woodruff, 5 McLean, 135, U. S. Dig. Amend., 442; Cassell *vs.* Cook,

8 Serg. & R., 287; Newlin *vs.* Palmer, 11 *id.*, 102; Haynes *vs.* Morgan, 3 Mass., 208; Eaton *vs.* Ogier, 2 Me., 46; Lake *vs.* Morse, 11 Ill., 587.)

To increase the *ad damnum* of the petition is not to add a new *res*, or in any sense to institute a new suit.

Mr. J. A. J. Creswell for the respondent.

The court, under the act creating it, has no power to allow amendments. To allow amendments after the time for filing claims has elapsed, is in effect to permit the new claims to be filed. (11th sec., act 23d June, 1874; Kidd *vs.* The United States, 8 Court of Claims, 259.)

PORTER, J., delivered the opinion of the court:

Motions have been made on behalf of the claimants, to amend the claims filed, respectively, in these cases. In some of them, it is proposed to describe certain articles of property altogether omitted. In others, it is sought to change the names of certain of the claimants, and to insert the names of other claimants. In a third class, leave is asked to state, at its value in currency, the amount of the demand originally claimed in gold. Lastly and chiefly, we are asked to allow a claimant to increase the amount of his claim, as set forth in his original petition. Some of these motions were argued soon after the court convened, and they have since been re-argued by some of the most eminent counsel who have appeared before us. The counsel of the United States has uniformly and earnestly opposed the motions. He insists that we have now no authority to allow amendments of this character. He points us to that part of the 11th section of the act of 23d June, 1874, which provides that all claims shall be "filed in said court within six months after the organization thereof," "and no claim shall be received, docketed or considered, that shall not have been so filed within the time aforesaid, but every such unrepresented claim shall be deemed and held to be finally and conclusively waived and barred." The time prescribed in this section, expired on the 22d of January, 1875. To allow such amendments, after the expiration of this period, the Government insists is, in effect, to allow the filing of new claims, in opposition to a prohibition of the act. This raises, in a distinct and definite form, the question of our authority to permit the filing of such amendments.

The power of courts of general jurisdiction to permit amendments of pleadings, has been generally favored by statute and by decision. The first English statute of *jeofaile* is more than five centuries old, having been passed in the reign of Edward III. Eleven statutes of similar purport have since been enacted, until in Great Britain scarcely any defect can now occur in pleading, at law or in equity, which the courts may not permit a party on reasonable terms to correct by proper amendment. In the following cases, some instructive examples of amendment may be found: Brown *vs.* Crump, 6 Taunton, 300; Taylor *vs.* Lyon, 2 Moore & Payne, 586; Carmarthin *vs.* Lewis, 6 Carrington & Payne, 608; Blunt *vs.* Cooke, 4 Manning & Granger, 458; Langford *vs.* Woods, 7 Manning & Granger, 625.

In almost every one of the United States, statutes and decisions have followed in the same direction. In Pennsylvania, for example, the names of the parties, the amount claimed, and even the form of the action, may be changed by amendment, on formal application to the court, but almost at the pleasure of the parties. (Cunningham *vs.* Day, 2 S. & R., 1; Franklin *vs.* Mackey, 16 S. & R., 117; Caldwell *vs.* Remmington, 2 Wharton, 132; Tassey *vs.* Church, 4 W. & S., 141; Good Intent Co. *vs.* Hartzell, 10 Harris, 277; Rangler *vs.* Hummell, 1 Wright, 130; Lycoming Ins. Co. *vs.* Shallerberger, 8 Wright, 259; Trego *vs.* Lewis, 8 P. F. Smith, 463.) Even after the jury has been sworn, such amendments are permitted in that State. (Cassell *vs.* Cooke, 8 S. & R., 268.) So in New York. (Merchant *vs.* Ins. Co., 2 Sanford, 669; Vibbard *vs.* Roderick, 51 Barbour, 616; Johnson *vs.* Brown, 57 Barbour, 118.) In the last-mentioned case, it was held that the amount of the damages claimed might be enlarged by an amendment of the complaint, at the discretion of the judge, and that no exception could be taken to such a decision. In Massachusetts, the plaintiff is allowed to amend his declaration in a real action by inserting a new and different description of the land. (Haynes *vs.* Morgan, 3 Mass., 208; Hill *vs.* Haskins, 8 Pickering, 83.) A declaration against one as maker of a promissory note may be amended so as to charge him as a guarantor. (Tenney *vs.* Price, 4 Pick., 385.) A new count for the enforcement of a claim growing out of the same transaction, act, or contract, on which the original declaration was founded, may generally be inserted as an amendment, however different the form of liability. (Smith *vs.* Palmer, 6 Cushing, 513.) In almost all of the Western States, similar powers of amendment exist.

It should be observed in the study of these cases, especially in England, but also in many of our own States, that the legislative statutes commonly relied on did not confer the power of amendment, but were merely declaratory of a power at common law to permit amendments to the same extent. In the case of the Harmony (1 Gallison, 124) Story, J., did not hesitate to act on this doctrine. In Tiernan *vs.* Woodruff, (5 McLean, 143,) Wilkins, J., holds this language: "From a careful, and I may say laborious, consideration of the cases, both in England and in this country, and from a solicitude to avoid, if possible, any innovation upon the settled practice of the courts, I have arrived at the conclusion that it is competent at common law to amend the declaration by a new count, introductive of a new cause of action, provided such amendment corresponds in character with the original count, is a kindred cause, admitting the same pleading and defense, and might have been included within the declaration originally filed, and *especially where such cause is outlawed by the statute.*" It could not have been otherwise. The pleadings were originally conducted orally, and justice could scarcely have been done in any case if the party had been held strictly to his first statement of it. Doubtless he varied it as often as he stated it. It is a part of the history of the law that amendments were allowed in England before any statute of *jeofail* was passed. Indeed, it is a necessary inference from all the authorities, ancient and modern, that such a power is inherent in every court.

The Court of Commissioners of Alabama Claims was, by the act of 23d June, 1874, constituted a court, not in form merely, but in every essential attribute of a court. It is called a court, and its members are designated as judges. It is required to meet and organize as a court. It is empowered to compel the attendance of parties and witnesses, to administer oaths, to preserve order, to punish for contempts, and to enforce the production of books and papers. It is required to hear and consider the allegations and proofs of the parties, to keep a record of its proceedings, to enter judgments, and to exercise, for certain purposes, the powers possessed by the circuit and district courts of the United States. Its jurisdiction is certainly limited to a particular class of subjects, but within the range of its jurisdiction its power to hear, to decide, and to enter judgment is as complete as could be claimed for any court of the most enlarged jurisdiction. If, therefore, nothing further was said in the act of Congress in regard to our powers, I would not have the least hesitation in holding that in respect to the amendment of pleadings, in cases cognizable by it, this court possessed the same power which we have found to belong generally to other courts.

But there is one provision which ought to be conclusive of the question. The third section of the act of 1874 authorizes the making of rules for regulating the forms and mode of procedure before the court, provides that "such rules and mode of procedure shall conform, as far as practicable, to the mode of procedure and practice of the circuit courts of the United States." This is the only test to which our powers are subjected. We are to do that which the circuit courts of the United States may do in everything relating to practice and procedure. The subject of amendment falls most naturally, both in a technical and popular sense, within what is known as the practice of a court. If there be any one who doubts whether such amendments as these, if proposed in any circuit of the United States, would be allowed, his doubt ought to be removed by reading these well-considered decisions: (Smith *vs.* Barker, 3 Day, 314; Gregg *vs.* Geir, 4 McLean, 208; Hilliard *vs.* Brevoort, 4 McLean, 24; Walden *vs.* Craig, 9 Wheaton, 576; Kennedy *vs.* The State Bank of Georgia, 8 Howard, 610.) But we are not left to mere judicial decision, however pertinent and authoritative. In the act of 24th September, 1789, (Revised Statutes, p. 180,) it is expressly provided that the circuit court "may, at any time, permit either of the parties to amend any defect in the process or pleadings, upon such conditions as it shall, in its discretion and by its rules, prescribe." If such a point were not settled by an express statute, and so many well-matured interpretations of it by eminent judges, then, indeed, we would be bound to concede that the point is most difficult of settlement.

What, then, was the object of Congress in fixing the limit prescribed in the eleventh section of the act of 1874? Certainly not to prevent any amendments to claims filed within the time, or Congress would have said so. Here it is noteworthy that the act does not contain one word on the subject of amendments. The object evidently was to fix some proper limit within which the business of the court should be transacted; to require those who had claims on the fund to come forward in some reasonable time and make them known; to prevent vigilant claimants from being delayed by the conduct of more negligent ones in participating in the *pro-rata* distribution provided for by the fourteenth section, in a certain important contingency; and then to leave claims filed within the appointed time subject to such rules as all courts, and especially the circuit courts of the United States, may prescribe on the subject of amendments.

It remains now only to notice the ruling in Kidd's case, (8 Court of Claims Reports, 259.) The plaintiff claimed, under the abandoned and captured property act, to recover the proceeds of 64 bales of cotton, and moved to amend his petition by increasing the demand to 197 bales, after the expiration of the time limited for filing the petition, namely, two years after the suppression of the rebellion. (12 Statutes at Large, 820, sec. 3.) The court refused to allow the amendment. There is a distinction between that case and the present. There was some ground for holding that, under the terms of the abandoned and captured property act, the claimant was required to state the amount of the property, the proceeds of which had found their way into the Treasury. A claimant is required under the act constituting this court to make his claim, undoubtedly in some proper form, but he is nowhere required to state its exact amount. This is required only by our own rules, which cannot override the act creating the court itself.

If this difference were not sufficient for a sound legal distinction between the cases, we must admit, after the fullest consideration of the views expressed in Kidd's case by judges whom we so highly respect, that our judgment is opposed to the conclusion reached by the court. Believing the allowance of amendments within proper limits better fitted to do justice between the parties before us, and bound to conform to the practice of the circuit courts, and to no other, we discharge our official duty, while we follow the lead of our own judgments, by departing from the course adopted by the Court of Claims in that case.

To what extent we shall exercise the power thus committed to us will depend upon the merits of each application. Merely formal changes ought to be allowed on motion, as of course. Amendments which touch the substance of the claim will also be allowed where we are satisfied that the original petition was filed in good faith; where the averment sought to be corrected originated in some error or want of information on the part of the claimant or his counsel; where the motion to amend is made within a reasonable time, and where the Government has not in the meanwhile been misled in some material point in the preparation of its proofs. For these reasons, we allow the amendments to be made, which were proposed in the cases noted at the commencement of this opinion.

WELLS, Presiding Judge, and BALDWIN, Judge, dissenting.

ANN ELIZA GANNETT, ADMINISTRATRIX, &C., *vs.* THE UNITED STATES. } No. 184.

RESPECTING THE PRACTICE OF THE COURT ON MOTIONS FOR REHEARING.

Mr. R. M. Corwine for the complainant.
Mr. J. A. J. Creswell for the respondent.

WELLS, Presiding Judge, delivered the opinion of the court:

Two motions have been submitted in this case by counsel for claimants, under the respective dates of March 15 and May 6, 1875. The first in order of date, that "the court will so far modify the judgment on demurrer entered in this case as that it may be made to apply only to so much of the petition as prays damages for the loss of the season's catch, and that so much of the petition as prays damages for the loss of the outfit, refit, and investment of said vessel, called the Splendid, is wholly unaffected by said judgment," &c. The second motion reading: "Now comes the above-named claimant, and asks leave to amend her petition herein by striking out so much thereof as states 'that the season's catch, covering a period of about one year, broken up by said rebel cruiser, was well worth, and would have realized the owners of said ship, the sum of fifty thousand dollars, which losses wholly and directly resulted from the damage caused by said rebel cruiser, in manner and under the circumstances aforesaid.'"

The court has carefully considered these motions, especially in view of the apparent large interest that is involved in this case, and also with the idea presented by counsel that this court had possibly erred in its opinion and judgment heretofore expressed. The very foundation of this claim, if it can be re-instated in court and re-argued, is "that the

Shenandoah drove the whale-ship Splendid from the fishing-grounds which she had secured, destroyed her outfits, refit, and investments, &c." Every principle and argument has been fully and ably stated by counsel to sustain the position taken as above, and yet all the facts of the case, gathered from the petition and statements of counsel, do not create with the court any desire to vary the rule established in the case of Brown *et al. vs.* Aspden *et al.*, (Howard's Rep., vol. 14, pages 26 and 27,) "that no re-argument will be heard in any case after judgment is entered, unless some member of the court who concurred in the judgment afterward doubts the correctness of his opinion, and desires a further argument on the subject." This case, decided A. D. 1852, was re-affirmed in A. D. 1869, in the case of The Public Schools *vs.* Walker, (9th Wallace, page 603,) where the court adds as follows:

When the court does not, on its own motion, order a rehearing, it will be proper for counsel to submit, without argument, a brief, written or printed, petition or suggestion of the point or points thought important. If, upon such petition or suggestion, any judge who concurred in the decision thinks proper to move for a rehearing, the motion will be considered.

In case No. 184 this course has been followed by attorneys for petitioners, in presenting a brief or printed argument in favor of the rehearing, carefully prepared, and doing full justice to the petitioners' important interests, but it has not induced any member of the court to request a further argument of the case. The motions of counsel for complainant are denied. On the rule here laid down, it is the intention of the court to act in the future.

APPENDIX.

APPENDIX.

RULES OF THE COURT OF COMMISSIONERS OF ALABAMA CLAIMS.

I. The clerk of the court is directed to file of record all claims which may be transmitted to him, and to enter the same on the docket in the order of time in which they may be received.

Claims transmitted by mail may be addressed to "John Davis, esq., clerk of the Court of Commissioners of Alabama Claims, Washington, D. C."

II. All claims must be verified by the affidavit of the claimant, and filed in this court within six months from the 22d day of July, 1871.

III. Every claim shall be stated in a petition addressed to the court, and signed by the claimant or his attorney.

The petition shall set forth—

1st. The title of the case, with the full Christian names and surnames of all the claimants, the places and times of their birth, and the places of their residence between the 13th day of April, 1861, and the 9th day of April, 1865, both inclusive.

If any of the claimants be naturalized citizens, an authenticated certificate of their naturalization shall be appended to the petition, and the petition shall also state whether the claimants, or any of them, have been naturalized in any other country than the United States; and, if not so naturalized, whether any and what steps have been taken toward being so naturalized.

2d. A plain and concise statement of the facts and circumstances, giving place and date, free from argument, and stating all assignments and transfers, whether in whole or in part.

3d. The prayer, in which the claimant shall state distinctly the amount of the actual loss or damage for which he asks judgment, and the date from which he claims interest thereon.

The claimant shall also give the post-office address of himself and of his attorney; and may append to his petition, as exhibits, the instruments or documents to which it refers, but shall not insert the same in the body of the petition. Immediately upon the filing of any petition, fifty copies of the same and the accompanying documents shall be printed in octavo form, under the direction of the clerk, for the use of the court and counsel.

IV. Parties having a common interest, growing out of the destruction of the same vessel or its cargo, may unite in one petition for the recovery of their respective claims, which may be heard together, but separate judgments shall be rendered in the case of each claimant.

V. Any person of good moral character admitted to practice as attorney or counsel in the supreme court of any State or Territory or the District of Columbia, or in any of the Federal courts, on filing with the clerk a written statement of the date and place of such admission, with his name and post-office address in full, may, on motion, be admitted to practice in this court.

VI. It shall not be necessary for the United States to deny, specially, in writing, the validity of any claim; but a general denial of every claim shall be entered of record by the clerk as of course, and thereby every material allegation shall be considered as put in issue by the United States.

Objections as to the law of the case may be raised by the United States at any stage of the proceedings by demurrer, stating the grounds of such objections with reasonable certainty.

VII. Testimony to be used in this court may be taken before a commissioner empowered by any circuit or district court of the United States to take testimony, on a rule entered of record in this court for that purpose by either party in any pending case, provided twenty days' notice be given to the adverse party; but nothing herein contained shall prevent the taking of testimony before any other person, with the leave of this court, nor prevent counsel from accepting, by agreement in writing, a shorter notice than twenty days.

VIII. It shall be the duty of the counsel of the claimant, at least ten days before the day of hearing, to file with the clerk of the court fifty copies of a brief (printed in octavo form) of the argument in behalf of the claimant.

IX. Claims supported by printed or written testimony shall be first heard in the order in which they stand on the docket, unless otherwise specifically ordered by the court; and afterward those claims shall be heard in support of which the claimant may desire to introduce oral testimony.

X. In cases where the amount claimed exceeds the sum of one thousand dollars, the claimant shall be at the expense of printing his own brief and testimony. In cases not exceeding that amount the printing shall be done, under the direction of the clerk of the court, at the expense of the United States.

XI. The time to be occupied in the oral arguments of counsel shall be regulated by the rule in force in the Supreme Court of the United States.

XII. Whenever any deposition or document shall have been filed in any case before this court, either party to any other case may use such testimony on the hearing thereof: *Provided*, That the party so desiring to use such testimony in a case in which the same was not originally taken shall file a notice in the case in which such testimony is sought to be used five days before the hearing thereof of his intention so to do, specifying therein particularly the depositions or documents sought to be used and the case or cases in which the same were originally taken.

SPECIAL RULE, (adopted March 7, 1876.)

In case of any claimant who may desire to present a claim under the provisions of an act entitled "An act to extend the time for claimants, under section eleven of chapter four hundred and fifty-nine of the laws of the Forty-third Congress, to prove their claims," approved March 6th, 1876, and who may be absent from the United States at the time of the making or of presenting his petition, such petition may be presented and verified by the attorney in fact of such claimant, or by any agent specially authorized thereto, or by any person acting as agent or next friend; but in every case of a petition filed without precedent authority specifically given, the court will require subsequent ratification of such petition or claim by the claimant. Such agency or ratification shall, in every case, be duly established by proof to the satisfaction of the court.

AN ACT* for the creation of a court for the adjudication and disposition of certain moneys received into the Treasury under an award made by the tribunal of arbitration constituted by virtue of the first article of the treaty concluded at Washington the eighth of May, anno Domini eighteen hundred and seventy-one, between the United States of America and the Queen of Great Britain.

Be it enacted by the Senate and House of Representatives of the United States of America in Congress assembled, That the President of the United States be, and he is hereby, authorized to nominate and, by and with the advice and consent of the Senate, appoint five suitable persons, who shall constitute a court, to be known as the "Court of Commissioners of Alabama Claims." Each of the judges and other officers of said court shall take the oath of office prescribed by law to be taken by all officers of the United States. The President shall designate, by appointment, one of said judges to be presiding judge of the court; and all vacancies which may occur in said court by reason of death, resignation, or inability, or refusal or neglect of any or either of said judges to discharge the duties of his position, shall be filled in the same manner as vacancies occurring in offices under the Constitution of the United States are filled.

SEC. 2. That the said judges shall meet and organize said court in the city of Washington, where the said court shall hold its sittings. Three judges of said court shall constitute a quorum for the transaction of business, and the agreement of three shall be necessary to decide any question arising before said court.

SEC. 3. That the said court be, and it is hereby, authorized to publish notice of its sessions, and to make all needful rules and regulations, not contravening the laws of the United States or the provisions of this act, for regulating the forms and mode of procedure before the said court, and for carrying into full and complete effect the provisions of this act. Such rules and mode of procedure shall conform, as far as practicable, to the mode of procedure and practice of the circuit courts of the United States; and the said court is hereby vested with the same powers now possessed by the circuit and district courts of the United States to compel the attendance and testimony of parties, claimants, and witnesses, to preserve order, and to punish for contempts; and in all claims which shall be presented before said court the person or persons prosecuting such claim shall be deemed the complainant and the United States shall be deemed the respondent. And said court shall have power to compel the production of any books or papers deemed material to the consideration of any claim or matter pending therein.

SEC. 4. That each of the said judges shall be paid monthly, at the rate of six thousand dollars per annum; and they shall have a clerk, who shall be appointed by the President, by and with the advice and consent of the Senate, to be paid at the rate of three thousand dollars per annum; and the said court shall have authority to appoint one short-hand reporter, to be paid monthly, at the rate of two thousand five hundred dollars per annum; and said court shall be further allowed the necessary actual expenses of office-rent, furniture, fuel, stationery, and printing, and other necessary incidental expenses, to be certified by the presiding judge of said court, and to be audited and paid on vouchers under the direction of the Secretary of State.

SEC. 5. That the President may designate a counselor at law, admitted to practice in the Supreme Court of the United States, to appear as counsel on behalf of the United States, and represent the interest of the Government in said suit, and in all claims filed for indemnity for

* Chap. 459 of the laws of the first session of the 43d Congress.

losses, as provided by this act, subject to the supervision and control of the Attorney-General. Such counsel shall receive for his services and expenses such reasonable allowance in each claim as may be approved by the court, to be apportioned in each claim adjudicated, and paid from said award upon the certificate of one of the judges.

SEC. 6. That the marshal of the United States for the District of Columbia, or his deputies, shall serve all process issued by said court, preserve order in the place of sitting, and execute the orders of said court.

SEC. 7. That the said court shall proceed immediately after its first meeting in the city of Washington, with all convenient dispatch, to arrange and docket the several claims admissible under this act, and to consider the evidence which shall have been or which may be offered by the respective claimants, and in opposition thereto, allowing such further time for the production of such further evidence as may be required and as it shall think reasonable and just, and shall thereupon proceed to determine and award upon each of said claims according to the provisions of this act.

SEC. 8. That the judges of the court created by this act shall convene in the city of Washington as soon as conveniently may be after their appointment; and the said court shall exist for one year from the date of its first convening and organizing; and should it be found impracticable to complete the work of the said court before the expiration of the said one year, the President may, by proclamation, extend the time of the duration thereof to a period not more than six months beyond the expiration of the said one year; and in such case all the provisions of this act shall be taken and held to be the same as though the continuance of the said court had been originally fixed by this act at the limit to which it may be thus extended.

SEC. 9. That all records, documents, or other papers which now or hereafter, during the continuance of the court, may come into the possession of the Department of State, in relation to such claims, and which shall be found necessary to the examination and adjudication of the same, shall, upon the order or requisition of said court, be delivered to the court for that purpose, and be given such weight as evidence as the court shall think just.

SEC. 10. That each of the said judges shall have authority to administer oaths and affirmations, and to take the depositions of claimants, parties, and witnesses, in all matters pertaining to the presentation or examination of said claims; and if any person shall knowingly and willfully swear or affirm falsely in such examination or deposition to any matter or fact material to the investigation of the claim touching which such person is examined, or if any person, whether claimant or witness, shall so swear or affirm falsely to the contents of any memorial, petition, affidavit, deposition, or other paper containing any matter or fact material in the examination of any claim pending before, or to be presented before, said court, or shall, in giving testimony, or in swearing or affirming to any deposition, affidavit, or other paper, before any officer authorized to administer oaths or to take such testimony, so swear or affirm falsely to any matter or thing material in the examination of any claim pending or to be presented before said court, every such person so swearing or affirming falsely as aforesaid shall be deemed guilty of perjury, the same as if such false oath or affirmation had been taken in a judicial proceeding in any of the courts of the United States, and shall be liable to indictment and trial in the district or circuit court of the United States for the district in which such perjury shall have been committed, or in the proper courts of the United States for the Territory or District of Columbia in which such perjury shall have been committed, and shall, upon conviction, suffer such punishment as is provided by the laws of the United States for that offense.

SEC. 11. That it shall be the duty of said court to receive and examine all claims admissible under this act that may be presented to it, directly resulting from damage caused by the so-called insurgent cruisers Alabama, Florida, and their tenders, and also all claims admissible under this act directly resulting from damage caused by the so-called insurgent cruiser Shenandoah after her departure from Melbourne on the eighteenth day of February, eighteen hundred and sixty-five, and to decide upon the amount and validity of such claims, in conformity with the provisions hereinafter contained, and according to the principles of law and the merits of the several cases. All claims shall be verified by oath of the claimant, and filed in said court within six months next after the organization thereof, as provided in section eight of this act; and no claim shall be received, docketed, or considered that shall have not been so filed within the time aforesaid; but every such unrepresented claim shall be deemed and held to be finally and conclusively waived and barred.

SEC. 12. That no claim shall be admissible or allowed by said court for any loss or damage for or in respect to which the party injured, his assignees or legal representatives, shall have received compensation or indemnity from any insurance company, insurer, or otherwise; but if such compensation or indemnity so received shall not have been equal to the loss or damage so actually suffered, allowance may be made for the difference. And in no case shall any claim be admitted or allowed for or in respect to unearned freights, gross freights, prospective profits, freights, gains, or advantages, or for wages of officers or seamen for a longer time than one year next after the breaking up of a voyage by the acts aforesaid. And no claim shall be admissible or allowed by said court by or in behalf of any insurance company or insurer, either in its or his own right, or as assignee or otherwise, in the right of a person or party insured as aforesaid, unless such claimant shall show to the satisfaction of said court that during the late rebellion the sum of its or his losses, in respect to its or his war-risks, exceeded the sum of its or his premiums or other gains upon or in respect to such war-risks; and in case of any such allowance, the same shall not be greater than such excess of loss. And no claim shall be admissible or allowed by said court arising in favor of any insurance company not lawfully existing at the time of the loss under the laws of some one of the United States. And no claim shall be admissible or allowed by said court, arising in favor of any person not entitled, at the time of his loss, to the protection of the United States in the premises, nor arising in favor of any person who did not at all times during the late rebellion bear true allegiance to the United States.

SEC. 13. That in estimating the compensation to claimants, interest shall be allowed, at the rate of four per centum per annum upon the amount of actual loss or damage which shall be ascertained in each case to have been sustained, from such date as the court shall, in each case, decide that the loss was sustained by the claimant: *Provided, however*, That the amount of such interest shall not be included in or added to the amount for which judgment may be rendered on said claim; but in each case a report of the amount of such interest, certified under the seal of the court, shall accompany the report of the judgment on the claim to the Secretary of State.

SEC. 14. That the said court shall report to the Secretary of State a list of the several judgments and decisions made by it, a certified copy of which shall, upon the conclusion of the business of the said court, be by him transmitted to the Secretary of the Treasury, who shall thereafter, as soon as may be and upon such notice and in such manner as he shall prescribe, pay the said judgments, together with interest at the rate of four per centum per annum on the amount of such judgments from the date certified, unto the persons, respectively, in whose favor the same shall have been made, or to their respective legal representatives, in full satisfaction and discharge of said judgments: *Provided*, That if the sum of all the judgments rendered by the said court, together with interest, shall exceed the amount received into the Treasury of the United States as proceeds of the sum to be paid by Great Britain, by virtue of said decision and award, then the Secretary of the Treasury shall distribute, in ratable proportion, among the parties in whose favor judgment shall have been rendered, or to their legal representatives, such moneys as have been received into the Treasury, according to the proportions which their respective judgments shall bear to the whole amount received into the Treasury as aforesaid, which payments shall be in full satisfaction and discharge of such claims and judgment.

SEC. 15. That the Secretary of the Treasury is hereby authorized and required to pay the said respective judgments of said court, out of any such money in the Treasury not otherwise appropriated; and for that purpose he is hereby authorized when necessary to issue and sell at public sale, after ten days' notice of the time and place of sale, at not less than par in coin, a sufficient amount of coupon or registered bonds of the United States, in such form as he may prescribe, of denominations of fifty dollars, or some multiple of that sum, redeemable in coin of the present standard value, at the pleasure of the United States after ten years from the date of their issue, and bearing interest payable quarterly in such coin at the rate of five per centum per annum; and upon the payment from time to time, of the said respective judgments of said court as before provided, the bonds of the United States mentioned in the act approved March third, eighteen hundred and seventy-three, entitled "An act for the creation of a court for the adjudication and disposition of certain moneys received into the Treasury under an award made by the tribunal of arbitration constituted by virtue of the first article of the treaty concluded at Washington the eighth of May, anno Domini eighteen hundred and seventy-one, between the United States of America and the Queen of Great Britain," shall be canceled and extinguished to the amount of such payments; and when all such payments shall have been made, any such bonds remaining shall also be canceled and extinguished; and after the payment of the said judgments, and the re-imbursement of the expenses as herein provided, if there shall remain any part of the said money, the same shall be and remain a fund from which Congress may hereafter authorize the payment of other claims thereon. And the moneys necessary for the payment of the salaries of the judges and other officers authorized by this act, and of the expenses of the said court as hereinbefore mentioned, are hereby appropriated out of any moneys in the Treasury not otherwise appropriated.

SEC. 16. That as soon as the business of said court shall be executed and completed, the records, documents, and all other papers in the possession of the court, or its officers, shall be deposited in the office of the Secretary of State.

SEC. 17. In ascertaining the amount of such losses, the memorials, affidavits, depositions, and any other papers in the several cases of losses claimed respectively, now filed in the State Department, or official copies thereof, may be read in evidence: *Provided*, That no affidavit shall be read except where it appears to the satisfaction of the tribunal that the affiant cannot be produced before it as a witness or his testimony taken by a commission upon interrogatories; and in the hearing of the cause, any party claiming shall produce all books, papers, letters, and documents that may be called for by a general description thereof by any opposing party, or satisfactorily account for their loss or non-production, or suffer such judgment as is prescribed in section fifteen of the act entitled "An act to establish the judicial courts of the United States," approved September twenty-ninth, seventeen hundred and eighty-nine; and on the hearing of the cause, any competent evidence may be produced by either party, either viva voce or by deposition taken upon interrogatories; and for this purpose depositions may be taken by either party de bene, or the court may admit affidavits where it is satisfactorily shown that the witness cannot be produced or his examination by interrogatories and cross-examination cannot be had.

SEC. 18. That in case any judgment is rendered by said court for indemnity for any loss or claim hereinbefore mentioned against the United States at the time of the giving of the judgment, the court shall, upon motion of the attorney or counsel for the claimant, allow, out of the amount thereby awarded, such reasonable counsel and attorney fees to the counsel and attorney employed by the claimant or claimants respectively as the court shall determine is just and reasonable, as compensation for the services rendered the claimant in prosecuting such claims, which allowance shall be entered as part of the judgment in such case, and shall be made specifically payable as a part of said judgment for indemnification to the attorney or counsel, or both, to whom the same shall be adjudged; and a warrant shall issue from the Treasury in favor of the person to whom such allowance shall be made respectively, which shall be in full compensation to the counsel or attorney for prosecuting such claim; and all other liens upon, or assignments, sales, transfers, either absolute or conditional, for services rendered or to be rendered about any claim or part or parcel thereof provided for in this bill heretofore or hereafter made or done before such judgment is awarded and the warrant issued therefor, shall be absolutely null and void and of none effect.

Approved June 23, 1874.

By the President of the United States of America.

A PROCLAMATION.

Whereas by the eighth section of the act of Congress entitled "An act for the creation of a court for the adjudication and disposition of certain moneys received into the Treasury under an award made by the tribunal of arbitration constituted by virtue of the first article of the treaty concluded at Washington on the 8th of May, anno Domini eighteen hundred and seventy-one, between the United States of America and the Queen of Great Britain," approved June twenty-three, eighteen hundred and seventy-four, it is provided that "the judges of the court created by this act shall convene in the city of Washington as soon as convenient after their appointment; and the said court shall exist for one year from the date of its first convening and organizing; and should it be found impracticable to complete the work of the said court before the expiration of the said one year, the President may, by proclamation, extend the time of the duration thereof to a period of not more than six months beyond the expiration of the said one year; and in such case all the provisions of this act shall be taken and held to be the same as though the continuance of the said court had been originally fixed by this act at the limit to which it may be thus extended;" and

Whereas it has been made satisfactorily to appear to me that the said court convened on the 22d of July, 1874, and that a large portion of the business of said court still remains undisposed of, and that it is found impracticable to complete the work of the said court before the expiration of the said year from its first convening and organizing:

Now, therefore, be it known that I, Ulysses S. Grant, President of the United States of America, by virtue of the authority vested in me by the provisions of the said eighth section of the act of Congress aforesaid, do hereby extend the time of the duration of said Court of Commissioners of Alabama Claims for a period of six months after the 22d day of July, A. D. 1875.

In testimony whereof I have hereunto signed my name and have caused the seal of the United States to be affixed.

Done at the city of Washington this 2d day of June, A. D. 1875, and of the Independence of the United States the ninety-ninth.

U. S. GRANT.

By the President:
HAMILTON FISH,
Secretary of State.

AN ACT to extend the duration of the Court of Commissioners of Alabama Claims.

Be it enacted by the Senate and House of Representatives of the United States of America in Congress assembled, That the existence of the Court of Commissioners of Alabama Claims, created by the act entitled "An act for the creation of a court for the adjudication and disposition of certain moneys received into the Treasury under an award made by the Tribunal of Arbitration constituted by virtue of the first article of the treaty concluded at Washington the eighth of May, anno Domini eighteen hundred and seventy-one, between the United States of America and the Queen of Great Britain," be, and the same is hereby, continued and extended to the twenty-second day of July next, with the same effect, and no other, as if said last-named day had been named in said act for the termination of the powers of said court; and said act is hereby continued in force during said period.

SEC. 2. That the powers of the clerk of said court are hereby extended for an additional period, not to exceed two months from and after the termination of the existence of the court, for the purpose of closing his accounts, depositing the records, documents, and all other papers in the possession of the court or its officers, in the office of Secretary of State, as provided in said act; and all disbursements made by him during this period shall be under the direction of the Secretary of State.

Approved December 24, 1875.

AN ACT providing for the payment of judgments rendered under section eleven of chapter four hundred and fifty-nine of the laws of the first session of the Forty-third Congress.

Be it enacted by the Senate and House of Representatives of the United States of America in Congress assembled, That the Court of Commissioners of Alabama Claims as soon after the twenty-second day of January, anno Domini eighteen hundred and seventy-six, as may be practicable, report to the Secretary of State the several judgments, which before, or on that day shall have been rendered by the said court pursuant to section eleven of chapter four hundred and fifty-nine, of the laws of the Forty-third Congress.

SEC. 2. That the said court, after the twenty-second day of July, eighteen hundred and seventy-six, in like manner report to the Secretary of State the several judgments it shall render, pursuant to said section eleven, from the said twenty-second day of January to, and including said twenty-second day of July.

SEC. 3. That when a report is made under this act to the Secretary of State he transmit the same or a copy thereof to the Secretary of the Treasury, who shall without unnecessary delay proceed, pursuant to said chapter 459, to pay the judgments specified therein, with interest on the principal, at the rate of four per centum per annum from the date of loss, as certified until the Secretary of the Treasury shall give notice for payment, as provided by section 14 of such act.

Approved February 15, 1876.

AN ACT to extend the time for claimants, under section eleven of chapter four hundred and fifty-nine of the laws of the Forty-third Congress, to prove their claims.

Be it enacted by the Senate and House of Representatives of the United States of America in Congress assembled, That it shall be the duty of the Court of Commissioners for the Alabama Claims to receive, examine, and pass upon all claims that may be admissible under the provisions of chapter four hundred and fifty-nine of the laws of the Forty-third Congress which may be presented and filed within three months after this act shall take effect: *Provided,* That it shall appear by the claimant's petition, and be proved to the satisfaction of the court, that, by reason of his absence from the United States, or his ignorance of the time limited for the filing of a petition by such claimant, or by reason of fraud, accident, or mistake, the claim of such claimant has not been previously presented to said court within the time limited by said act; and such claim, in cases where the claimant shall be absent from the United States at the time of presenting the petition, may be presented and verified in such manner as the court shall by rule have provided.

Approved March 6, 1876.

AN ACT to enable the Secretary of the Treasury to pay judgments provided for in an act approved February fifteen, eighteen hundred and seventy-six, entitled "An act providing for the payment of judgments rendered under section eleven of chapter four hundred and fifty-nine of the laws of the first session of the Forty-third Congress."

Be it enacted by the Senate and House of Representatives of the United States of America in Congress assembled, That the Secretary of the Treasury, for the purpose of paying the judgments provided for in an act approved February fifteenth, eighteen hundred and seventy-six, entitled

"An act providing for the payment of judgments rendered under section eleven of chapter four hundred and fifty-nine of the laws of the first session of the Forty-third Congress" is hereby authorized to convert into coupon-bonds, and to sell after five days' notice, so many as may be necessary for this purpose of the five per centum registered bonds of the United States now held subject to the disposition of Congress under the provisions of the act approved March third, eighteen hundred and seventy-three, chapter two hundred and sixty-one.

SEC. 2. That so much of section fifteen of the act approved June twenty-third, eighteen hundred and seventy-four, chapter four hundred and fifty-nine, as conflicts with this act is hereby repealed.

Approved April 11, 1876.

AN ACT to extend the duration of the Court of Commissioners of Alabama Claims.

Be it enacted by the Senate and House of Representatives of the United States of America in Congress assembled, That the existence of the Court of Commissioners of Alabama Claims, created by the act entitled "An act for the creation of a court for the adjudication and disposition of certain moneys received into the Treasury under an award made by the Tribunal of Arbitration constituted by virtue of the first article of the treaty concluded at Washington the eighth of May, anno Domini eighteen hundred and seventy-one, between the United States of America and the Queen of Great Britain," be, and the same is hereby, continued and extended to the first day of January next, with the same effect and no other as if said last-named day had been named in said act for the termination of the powers of said court, and said act is hereby continued in force during said period.

SEC. 2. That the powers of the clerk of said court are hereby extended for an additional period, not to exceed two months from and after the termination of the existence of the court, for the purpose of closing his accounts, depositing the records, documents, and all other papers in the possession of the court or its officers in the office of the Secretary of State, as provided in said act; and all disbursements made by him during this period shall be under the direction of the Secretary of State.

Approved July 22, 1876.

[Extract.]

TREATY BETWEEN THE UNITED STATES AND GREAT BRITAIN.

CLAIMS, FISHERIES, NAVIGATION OF THE SAINT LAWRENCE, &C., AMERICAN LUMBER ON THE RIVER SAINT JOHN, BOUNDARY.

(Concluded May 8, 1871; ratifications exchanged June 17, 1871; proclaimed July 4, 1871.)

By the President of the United States of America.

A PROCLAMATION.

Whereas a treaty between the United States of America and Her Majesty the Queen of the United Kingdom of Great Britain and Ireland, concerning the settlement of all causes of difference between the two countries, was concluded and signed at Washington by the High

Commissioners and plenipotentiaries of the respective Governments, on the eighth day of May last, which Treaty is, word for word, as follows:

The United States of America and Her Britannic Majesty being desirous to provide for an amicable settlement of all causes of difference between the two countries, have for that purpose appointed their respective plenipotentiaries, that is to say, the President of the United States has appointed on the part of the United States as Commissioners in a Joint High Commission and Plenipotentiaries, Hamilton Fish, Secretary of State; Robert Cumming Schenck, Envoy Extraordinary and Minister Plenipotentiary to Great Britain; Samuel Nelson, an Associate Justice of the Supreme Court of the United States; Ebenezer Rockwood Hoar, of Massachusetts, and George Henry Williams, of Oregon. And Her Britannic Majesty, on her part, has appointed as her High Commissioners and Plenipotentiaries the Right Honorable George Frederick Samuel, Earl De Grey and Earl of Ripon, Viscount Goderich, Baron Grantham, a Baronet, a Peer of the United Kingdom, Lord President of Her Majesty's Most Honorable Privy Council, Knight of the Most Noble Order of the Garter, &c., &c.; the Right Honorable Sir Stafford Henry Northcote, Baronet, one of Her Majesty's Most Honorable Privy Council, a Member of Parliament, a Companion of the Most Honorable Order of the Bath, &c., &c.; Sir Edward Thornton, Knight Commander of the Most Honorable Order of the Bath, Her Majesty's Envoy Extraordinary and Minister Plenipotentiary to the United States of America; Sir John Alexander Macdonald, Knight Commander of the Most Honorable Order of the Bath, a Member of Her Majesty's Privy Council for Canada, and Minister of Justice and Attorney-General of Her Majesty's Dominion of Canada; and Mountague Bernard, Esq., Chichele Professor of International Law in the University of Oxford.

And the said plenipotentiaries, after having exchanged their full powers, which were found to be in due and proper form, have agreed to and concluded the following articles:

Article I.

Whereas differences have arisen between the Government of the United States and the Government of Her Britannic Majesty, and still exist, growing out of the acts committed by the several vessels which have given rise to the claims generically known as the "Alabama Claims;"

And whereas her Britannic Majesty has authorized Her High Commissioners and Plenipotentiaries to express, in a friendly spirit, the regret felt by Her Majesty's Government, for the escape, under whatever circumstances, of the Alabama and other vessels from British ports and for the depredations committed by those vessels:

Now, in order to remove and adjust all complaints and claims on the part of the United States, and to provide for the speedy settlement of such claims, which are not admitted by Her Britannic Majesty's Government, the High Contracting Parties agree that all the said claims, growing out of acts committed by the aforesaid vessels and generically known as the "Alabama claims," shall be referred to a Tribunal of Arbitration, to be composed of five Arbitrators, to be appointed in the following manner, that is to say: One shall be named by the President of the United States; one shall be named by Her Britannic Majesty; His Majesty the King of Italy shall be requested to name one; the President of the Swiss Confederation shall be requested to name one, and His Majesty the Emperor of Brazil shall be requested to name one.

In case of the death, absence, or incapacity to serve of any or either of the said Arbitrators, or in the event of either of the said arbitrators omitting or declining or ceasing to act as such, the President of the United States, or Her Britannic Majesty, or His Majesty the King of Italy, or the President of the Swiss Confederation, or His Majesty the Emperor of Brazil, as the case may be, may forthwith name another person to act as Arbitrator in the place and stead of the Arbitrator originally named by such Head of a State.

And in the event of the refusal or omission for two months after receipt of the request from either of the High Contracting Parties, of His Majesty the King of Italy, or the President of the Swiss Confederation, or His Majesty the Emperor of Brazil, to name an Arbitrator either to fill the original appointment or in the place of one who may have died, be absent, or incapacitated, or who may omit, decline, or from any cause cease to act as such Arbitrator, His Majesty the King of Sweden and Norway shall be requested to name one or more persons, as the case may be, to act as such Arbitrator or Arbitrators.

ARTICLE II.

The Arbitrators shall meet at Geneva, in Switzerland, at the earliest convenient day after they shall have been named, and shall proceed impartially and carefully to examine and decide all questions that shall be laid before them on the part of the Governments of the United States and Her Britannic Majesty respectively. All questions considered by the Tribunal, including the final award, shall be decided by a majority of all the Arbitrators.

Each of the High Contracting Parties shall also name one person to attend the Tribunal as its agent, to represent it generally in all matters connected with the arbitration.

ARTICLE III.

The written or printed case of each of the two Parties, accompanied by the documents, the official correspondence, and other evidence on which each relies, shall be delivered in duplicate to each of the arbitrators and to the agent of the other party as soon as may be after the organization of the Tribunal, but within a period not exceeding six months from the date of the exchange of the ratifications of this Treaty.

ARTICLE IV.

Within four months after the delivery on both sides of the written or printed case, either Party may, in like manner, deliver in duplicate, to each of the said Arbitrators and to the agent of the other party, a counter-case and additional documents, correspondence, and evidence, in reply to the case, documents, correspondence, and evidence so presented by the other Party.

The Arbitrators may, however, extend the time for delivering such counter-case, documents, correspondence, and evidence, when in their judgment it becomes necessary, in consequence of the distance of the place from which the evidence to be presented is to be procured.

If, in the case submitted to the Arbitrators, either Party shall have specified or alluded to any report or document in its own exclusive possession, without annexing a copy, such Party shall be bound, if the other Party thinks proper to apply for it, to furnish that Party with a copy thereof; and either Party may call upon the other, through the Arbitrators, to produce the originals or certified copies of any papers adduced as evidence, giving in each instance such reasonable notice as the Arbitrators may require.

ARTICLE V.

It shall be the duty of the agent of each Party, within two months after the expiration of the time limited for the delivery of the counter-case on both sides, to deliver in duplicate, to each of the said Arbitrators, and to the agent of the other Party, a written or printed argument showing the points and referring to the evidence upon which his Government relies; and the Arbitrators may, if they desire further elucidation with regard to any point, require a written or printed statement or argument, or oral argument by counsel upon it; but in such case the other Party shall be entitled to reply either orally or in writing, as the case may be.

ARTICLE VI.

In deciding the matters submitted to the arbitrators, they shall be governed by the following three rules, which are agreed upon by the High Contracting Parties as rules to be taken as applicable to the case, and by such principles of International Law, not inconsistent therewith, as the Arbitrators shall determine to have been applicable to the case.

RULES.

A neutral government is bound—

First, to use due diligence to prevent the fitting out, arming, or equipping, within its jurisdiction, of any vessel which it has reasonable ground to believe is intended to cruise or to carry on war against a Power with which it is at peace; and also to use like diligence to prevent the departure from its jurisdiction of any vessel intended to cruise or carry on war as above, such vessel having been specially adapted, in whole or in part, within such jurisdiction, to warlike use.

Secondly, not to permit or suffer either belligerent to make use of its ports or waters as the base of naval operations against the other, or for the purpose of the renewal or augmentation of military supplies or arms, or the recruitment of men.

Thirdly, to exercise due diligence in its own ports and waters, and as to all persons within its jurisdiction, to prevent any violation of the foregoing obligations and duties.

Her Britannic Majesty has commanded her High Commissioners and Plenipotentiaries to declare that Her Majesty's Government cannot assent to the foregoing rules as a statement of principles of International Law, which were in force at the time when the claims mentioned in Article I arose, but that Her Majesty's Government, in order to evince its desire of strengthening the friendly relations between the two countries, and of making satisfactory provision for the future, agrees that in deciding the questions between the two countries arising out of those claims, the Arbitrators should assume that Her Majesty's Government had undertaken to act upon the principles set forth in these rules.

And the High Contracting Parties agree to observe those rules as between themselves in future, and to bring them to the knowledge of other maritime Powers, and to invite them to accede to them.

ARTICLE VII.

The decision of the Tribunal shall, if possible, be made within three months from the close of the argument on both sides.

It shall be made in writing and dated, and shall be signed by the Arbitrators who may assent to it.

The said Tribunal shall first determine as to each vessel separately whether Great Britain has, by any act or omission, failed to fulfill any of the duties set forth in the foregoing three rules, or recognized by the principles of International Law not inconsistent with such rules, and shall certify such fact as to each of the said vessels. In case the Tribunal find that Great Britain has failed to fulfill any duty or duties as aforesaid, it may, if it think proper, proceed to award a sum in gross to be paid by Great Britain to the United States for all the claims referred to it; and in such case the gross sum so awarded shall be paid in coin by the Government of Great Britain to the Government of the United States, at Washington, within twelve months after the date of the award.

The award shall be in duplicate, one copy whereof shall be delivered to the agent of the United States for his Government, and the other copy shall be delivered to the agent of Great Britain for his Government.

ARTICLE VIII.

Each Government shall pay its own agent and provide for the proper remuneration of the counsel employed by it, and of the Arbitrator appointed by it, and for the expense of preparing and submitting its case to the Tribunal. All other expenses connected with the Arbitration shall be defrayed by the two Governments in equal moieties.

ARTICLE IX.

The Arbitrators shall keep accurate record of their proceedings, and may appoint and employ the necessary officers to assist them.

ARTICLE X.

In case the Tribunal finds that Great Britain has failed to fulfill any duty or duties as aforesaid, and does not award a sum in gross, the High Contracting Parties agree that a Board of Assessors shall be appointed, to ascertain and determine what claims are valid, and what amount or amounts shall be paid by Great Britain to the United States on account of the liability arising from such failure, as to each vessel, according to the extent of such liability as decided by the Arbitrators.

The Board of Assessors shall be constituted as follows: One member thereof shall be named by the President of the United States, one member thereof shall be named by Her Britannic Majesty; and one member thereof shall be named by the Representative at Washington of His Majesty the King of Italy; and in case of a vacancy happening from any cause, it shall be filled in the same manner in which the original appointment was made.

As soon as possible after such nominations the Board of Assessors shall be organized in Washington, with power to hold their sittings there, or in New York, or in Boston. The members thereof shall severally subscribe a solemn declaration that they will impartially and carefully examine and decide, to the best of their judgment and according to justice and equity, all matters submitted to them, and shall forthwith proceed, under such rules and regulations as they may prescribe, to the investigation of the claims which shall be presented to them by the Government of the United States, and shall examine and decide upon them in such order and manner as they may think proper, but upon such evidence or information only as shall be furnished by or on behalf of the Governments of the United States and of Great Britain respectively. They shall be bound to hear on each separate claim, if required, one person on behalf of each Government, as counsel or agent. A majority of the Assessors in each case shall be sufficient for a decision.

The decision of the Assessors shall be given upon each claim in writing, and shall be signed by them respectively and dated.

Every claim shall be presented to the Assessors within six months from the day of their first meeting, but they may, for good cause shown, extend the time for the presentation of any claim to a further period, not exceeding three months.

The Assessors shall report to each Government, at or before the expiration of one year from the date of their first meeting, the amount of claims decided by them up to the date of such report; if further claims then remain undecided, they shall make a further report at or before the expiration of two years from the date of such first meeting; and in case any claims remain undetermined at that time, they shall make a final report within a further period of six months.

The report or reports shall be made in duplicate, and one copy thereof shall be delivered to the Secretary of State of the United States, and one copy thereof to the Representative of Her Britannic Majesty at Washington.

All sums of money which may be awarded under this Article shall be payable at Washington, in coin, within twelve months after the delivery of each report.

The Board of Assessors may employ such clerks as they shall think necessary.

The expenses of the Board of Assessors shall be borne equally by the two Governments, and paid from time to time, as may be found expedient, on the production of accounts certified by the Board. The remuneration of the Assessors shall also be paid by the two Governments in equal moieties in a similar manner.

ARTICLE XI.

The High Contracting Parties engage to consider the result of the proceedings of the Tribunal of Arbitration and of the Board of Assessors, should such Board be appointed, as a full, perfect, and final settlement of all the claims hereinbefore referred to; and further engage that every such claim, whether the same may or may not have been presented to the notice of, made, preferred, or laid before, the Tribunal or Board, shall, from and after the conclusion of the proceedings of the Tribunal or Board, be considered and treated as finally settled, barred, and thenceforth inadmissible.

* * * * * * *

ARTICLE XLIII.

The present treaty shall be duly ratified by the President of the United States of America, by and with the advice and consent of the Senate thereof, and by Her Britannic Majesty, and the ratifications shall be exchanged either at Washington or at London within six months from the date hereof, or earlier if possible.

In faith whereof, we, the respective Plenipotentiaries, have signed this Treaty and have hereunto affixed our seals.

Done in duplicate at Washington the eighth day of May, in the year of our Lord one thousand eight hundred and seventy-one.

[L. S.] HAMILTON FISH.
[L. S.] ROBT. C. SCHENCK.
[L. S.] SAMUEL NELSON.
[L. S.] EBENEZER ROCKWOOD HOAR.
[L. S.] GEO. H. WILLIAMS.
[L. S.] DE GREY & RIPON.
[L. S.] STAFFORD H. NORTHCOTE.
[L. S.] EDWD. THORNTON.
[L. S.] JOHN A. MACDONALD.
[L. S.] MOUNTAGUE BERNARD.

And whereas the said Treaty has been duly ratified on both parts and the respective ratifications of the same were exchanged in the city of London, on the seventeenth day of June, 1871, by Robert C. Schenck, Envoy Extraordinary and Minister Plenipotentiary of the United States, and Earl Granvill, Her Majesty's Principal Secretary of State for Foreign Affairs, on the part of their respective Governments:

Now, therefore, be it known that I, ULYSSES S. GRANT, President of the United States of America, have caused the said Treaty to be made public, to the end that the same, and every clause and article thereof, may be observed and fulfilled with good faith by the United States and the citizens thereof.

In witness whereof I have hereunto set my hand and caused the seal of the United States to be affixed.

Done at the city of Washington this fourth day of July, in the year of our Lord one thousand eight hundred and seventy-one and of [SEAL.] the Independence of the United States the ninety-sixth.

U. S. GRANT.

By the President:
HAMILTON FISH,
Secretary of State.

DECISION AND AWARD MADE BY THE TRIBUNAL OF ARBITRATION CONSTITUTED BY VIRTUE OF THE FIRST ARTICLE OF THE TREATY CONCLUDED AT WASHINGTON THE 8TH OF MAY, 1871, BETWEEN THE UNITED STATES OF AMERICA AND HER MAJESTY THE QUEEN OF THE UNITED KINGDOM OF GREAT BRITAIN AND IRELAND.

The United States of America and Her Britannic Majesty having agreed by Article I of the treaty concluded and signed at Washington the 8th of May, 1871, to refer all the claims "generically known as the Alabama claims" to a tribunal of arbitration to be composed of five arbitrators named:

One by the President of the United States,
One by Her Britannic Majesty,
One by His Majesty the King of Italy,
One by the President of the Swiss Confederation,
One by His Majesty the Emperor of Brazil;

And the President of the United States, Her Britannic Majesty, His

Majesty the King of Italy, the President of the Swiss Confederation, and His Majesty the Emperor of Brazil having respectively named their arbitrators, to wit:

The President of the United States, Charles Francis Adams, esquire;

Her Britannic Majesty, Sir Alexander James Edmund Cockburn, baronet, a member of Her Majesty's privy council, lord chief justice of England;

His Majesty, the King of Italy, His Excellency Count Frederick Sclopis, of Salerano, a knight of the Order of the Annunciato, minister of state, senator of the Kingdom of Italy;

The President of the Swiss Confederation, M. James Stämpfli;

His Majesty the Emperor of Brazil, His Excellency Marcos Antonio d'Aranjó, Viscount d'Itajaubá, a grandee of the Empire of Brazil, member of the council of H. M. the Emperor of Brazil, and his Envoy Extraordinary and Minister Plenipotentiary in France.

And the five arbitrators above named having assembled at Geneva (in Switzerland) in one of the chambers of the Hôtel de Ville on the 15th of December, 1871, in conformity with the terms of the second article of the treaty of Washington of the 8th of May of that year, and having proceeded to the inspection and verification of their respective powers, which were found duly authenticated, the Tribunal of Arbitration was declared duly organized.

The agents named by each of the High Contracting Parties, by virtue of the same Article II, to wit:

For the United States of America, John C. Bancroft Davis, esquire;

And for Her Brittannic Majesty, Charles Stuart Aubrey, Lord Tenderden, peer of the United Kingdom, companion of the most honorable Order of the Bath, assistant under secretary of state for foreign affairs;

Whose powers were found likewise duly authenticated, then delivered to each of the arbitrators the printed case prepared by each of the two parties, accompanied by the documents, the official correspondence, and other evidence on which each relied, in conformity with the terms of the third article of the said treaty.

In virtue of the decision made by the tribunal at its first session, the counter-case and additional documents, correspondence, and evidence referred to in Article IV of the said treaty were delivered by the respective agents of the two parties to the secretary of the tribunal on the 15th of April, 1872, at the chamber of conference, at the Hôtel de Ville of Geneva.

The tribunal, in accordance with the vote of adjournment passed at their second session, held on the 16th of December, 1871, re-assembled at Geneva on the 15th of June, 1872; and the agent of each of the parties duly delivered to each of the arbitrators, and to the agent of the other party, the printed arguments referred to in Article V of the said treaty.

The tribunal having since fully taken into their consideration the treaty, and also the cases, counter-cases, documents, evidence, and arguments, and likewise all other communications made to them by the two parties during the progress of their sittings, and having impartially and carefully examined the same, has arrived at the decision embodied in the present award.

Whereas, having regard to the sixth and seventh articles of the said treaty, the arbitrators are bound under the terms of the said sixth article, "in deciding the matters submitted to them, to be governed by the three rules therein specified, and by such principles of international law not inconsistent therewith, as the arbitrators shall determine to have been applicable to the case;"

And whereas the "due diligence" referred to in the first and third of the said rules ought to be exercised by neutral governments in exact proportion to the risks to which either of the belligerents may be exposed from a failure to fulfill the obligations of neutrality on their part;

And whereas the circumstances out of which the facts constituting the subject-matter of the present controversy arose were of a nature to call for the exercise on the part of Her Britannic Majesty's government of all possible solicitude for the observance of the rights and the duties involved in the proclamation of neutrality issued by Her Majesty on the 13th day of May, 1861;

And whereas the effects of a violation of neutrality committed by means of the construction, equipment, and armament of a vessel are not done away with by any commission which the government of the belligerent power, benefited by the violation of neutrality, may afterward have granted to that vessel, and the ultimate step by which the offense is completed, cannot be admissible as a ground for the absolution of the offender, nor can the consummation of his fraud become the means of establishing his innocence;

And whereas the privilege of exterritoriality accorded to vessels of war has been admitted into the law of nations, not as an absolute right, but solely as a proceeding founded on the principle of courtesy and mutual deference between different nations, and therefore can never be appealed to for the protection of acts done in violation of neutrality;

And whereas the absence of a previous notice cannot be regarded as a failure in any consideration required by the law of nations, in those cases in which a vessel carries with it its own condemnation;

And whereas, in order to impart to any supplies of coal a character inconsistent with the second rule, prohibiting the use of neutral ports or waters, as a base of naval operations for a belligerent, it is necessary that the said supplies should be connected with special circumstances of time, of persons, or of place, which may combine to give them such character;

And whereas, with respect to the vessel called the Alabama, it clearly results from all the facts relative to the construction of the ship at first designated by the number "290" in the port of Liverpool, and its equipment and armament in the vicinity of Terceira through the agency of the vessels called the Agrippina and the Bahama, dispatched from Great Britain to that end, that the British government failed to use due diligence in the performance of its neutral obligations; and especially that it omitted, notwithstanding the warnings and official representations made by the diplomatic agents of the United States during the construction of the said number "290," to take in due time any effective measures of prevention, and that those orders which it did give at last, for the detention of the vessel, were issued so late that their execution was not practicable;

And whereas, after the escape of that vessel, the measures taken for its pursuit and arrest were so imperfect as to lead to no result, and therefore cannot be considered sufficient to release Great Britain from the responsibility already incurred;

And whereas, in spite of the violations of the neutrality of Great Britain committed by the "290," this same vessel, later known as the confederate cruiser Alabama, was on several occasions freely admitted to the ports of colonies of Great Britain, instead of being proceeded against as it ought to have been in any and every port within British urisdiction in which it might have been found;

And whereas the government of Her Britannic Majesty cannot justify itself for a failure in due diligence on the plea of insufficiency of the legal means of action which it possessed:

Four of the arbitrators, for the reasons above assigned, and the fifth, for reasons separately assigned by him,

Are of opinion—

That Great Britain has in this case failed, by omission, to fulfill the duties prescribed in the first and the third of the rules established by the sixth article of the treaty of Washington.

And whereas, with respect to the vessel called the Florida, it results from all the facts relative to the construction of the Oreto in the port of Liverpool, and to its issue therefrom, which facts failed to induce the authorities of Great Britain to resort to measures adequate to prevent the violation of the neutrality of that nation, notwithstanding the warnings and repeated representations of the agents of the United States, that Her Majesty's government has failed to use due diligence to fulfill the duties of neutrality;

And whereas it likewise results from all the facts relative to the stay of the Oreto at Nassau, to her issue from that port, to her enlistment of men, to her supplies, and to her armament, with the co-operation of the British vessel Prince Alfred, at Green Cay, that there was negligence on the part of the British colonial authorities;

And whereas notwithstanding the violation of the neutrality of Great Britain committed by the Oreto, this same vessel, later known as the confederate cruiser Florida, was nevertheless on several occasions freely admitted into the ports of British colonies;

And whereas the judicial acquittal of the Oreto at Nassau cannot relieve Great Britain from the responsibility incurred by her under the principles of international law; nor can the fact of the entry of the Florida into the confederate port of Mobile, and of its stay there during four months, extinguish the responsibility previously to that time incurred by Great Britain:

For these reasons,

The tribunal, by a majority of four voices to one, is of opinion—

That Great Britain has in this case failed, by omission, to fulfill the duties prescribed in the first, in the second, and in the third of the rules established by Article VI of the treaty of Washington.

And whereas, with respect to the vessel called the Shenandoah, it results from all the facts relative to the departure from London of the merchant vessel the Sea King, and to the transformation of that ship into a confederate cruiser under the name of the Shenandoah, near the island of Madeira, that the government of Her Britannic Majesty is not chargeable with any failure, down to that date, in the use of due diligence to fulfill the duties of neutrality;

But whereas it results from all the facts connected with the stay of the Shenandoah at Melbourne, and especially with the augmentation which the British government itself admits to have been clandestinely effected of her force, by the enlistment of men within that port, that there was negligence on the part of the authorities at that place:

For these reasons,

The tribunal is unanimously of opinion—

That Great Britain has not failed, by any act or omission, "to fulfill any of the duties prescribed by the three rules of Article VI in the treaty of Washington, or by the principles of international law not inconsistent therewith," in respect to the vessel called the Shenandoah, during the period of time anterior to her entry into the port of Melbourne;

And, by a majority of three to two voices, the tribunal decides that Great Britain has failed, by omission, to fulfill the duties prescribed by the second and third of the rules aforesaid, in the case of this same vessel, from and after her entry into Hobson's Bay, and is therefore responsible for all acts committed by that vessel after her departure from Melbourne, on the 18th day of February, 1865.

And so far as relates to the vessels called—

The Tuscaloosa, (tender to the Alabama,)

The Clarence,

The Tacony, and

The Archer, (tenders to the Florida,)

The tribunal is unanimously of opinion—

That such tenders or auxiliary vessels, being properly regarded as accessories, must necessarily follow the lot of their principals, and be submitted to the same decision which applies to them respectively.

And so far as relates to the vessel called Retribution,

The tribunal, by a majority of three to two voices, is of opinion—

That Great Britain has not failed by any act or omission to fulfill any of the duties prescribed by the three rules of Article VI in the treaty of Washington, or by the principles of international law not inconsistent therewith.

And so far as relates to the vessels called—

The Georgia,

The Sumter,

The Nashville,

The Tallahassee, and

The Chickamauga, respectively,

The tribunal is unanimously of opinion—

That Great Britain has not failed, by any act or omission, to fulfill any of the duties prescribed by the three rules of Article VI in the treaty of Washington, or by the principles of international law not inconsistent therewith.

And so far as relates to the vessels called—

The Sallie,

The Jefferson Davis,

The Music,

The Boston, and

The V. H. Joy, respectively,

The tribunal is unanimously of opinion—

That they ought to be excluded from consideration for want of evidence.

And whereas, so far as relates to the particulars of the indemnity claimed by the United States, the costs of pursuit of the confederate cruisers are not, in the judgment of the tribunal, properly distinguishable from the general expenses of the war carried on by the United States:

The tribunal is, therefore, of opinion, by a majority of three to two voices—

That there is no ground for awarding to the United States any sum by way of indemnity under this head.

And whereas prospective earnings cannot properly be made the subject of compensation, inasmuch as they depend in their nature upon future and uncertain contingencies:

That there is no ground for awarding to the United States any sum by way of indemnity under this head.

And whereas, in order to arrive at an equitable compensation for the damages which have been sustained, it is necessary to set aside all double claims for the same losses, and all claims for "gross freights," so far as they exceed "net freights;"

And whereas it is just and reasonable to allow interest at a reasonable rate;

And whereas, in accordance with the spirit and letter of the treaty of Washington, it is preferable to adopt the form of adjudication of a sum in gross, rather than to refer the subject of compensation for further discussion and deliberation to a board of assessors, as provided by Article X of the said treaty:

The tribunal, making use of the authority conferred upon it by Article VII, of the said treaty, by a majority of four voices to one, awards to the United States a sum of $15,500,000 in gold, as the indemnity to be paid by Great Britain to the United States, for the satisfaction of all the claims referred to the consideration of the tribunal, conformably to the provisions contained in Article VII of the aforesaid treaty.

And in accordance with the terms of Article XI of the said treaty, the tribunal declares that "all the claims referred to in the treaty as submitted to the tribunal are hereby fully, perfectly, and finally settled."

Furthermore it declares that "each and every one of the said claims, whether the same may or may not have been presented to the notice of, or made, preferred, or laid before the tribunal, shall henceforth be considered and treated as finally settled, barred, and inadmissible."

In testimony whereof this present decision and award has been made in duplicate, and signed by the arbitrators who have given their assent thereto, the whole being in exact conformity with the provisions of Article VII of the said treaty of Washington.

Made and concluded at the Hotel de Ville of Geneva, in Switzerland, the 14th day of the month of September, in the year of our Lord one thousand eight hundred and seventy-two.

CHARLES FRANCIS ADAMS.
FREDERICK SCLOPIS.
STÄMPFLI.
VICOMTE D'ITAJUBA.

RULES FOR TAKING TESTIMONY.

COURT OF COMMISSIONERS OF ALABAMA CLAIMS,
Washington, D. C., ——, 1875.

SIR: I inclose herewith interrogatories and cross-interrogatories to be used in the examination of —— ——, of ——, in the claim of —— —— against the United States, No. ——.

In the examination of this witness, you will be pleased to conform to the following rules.

I am, sir, your obedient servant,

—— ——,
Clerk.

To —— ——, esq.,
Commissioner, &c.

RULES.

1. You will require the witness to hold up his right hand, and make solemn oath [or if he have conscientious scruples against taking an oath, to affirm] to "tell the truth, the whole truth, and nothing but the truth relative to the matters now to be inquired of."

2. You will allow no person to be present except the witness, unless it be needful for you to employ a third person to write down for you the witness's answers.

3. You will put each interrogatory, and write down in full the answer thereto, before proceeding to the next succeeding interrogatory. Endeavor to reduce to writing, so far as possible, the exact words of the witness. Should any alteration be necessary, note it over your initials, without making erasure or interlineation.

4. After the witness has fully answered all the interrogatories, and you have reduced his answers to writing, you will read over to him each question and his answer thereto, and permit him to make at the end of his deposition such correction as he may desire, and give reason for. He will then sign his deposition, as will you, with your full name and title.

5. You will begin the deposition as directed in the accompanying form A.

6. You will add to the deposition a certificate, as per accompanying form B.

7. Should it be necessary to adjourn the hearing, you will make a note of it in the deposition.

8. The sheets should be carefully connected, and the interrogatories which you receive with the deposition should be mailed to my address.

9. You will also sign your name at the bottom of each page of the deposition.

FORM A.

The deposition of ——— ———, taken in the case of ——— ———, claimant, *vs.* The United States, No. ——, upon written interrogatories filed by the claimant, and cross-interrogatories filed by the United States, at ———, before me, ——— ———, a duly-appointed commissioner, on the —— day of ———, 1875, to be used in the Court of Commissioners of Alabama Claims.

FORM B.

———, ———, 187–.

I, ——— ———, a commissioner duly appointed by the Court of Commission r of Alabama Claims to take the testimony of ——— ———, to be used in the case of ——— ——— *vs.* The United States, before the said court, do hereby certify that on the —— day of ———, 187–, I caused the said ——— ——— to appear before me at the said ———, and permitted no other person than himself to be present except ——— ——— before me; that I administered an oath to said ——— ———, that he would tell the truth, the whole truth, and nothing but the truth relative to the matters to be inquired of; that his deposition was then reduced to writing by me, [by a clerk appointed by me for that purpose,] and no interrogatory was put to the witness until the previous interrogatory had been answered by him; that the whole deposition was carefully read by him, and that he subscribed the same.

And I do further certify that I have no interest whatever in any of the claims referred to in this deposition.

In testimony whereof, I have hereunto set my hand and seal this —— day of ———, 187–.

[SEAL.]

——— ———.
——— ———.

[No. 30.] COURT OF COMMISSIONERS OF ALABAMA CLAIMS,
1514 *H street N. W., Washington, D. C.*, ———, 187—.

——— ———,
——— ———:

SIR: Owing to a very general misunderstanding as to the manner of taking testimony to be used before this court, I would call your attention to the annexed rules, which must be observed in every case except where a special order of the court is obtained to the contrary. No testimony will be placed on file until all the requirements of these rules shall have been complied with.

I am, sir, your obedient servant,

JOHN DAVIS,
Clerk.

RULES.

1. No commissioner shall take testimony except after receipt of a certificate of record of a rule for that purpose, as per inclosed blank.
2. The certificate must be filled out on the face, and signed by the clerk of the Court of Commissioners of Alabama Claims, and must have the seal of said court attached.
3. The certificate must show on the back a notice to the counsel on behalf of the United States for the *full twenty* days required by rule VII of the Court of Commissioners of Alabama Claims.
4. The certificate must show on the back also the acceptance of said notice by said counsel on behalf of the United States.
5. When testimony is taken in the same case before different commissioners, a certificate must be filed with each commissioner.
6. When the testimony in any case has been filed with the clerk of this court, further testimony may be taken in the same case before the same commissioner without another certificate; *provided* a written agreement to that effect is filed with the said commissioner, signed by the assistant counsel of the United States present when the testimony was first taken, and the counsel for the claimant.
7. After the certificate shall have been obtained, and the counsel on behalf of the United States shall have received and accepted notice for the *full twenty days*, special agreements in writing may be made by the assistant counsel of the United States in charge of any case, and the counsel of the claimant, changing the date of taking testimony.
8. The certificate of record and all written agreements of counsel must be forwarded to the clerk of the Court of Commissioners of Alabama Claims with the testimony.

EXTRACTS FROM THE RECORD OF THE COURT OF COMMISSIONERS OF ALABAMA CLAIMS.

* * * * * * *

The following resolutions were presented to the court on behalf of the bar by the Hon. JOHN A. J. CRESWELL, counsel on behalf of the United States, and * * * the clerk was directed to enter them among the records, and to send a copy of them to the family of the late MARTIN RYERSON.

RESOLUTIONS.

The Hon. MARTIN RYERSON, of New Jersey, lately a judge of this court, having departed this life, it is hereby resolved—

1. That the members of this bar have received with unfeigned sorrow intelligence of the death of Judge RYERSON.

2. That his well-established reputation for ability and integrity justify the opinion that if his life and health had been spared he would have brought to the discharge of his duties as a member of this court the highest qualifications of an upright, fearless, and impartial judge.

3. That the heart-felt sympathy of this bar is extended to the family and relatives of the deceased.

4. That this court be requested to order these resolutions to be entered among the records of the court, and that a copy thereof be sent to the family; and, as a further mark of respect, that this court do now adjourn.

June 24, 1875.

---

* * * * * * *

JOHN A. J. CRESWELL, esq., counsel of the United States, on behalf of the bar of this court, announced the death of CALEB BALDWIN, of Iowa, recently a judge of this court, and presented a series of resolutions, which he moved to have entered on the records of the court.

JAMES LOWNDES, esq., seconded the motion.

After remarks by Mr. CRESWELL and Mr. LOWNDES, the court ordered that the resolutions be placed on the records, and the clerk was directed to send a copy thereof to the family.

RESOLUTIONS.

The Hon. CALEB BALDWIN, of Iowa, recently a judge of this court' having departed this life, it is hereby resolved—

1. That the members of the bar of this court have received with unfeigned sorrow intelligence of the death of Judge BALDWIN.

2. That in the discharge of his duties as a member of this court, he not only displayed a high order of ability, but always bore himself as became an upright, learned, and impartial judge.

3. That the heart-felt sympathy of this bar is extended to the family and relatives of the deceased.

4. That the court is hereby requested to order that these resolutions be entered on its minutes, and that a copy thereof be sent to the family; and, as a further mark of respect, that this court do now adjourn.

December 29, 1876.

---

* * * * * * *

The court desires to place upon record an expression of their sense of the value of the services of the Hon. JOHN A. J. CRESWELL in the discharge of his duties of counsel on behalf of the United States. He has exhibited unwearied industry in the investigation of the facts of the several cases, great research in examination of the difficult questions of law often arising, and great ability in presenting to the court his views both of the facts and law; with an earnest zeal to protect the rights of the Government, he has yet been entirely fair and just to claimants.

His uniform courtesy and kindness of manner has made his official intercourse with the members of the court peculiarly agreeable to them. It is therefore alike proper and just that this expression of our opinion of his ability, fidelity, and integrity should be placed upon the record.

December 29, 1876.

---

* * * * * * *

The court also place upon record their sense of the value of the services of JOHN DAVIS, esq., the clerk of the court. Nothing could have exceeded his industry, his fidelity, and his careful attention to his duties, including not only the keeping of the records, but the management of all the financial business of the court; and the very moderate expenses of the court are in a great measure due to his watchfulness.

In all the various duties of his office he has exhibited very marked executive and administrative ability.

December 29, 1876.

Mr. Fish to Mr. Davis.

WASHINGTON, *January* 18, 1877.

SIR: I have received your letter of the 5th instant, with which you transmit a report of the business of the Court of Commissioners of Alabama Claims, together with several of the opinions of the judges of the court delivered in the more important cases brought before that body. You also state that the court, having examined and decided all claims submitted to it in accordance with the several acts prescribing its jurisdiction, adjourned on the 29th December last.

The complimentary reference made by you to the gentlemen employed in the discharge of the work of the office is very gratifying, and I cannot permit the present occasion to pass without adding an expression of my own high appreciation of the intelligence and fidelity displayed by you in discharging the important trust confided to your care, and of my regret at the close of your long official connection with the Department.

I am, &c.,

HAMILTON FISH.

INDEX.

ERRATA.

Pages 23, 24, and 25, for *post* read *infra.*

www.ingramcontent.com/pod-product-compliance
Lightning Source LLC
LaVergne TN
LVHW021401110826
845150LV00007B/1742
9781425512521